Clifford Young, Kirby Goidel
Nativist Nation

De Gruyter Series in Race, Ethnicity, and Political Communication

Edited by
Stephen Maynard Caliendo and Charlton D. McIlwain

Volume 2

Clifford Young, Kirby Goidel

Nativist Nation

———

Populism, Grievance, Identity, and the
Transformation of American Politics

DE GRUYTER

ISBN (Paperback) 978-3-11-138222-7
ISBN (Hardcover) 978-3-11-138453-5
e-ISBN (PDF) 978-3-11-138404-7
e-ISBN (EPUB) 978-3-11-138426-9
ISSN 2942-6618

Library of Congress Control Number: 2025942658

Bibliographic information published by the Deutsche Nationalbibliothek
The Deutsche Nationalbibliothek lists this publication in the Deutsche Nationalbibliografie;
detailed bibliographic data are available on the internet at http://dnb.dnb.de.

© 2026 Walter de Gruyter GmbH, Berlin/Boston, Genthiner Straße 13, 10785 Berlin
Cover image: Robert Llewellyn/Photodisc/Getty Images
Typesetting: Integra Software Services Pvt. Ltd.

www.degruyterbrill.com
Questions about General Product Safety Regulation:
productsafety@degruyterbrill.com

Contents

List of Figures and Tables

Figures

https://doi.org/10.1515/9783111384047-203

Tables

Chapter 1
An Introduction to a Nativist Nation: Building a Wall to the Trump Presidency?

Nativist Utterances over time

> I would build a great wall, and nobody builds walls better than me, believe me, and I'll build them very inexpensively. I will build a great great wall on our southern border and I'll have Mexico pay for that wall.[1]

> We have people coming into the country, or trying to come in – and we're stopping a lot of them – but we're taking people out of the country. You wouldn't believe how bad these people are. These aren't people. These are animals.[2]

> Nobody has ever seen anything like we're witnessing right now. It is a very sad thing for our country. It's poisoning the blood of our country. It's so bad, and people are coming in with disease. People are coming in with every possible thing that you could have.[3]

During an answer to a question about immigration, Trump said:

> They're eating the dogs, the people that came in, they're eating the cats. They're eating the pets of the people that live there, and this is what's happening in our country, and it's a shame.[4]

Donald J. Trump's path to Republican nomination and the presidency in 2016 was built on a simple appeal. If elected, he would build a wall on the US-Mexico border that Mexico would pay for, securing the border, reducing illegal immigration into the United States, and restoring economic security to the American worker. In a crowded Republican primary populated with focus-group-tested, cookie-cutter politicians, Trump's vitriolic rhetoric stood out and found resonance. As a presidential candidate, Trump was willing to say the quiet parts out loud. At his

---

[1] Politifact (2020, July 15). Trump-O-Meter: Build a wall—and make Mexico pay for it. https://www.politifact.com/truth-o-meter/promises/trumpometer/promise/1397/build-wall-and-make-mexico-pay-it/ (retrieved May 5, 2025).
[2] Blake, A. (2018, May 16). Trump's 'animals' comment on undocumented immigrants earns backlash, historical comparisons. The Washington Post. https://www.washingtonpost.com/news/the-fix/wp/2018/05/16/trumps-animals-comment-on-undocumented-immigrants-earn-backlash-historical-comparisons/.
[3] Collinson, S. (2023, October 6). Trump's anti-immigrant comments take center stage in 2024 campaign. CNN. https://www.cnn.com/2023/10/06/politics/trump-anti-immigrant-comments/index.html.
[4] Garsd, Jasmine. (2024, September 11). Donald Trump's debate comment about immigrants eating dogs and cats is a false stereotype. NPR. https://www.npr.org/2024/09/11/nx-s1-5108401/donald-trump-debate-eating-dogs-cats-immigrants-false-stereotype.

https://doi.org/10.1515/9783111384047-001

2016 rallies, often broadcast on CNN from start to finish,[5] he repeated his promise to build a wall, always to great applause, often followed by a promise that only he could *Make America Great Again*. It is a refrain he has returned to repeatedly since his initial descent down a Trump Tower escalator to give a thumbs up and announce his 2016 run for the presidency. He immediately connected to two themes that defined his presidential campaign, his presidency, and his 2024 return. First, the United States of America was losing its place in the world, losing economically to China, Japan, and others because of bad trade deals, and losing militarily by fighting unnecessary wars and contributing more than its share to international security. Second, at home, America was losing its identity because of immigration, because immigrants were changing the culture, because the immigrants who were arriving did not share in American values. Both themes connect to the pervading sense of status threat, the fear among White Americans that their place in the world was being undermined, resulting in a desire to protect (or conserve) the status quo and nostalgia for the past (Mutz, 2018).

In that initial speech announcing his presidential run in 2015, Trump spoke clearly and unequivocally. "When Mexico sends its people, they're not sending their best. They're not sending you. They're not sending you. They're sending people that have lots of problems, and they're bringing those problems with us. They're bringing drugs. They're bringing crime. They're rapists."[6] In doing so, Trump tapped into a deeply visceral sentiment among so many, who felt they were being left behind in their own country. Their future was no longer secure, elected officials were unresponsive to their demands, and their culture and way of life were slipping away. Fairly or not, many of these Americans worried that this was no longer the country they grew up in. It was no longer the country they wanted their kids to grow up in. They were losing the America they loved, and they increasingly felt like "strangers in the land" (Higham, 1955).

What was this? What was Trump tapping into? Was it just Trump or something that would outlast him? These were questions that we would come back to again and again over the years. We can say unequivocally that the puzzle is com-

---

5 According to estimates, Trump received $5 billion in free media coverage during the 2016 campaign. His strategy was relatively simple: Make controversial statements that attracted media coverage. Perhaps more than any candidate in the history of American politics, Trump played into the structural media biases that how the media decide what to cover. La Monica, P. R. (2016, November 29). Donald Trump rode $5 billion in free media to the White House. TheStreet. https://www.thestreet.com/politics/donald-trump-rode-5-billion-in-free-media-to-the-white-house-13896916.
6 Time Staff. (2015, June 16). Read Donald Trump's presidential announcement speech. Time. https://time.com/3923128/donald-trump-announcement-speech/.

plex but the answer is simple: Trump was surfing a nativist wave. Here, we define nativism as *a predisposition to support policies that favor native-born populations and disadvantage foreign-born ones.*

This book challenges the dominant story of contemporary politics. While others have focused on populism, authoritarianism, economic anxiety or racism, we argue that nativism—a deep-seated structure of belonging—is the defining constraint of our political age.

So, what big picture did Trump divine?

In a divided America, Trump understood America's fundamental division and how to play to it. The American population was rapidly changing. Immigration was a large part of the story. In 2022, the foreign-born population reached a record 46.1 million, increasing as a percentage of the population from 4.7 percent in 1970 to 13.8 percent in 2022 (Moslimani & Passel, 2024). With this shift, the demographic makeup of the country was also shifting. Non-Hispanic Whites decreased from 63.8 percent of the population in 2010 to 58.9 percent in 2022. Based on current projections, by 2045, the non-Hispanic White population will no longer be a majority (Vespa et al., 2018). For many Americans, these population shifts are perceived as a threat to their status as a group, subsequently giving rise to intolerant reactions toward immigrant groups and support for right-wing populist parties and candidates (Bai & Federico, 2020, 2021; Blumer, 1958; Bobo & Hutchings, 1996; Craig & Richeson, 2014, 2017; Major et al., 2018).

Seen in this light, nativism exposes the fundamental division of American society. But, it is not merely about nativism. It is also about what it means to be an American. On one side, there is a shrinking majority non-Hispanic White population that defines American identity in exclusive terms. This means being an American to them is about birthplace, racial and ethnic identity, and the American creed. Such Americans look back and root themselves in the past. They seek to make America great again by returning to founding principles. On the other side, there is an ascendant majority, racially diverse, with a less restrictive understanding of American identity. For this group, what it means to be an American is not rooted in ethnicity, nor is it predetermined by birthplace, but is instead evolving and aspirational. These Americans look to the future. For them, American ideals—individual freedom, self-determination, and economic opportunity—are not set but are instead constantly shifting. Contemporary politics is rooted in a conflict over these definitional rights. Who gets to define what it means to be an American? More fundamentally, nativist beliefs are the cornerstone of this conflict.

This is not merely a story of opinion shifts or campaign tactics. It is a fight over the soul of the nation—over who gets to define what America is, and who belongs. These are not secondary questions. They are the central political conflict of our time.

Riding the Wave of Nativist Politics

The story of how disaffected White rural Americans found affinity with New York billionaire Donald J. Trump has already been told.[7] We will not retell it here. Instead, we dive deeper and build an explanation for why Donald Trump's nativist appeals found resonance in 2016 and why the politics of nativism has transformed American politics. This is our origin story.

We also will explain why nativism continues to find resonance in 2024. We believe that nativism has been missing from most explanations of the seismic shifts that have redefined contemporary politics. We argue that nativism is the most important driver in this realignment, shifting the Republican Party from the party of America's business class to a (mostly) White nativist party.

So, what drives this? Let's dissect this piece by piece.

Nativism has always been with us, though it is often lurking beneath the political surface. When nativism fades from the political agenda, it does not disappear, it only ceases to be politically relevant in the current moment. Nativism can be latent or manifest at any given moment. Nativism's role in politics ultimately is conditional on other factors.

If Trump was the spark, what was the fuel? What explained the sudden ferocity of nativist politics—not just in America, but around the world? The answer, we argue, lies in a structural alignment: latent beliefs, catalytic conditions, and political entrepreneurship. We call this the **Nativism Activation Model (NAM)** which we display in Figure 1.1.

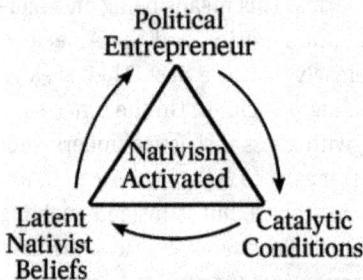

Figure 1.1: Nativism Activation Model.

---

7 There are conflicting accounts about Trump's net worth, in no small part because Trump has deflated his worth for tax purposes and inflated it for banks and insurers. Gerstein, J. (2023, September 26). Trump fraud trial to focus on inflated net worth claims. Politico. https://www.politico.com/news/2023/09/26/trump-fraud-trial-inflate-net-worth-00118269.

The Nativism Activation Model (NAM)

To truly understand why nativism becomes a dominant force in some moments and fades in others, we must look beyond individual politicians and instead focus on the conditions that bring nativism to life. This is the essence of **NAM**—a framework that reveals how nativism transitions from a dormant sentiment to a driving force in politics.

At the heart of this model are three interconnected forces, each a necessary but not sufficient condition for the rise of nativism. When these three elements align, nativism becomes politically powerful, capable of shaping elections, defining political parties, and even transforming national identities.

The First Force: Latent Nativist Beliefs

Nativism begins as a quiet undercurrent—an instinctual preference for native-born citizens over foreign-born ones. These beliefs are not always visible. They lie dormant, often unexpressed, a low hum beneath the noise of everyday politics. For most of American history, this hum has been present, sometimes louder, sometimes barely audible. It is the sense that America should belong to those who were here first, that newcomers must assimilate, or that the culture must be preserved against foreign influence.

These beliefs are as old as the nation itself. In the 1840s, they appeared in the anti-Catholic sentiment of the Know Nothing Party, which feared that Catholic immigrants would undermine American democracy. They reappeared in the 1920s with the rise of immigration restrictions, driven by fears of Eastern European and Asian immigrants. And they have never truly disappeared.

The Second Force: Catalytic Conditions

But latent beliefs alone are not enough. They must be awakened by events—by catalytic conditions that make nativism not just a private sentiment but a public force. These conditions can take many forms, but they share one thing in common: they create a sense of threat.

Sometimes the threat is economic—rising inequality, job losses, or industrial decline that leave whole communities struggling. Sometimes it is cultural—a demographic shift that transforms the face of a neighborhood, or the rise of cultural symbols seen as foreign. Sometimes it is political—a crisis that shakes confidence in national identity.

These shifts can be subtle, overhearing foreign language in the grocery store or witnessing the increasing diversity of local schools or local community events. But they are ever-present and inescapable. Such micro signals can interact with larger shifts in entertainment media to challenge the prevailing social norms.

In the United States, the 2016 election was marked by two such catalytic conditions. First, the foreign-born population reached record levels, with nearly 14% of Americans born outside the country, the highest level since the 1890s. Second, the American economy was shifting from manufacturing to a digital, information-based system, leaving traditional working-class communities behind. In this context, the quiet buzz of nativist beliefs began to grow louder.

The Third Force: Political Entrepreneur

Even with a reservoir of latent beliefs and a catalytic context, nativism does not emerge on its own. It requires a voice—a political entrepreneur—whether individual or organizational—who can identify these conditions, articulate the fears they produce, and transform them into a political force.

In the 1850s, the Know Nothing Party built a political movement out of nativist sentiments. In the 1890s, the Immigration Restriction League gave voice to nativist sentiments.

Donald Trump was this catalyst in 2016. Where other politicians used carefully coded language, Trump spoke directly and without restraint. He framed immigration as an existential threat, promising to build a wall, to deport millions, and to put 'America First.' He gave nativism a voice, and millions responded.

But Trump was not the first, nor will he be the last. Jair Bolsonaro in Brazil, Marine Le Pen in France, Viktor Orbán in Hungary—each has played this role, recognizing the latent power of nativism and bringing it to life.

Nativism Activated: When Three Forces Converge

Our Nativism Activation Model is a lens for understanding how nativism moves from the shadows into the spotlight, from a quiet sentiment to a political wave. It requires the convergence of three forces: the ever-present latent beliefs, the sense of crisis created by catalytic conditions, and the voice of a political entrepreneur who can bring those beliefs to life.

When these three forces align, nativism becomes a dominant force in politics. It shapes voter behavior, defines political parties, and transforms the national de-

bate over who belongs. It is a force that can lie dormant for decades, only to reemerge with sudden, explosive power.

In the chapters that follow, this framework will be our guide. It will help us
understand how nativism became the defining force in American politics, why it
has returned with such intensity, and why it may continue to shape our political
future. We will see that nativism is not just a product of angry voters or manipu-
lative politicians—it is a recurring force, a deep and enduring current that shapes
the very idea of what it means to be an American.

American Identity and Nativism

This is fundamentally a book about what it means to be an American. It is written by two pollsters, one working in industry, the other working in academics,
who witnessed the emergence of nativism as a driving force in American politics. Existing explanations of our shifting political landscape, we felt, only
scratched the surface of how deeply nativism was transforming politics. In this
book, we take a deeper dive, exploring the role of national identity, who counts
as a 'real American,' and why these debates are inescapable in contemporary
politics.

The primary political cleavage in American society today revolves around
this very definition. Roughly speaking, two groups—Republicans and Democrats
—vie for power over these definitional rights—one that longs for an America that
'once was' and the other that imagines what America might become. One group
finds itself in ascension, growing and diversifying, and the other in decline, dwin-
dling and fighting to remain unchanged. Nativist beliefs serve as the cornerstone
of this conflict. They cut to the essence of American identity and what it means to
be American. Ultimately, societal change can threaten identity which, in turn, engenders strong visceral reactions.

Our exploration into this dynamic process starts, but does not end, with the
role that nativism has played in reshaping contemporary American politics. In
Chapter 2, we distinguish nativism from related concepts (e.g., populism, nationalism, and xenophobia). For present purposes, it is enough to note that politicians have historically (and routinely) used nativist appeals as wedge issues, polarizing and dividing the electorate. Donald Trump—with his call to build a big,
beautiful wall that Mexico would pay for—hardly originated this type of campaign appeal. Indeed, much of Trump's 2016 presidential campaign echoed Pat
Buchanan's insurgent primary challenge to President George H.W. Bush in 1992.
In 1992, in a campaign that foreshadowed Trump's 2016 campaign, Buchanan's

America First campaign called for building a fence along the US-Mexico border. In 2024, the Republican vice-presidential nominee, J.D. Vance, echoed Trump's nativist appeals. "What happens when you have massive amounts of illegal immigration?" Vance queried and then answered, citing the movie *Gangs of New York*. "It actually starts to create ethnic conflict. It creates higher crime rates."[8]

Why did Trump succeed, while Buchanan failed, despite running a similar campaign? Context matters. Buchanan was challenging an incumbent president while Trump successfully ran in a crowded but largely homogeneous Republican primary. In a field of professionally vanilla Republican candidates, Trump stood out for his brashness, his authenticity, and his difference. By 2016, the Republican Party had also moved to the right, creating an opening for Donald Trump that eluded Pat Buchanan. Barack Obama's Presidency, once welcomed as a sign of a post-racial America, also racialized politics even on issues like health care that were not previously associated with race (Tesler, 2015, 2019).

True to historical form, Trump's nativist appeals mostly resonated with White, rural voters troubled by what they perceived as threats to an American identity grounded in the Christian religious faith, the disappearance of the American dream, and the loss of a simpler, but more meaningful, way of life. As we will show in subsequent analyses, nativists believe strongly in a traditional American identity but see that identity being undermined by contemporary culture and shifting population demographics. Racial resentment is unquestionably a large part of this story, but it is not the story.

Nativist messages proved to be effective in 2016 and continue to find resonance because social, economic, and political conditions were ripe for such appeals, because they were championed by a political entrepreneur who understood and tapped into the prevailing zeitgeist. According to the estimates we present in Chapter 3, nativists consistently comprise a third of the American electorate. These estimates do not include voters, who we do not categorize as nativists, but are potentially mobilized or persuaded by nativist appeals. Perhaps even more to the point, nativism has increased in electoral importance as the parties have sharply divided along nativist lines. The Republican Party is of increasingly nativist composition; the Democratic Party, in response, is increasingly pro-immigration.

---

8 Flegenheimer, M. (2024, August 18). Vance's immigration stance echoes *Gangs of New York*. The New York Times. https://www.nytimes.com/2024/08/18/us/politics/vance-immigration-gangs-of-new-york.html.

Nativism in America and Around the World

Our starting point is deceptively simple. Nativism is deeply rooted and ever-present, but often dormant. We are hardly the first to make this claim. In his seminal and magisterial work *Strangers in the Land*, John Higham argues that nativism goes through periods of ascendency and dormancy, depending on Americans' confidence that the political system can absorb and assimilate 'new' waves of immigrants (Higham, 1955). A confident America is a welcoming and cosmopolitan nation that believes immigrants can be socialized into America's civic creed and that they can (and will) become Americans. This confidence is rooted in the power of the American ideal, the belief that America is exceptional and that it plays a special role in the contemporary world as beacon of rationality, self-determination, and individual freedom. The power of America is the power to transform immigrants into Americans.

A less confident America, where American identity is less firmly rooted and more subject to challenge, is less welcoming and more fearful of immigrants. If immigrants are often the root source of that fear, the rationalization changes over time. Nativist movements isolate race, religion, or political ideology or some combination of the three as the reason why immigrants cannot (or will not) become Americans. The perceived threats fade with time—Italian and Irish immigrants were once seen as threatening—but, in the moment, they create the necessary (but not sufficient) conditions for nativist political movements. Immigration increases amidst a political and social context defined by economic uncertainty and cultural loss, and among ethnic groups perceived as unlikely to be socialized into the America's foundational beliefs.

While our focus is on American politics, this pattern is hardly unique to the United States. Globalization flattens the world, eases the movement of populations across borders, and, in doing so, presents fundamental challenges to national identity throughout the world. Each nation, we argue, must grapple with questions about who counts as a citizen, who is allowed entry into the country, and what this means for prevailing understandings of national identity. The politics of immigration, to put it bluntly, are battles over the meaning of a nation, and they are as inevitable as they are divisive. In the United States, this battle takes place in the arena of immigration politics. It is fought over who counts as a 'real American.'

The American case is special in this sense. Under the tenets of the American creed, the belief in economic and political freedom, self-governance, and equality of opportunity, what it means to be American has not been as explicitly tied to race and ethnicity. America, with its symbolism reflected by the Statue of Liberty, is a nation of immigrants. Where you were born or who your parents are have, at least in the abstract, mattered much less than what you believed. Historically, the American political identity has been rooted in classic liberal political ideology and individual beliefs in individual freedom, economic markets, equality of opportunity, limited government, and self-governance.

In contemporary politics, each of these ideas has been challenged, as has the myth of American exceptionalism—the belief that America occupies a special place in world. Nativism arises as a reaction to a changing American national identity, just as the unraveling of the American national identity increased the resonance of nativist appeals. The causal arrows run in both directions. If the ideas that define a traditional understanding of what it means to be an American are in question, what does it mean to be an American? This, we contend, is the defining political question of contemporary politics.

Question for our Book

Our reflections above beg very fundamental questions by making simplifying assumptions. To wit, we ask and attempt to answer three questions:
1. What is nativism?
2. How has it shaped, and how does it continue to shape, contemporary US politics?
3. What does a politics rooted in nativism mean for the future of American politics?

Pollster as Cartographer

Our objective is to tell the contemporary story of nativism in the United States and to place it within a broader historical and global context. We aim to map the contours of nativism in America today. In pursuit of this goal, we have conducted over 40 polls in more than 30 countries over the last decade. Our work has generated dozens of papers, op-eds, and reports—built on a foundation of blood, sweat, and intellectual investment.

This project has two core tasks: definition and measurement. The first is to define nativism and establish a reliable metric for capturing it. Since the early moments of Trump's rise in 2015, we have tested a nativist index—proven effective across contexts, both in the United States and globally. The second task is to show nativism's impact—how it shapes politics, evolves over time, and extends across borders. Our focus is not just on identifying nativism but on understanding its dynamic presence as a force that transcends national boundaries.

This book embodies the highest aspirations of the polling profession. Pollsters are not just technicians fixated on nailing the next election. They are cartographers of public opinion, mapping the unseen terrain of beliefs, fears, and hopes that drive societies. Our work is not just about data collection; it is about making sense of complex realities. We ask fundamental questions: Why did Trump's rise resonate with such intensity? What makes nativism endure? Our analysis goes beyond measurement—it brings these questions to life through narrative context and vivid examples.

In the chapters that follow, we define nativism and show how to measure it. We demonstrate its influence on vote choice and identity, disentangle it from racism, authoritarianism, and populism, and trace its global spread. We explore how it rises, when it recedes, and why it endures. Ultimately, we argue that nativism is not a temporary fever—it is a permanent structure within American and global politics.

Nativist Nation: Book Outline

In this book, we unpack the underlying belief system that brought Trump to power and connect nativism to fundamental questions about American identity. The primary political cleavage in American society today revolves around the definition of what America is and is not. Our present politics is defined by this cleavage and the partisan split between a Republican Party that defines what it means to be an American by looking to the past and a Democratic Party that defines what it means to be an American by looking to the future. Our thesis is relatively straightforward: Nativist sentiments are ever-present but often lay dormant. Economic and social conditions bring these sentiments bubbling to the surface until, recognizing the opportunity, a political entrepreneur, alert to the possibilities of changing political conditions, awakens and mobilizes them. Waves of immigration, as indicated by increases in the foreign-born population, create the necessary (but not sufficient) condition for nativist politics. To fully emerge, nativist politics demands a conducive social, economic, and political context, and a political entrepreneur willing and able to take advantage of that context.

Contemporary politics revolves around the conflict over who counts (and who does not) as an American. Nativist beliefs are the cornerstone of this conflict. They cut to the essence of American identity. By nativism, we mean a predisposition to favor native-born citizens over foreign ones. Nativism has always been part of the American experience. At times, it has manifested itself more strongly; at other times, it has waited patiently in the background. The ebbs and flows of nativist expression have typically followed broader immigration patterns—when immigration was up, nativist expression was manifest in politics. Take the Know Nothing movement of the 1840s or the Chinese restriction acts of the 1880s as examples.

Today, America finds itself again confronted with historically high immigration levels. The number of foreign-born residents is higher than at any time in American history, while the proportion of foreign-born residents is higher than at any time since the 1890s, a period of industrialization, rapid population growth, and demographic change (Hirschman & Mogford, 2009). As was the case then, the nativist backlash today has been fierce. Writing in 1908, for example, Henry Cabot Lodge observed that "Every day we read in newspapers of savage murders by members of secret societies composed of alien immigrants. Can we doubt in the presence of such horrible facts as these, the need of stringent laws and rigid enforcement, to exclude the criminals and anarchists of foreign countries from the United States?"[9] Interestingly, Europe is experiencing a profound influx of immigration and there we see an emergent nativist politics as well. The social forces that bind our world have well-grounded truths that lead to similar manifestations. Ultimately, immigration threatens identity, which engenders strong visceral reactions.

Nativism maps neatly, but imperfectly, on to the underlying racial resentments that mark contemporary American politics. Conventional wisdom, prior to Trump's candidacy, was that race-based appeals needed to be implicit, more of a dog whistle than a bullhorn. By focusing on immigration, especially illegal immigration, nativism allows racial grievance to be expressed explicitly in a more socially acceptable way and at an unprotected target (illegal immigrants). Trump's nativist rhetoric, seen in this light, gave voters permission to express prejudice forcefully and openly. Racism and nativism are not, however, interchangeable. Nativism casts a much wider net and extols a much smaller penalty as a violation of social norms.

The past decade has witnessed a seismic shift in American politics, giving rise to populist political leaders and threatening the pluralistic foundations of American democracy. This shift was the result of a politics rooted in nativist public opinion; activated by nativist political appeals and articulated by strategic political leaders; and given resonance by globalization, the cultural backlash against globalization, and the loss of the American identity caused by shifting population demographics. In the following chapters, we tell this story using original survey data collected by Ipsos, one of the world's leading public opinion firms and a leader in recognizing and identifying the importance in nativism in contemporary politics. We supplement our survey data with contextual data that helps tell the story of how (and why) conditions ripened, how Donald Trump successfully

---

9 Speech by Henry Cabot Lodge on immigration. *The North American Review. 161*(2). https://nrs.lib.harvard.edu/urn-3:fhcl:1076595.

tapped into the undercurrent of nativist opinion, and why Trump's defeat in 2020 failed to mitigate the critical role nativism plays in contemporary politics. In what follows we provide a brief outline of the book:

– Chapter 2, 'What Nativism Is (and What It Isn't) Conceptual Definitions and Origins' provides a brief history of nativism in American politics, defines nativism, and compares our definition of nativism to related terms (e.g., nationalism, xenophobia, racism). Connecting that history to the contemporary context helps explain why, even though nativist appeals were hardly new, Donald Trump's appeals resonated in 2016. Nativism has a long history in American politics beginning with the American founding and Benjamin Franklin's concerns about German influence over the emerging republic. It continues into the progressive movement and the Know Nothing Party, extends into prohibition, World War I and World War II, and reemerges in the 1990s and early 2000s. Chapter 2 provides a brief overview of this history to help set the stage for Trump's emergence in 2016. We more fully address Trump's emergence in Chapter 4.

We also define our terms in Chapter 2, providing a conceptual definition of nativism and distinguishing it from other related concepts. A conceptual definition is, at first glance, relatively straightforward. Nativism refers to the general orientation that gives preference to native-born populations over foreign-born populations. But who counts as 'native-born'? The origins of the American polity as a nation of immigrants confounds simple definitions. In the 1840s, for example, nativist movements were decidedly anti-Catholic. Catholicism was seen as a threat to the American way of life when national identity was defined largely as Protestant and Anglo-Saxon. As this example shows, who counts (and who doesn't count) as an American has shifted over time.

Because nativism is closely related to other concepts (e.g., authoritarianism, populism, and racism) we also take time to draw conceptual distinctions between these terms. In doing so, we explain why describing the United States as a 'nativist nation' makes more sense than describing it as an authoritarian or populist nation, and why nativism reaches beyond racism as an influence in contemporary American politics.

– In Chapter 3, 'Who is a Nativist? The Contours of a Nativist Nation,' we move beyond conceptual definitions and into the empirics, providing an operational definition of nativism in the United States. Operationally, nativism is defined as a set of attitudes toward foreign-born populations, including whether the country would be better off if 'we stopped immigration,' whether employers should prioritize the hiring of native-born Americans over foreign-born populations, and whether immigrants take jobs from 'real Americans.' We demonstrate that our measure of nativism is valid, meaning it accurately measures anti-immigrant attitudes, and reliable, meaning it consistently measures these attitudes across space and time. While nativism is correlated with other related concepts (populism/anti-elite attitudes, perceptions the system is broken, authoritarianism, and White grievance), it remains conceptually distinct. We show in Chapter 5 that nativism is a powerful explanation for the shifts in contemporary politics. We conclude the chapter distinguishing between nativists and non-nativists on a range of demographic indicators, political orientations, and policy preferences, and we define the size and scope of the nativist nation.

– In Chapter 4, 'Why Now? The (Re)Emergence of Nativism' we explore the reemergence of nativism during the 2016 campaign and provide an explanation for why nativism has resurfaced now. First, while the economy was relatively strong in 2016 when measured by objective economic indicators, economic growth and prosperity were unevenly distributed. Longer term, the transformation of the economy from a manufacturing to a digital information-based economy, left traditional working-class communities unsettled. Rural, mostly White, communities throughout the country were mired in economic insecurity and job loss while simultaneously experiencing population stagnation and loss. Second, and perhaps even more importantly, there was a pervasive sense that what it meant to be American was shifting in ways that excluded many of these residents. They no longer recognized the America they grew up in and nostalgically longed for a mythical America of their past. This mythical America may have never really existed, but it loomed large in the political consciousness of Americans who longed to 'make America great again.' Overall, the political, social, and economic conditions provided fertile ground for nativist political appeals. To take root, however, the movement demanded a political entrepreneur able to recognize and take advantage of the moment. When Donald Trump declared his candidacy for President of the United States, he stepped squarely and firmly into a political context ready to embrace his populist and nativist appeals.

In this chapter, we explain why Trump's nativist appeals found resonance in 2016, how nativism fundamentally reshaped politics in the United States, and how it continues to influence public opinion during the Biden Administration. Trump neither created the nativist sentiments he exploited, nor have they disappeared with his 2020 election loss. In concluding the chapter, we show the continued relevance of nativism as a political force.

– In Chapter 5, 'Why Nativism Matters? How Nativism Conditions Politics' we explore the political consequences of nativism. Over the past decade, nativism has defined contemporary politics. In this chapter, we begin by tracing the origins of this shift to the fight over Barack Obama's birth certificate led by Donald Trump.

By questioning the legitimacy of President Obama's birth, Trump raised questions about whether Obama was a real American and, subsequently, whether his presidency was legitimate. If this mostly seemed like a curious and clownish sideshow, it helped set the stage for the nativist politics that followed. If a subset of voters were willing to question the legitimacy of a duly elected president, was it unreasonable to think that they would also question the legitimacy of their fellow citizens? Of elections won by 'illegal votes'? Of an economy rigged against 'real Americans'?

Nativist appeals flowed seamlessly out of the conspiracy theories over President Barack Obama's birthplace and legitimacy as president, and they resonated among voters who feared 'hope and change,' preferring instead an America they remembered nostalgically from their childhood. Using original survey data, we show the powerful effects nativism has had on voter turnout and voting behavior, mobilizing voters angry about a changing political culture, and aligning them with the Donald Trump-led Republican Party. Nativism, we contend, was not part of the story explaining Trump's hostile takeover of the Republican Party and ascendency to the US presidency, it was the story. Nor were the effects limited to Donald Trump; instead, they influenced Republican voting in down-ballot races, including congressional and statewide elections.

In reshaping contemporary politics, nativist attitudes do more than influence individual voting decisions, they influence a range of other attitudes and behaviors, including support for government spending, populist/anti-elite beliefs, and confidence in the political system. In this chapter, we explore these consequences to explain why nativism is a such a powerful force in contemporary politics.

With Donald Trump's defeat in 2020, one might have expected nativism to recede as a political force. Such an interpretation, we contend, is a misreading of our current political environment. As the 2024 presidential election illustrates, The forces that gave rise to nativism—economic globalization, population shifts, and cultural change—have not receded. We should not expect nativism as political current to fade soon. Moreover, it powerfully affects other attitudes and behaviors that define contemporary politics. A nativist nation is an aggrieved nation. Nativism gives grievances force and direction that extends beyond racism, captures populist anti-elite sentiments, and animates authoritarian impulses.

– Because race has played such a central chapter in American politics, we address the relationship between racial resentment and nativism in greater detail Chapter 6, 'Racism by Another Name? The Politics of Nativism and White Grievance.' Is nativism just racism by another name? Nativism does not exist in a vacuum. It festers with other beliefs. The politics of grievance is multifaceted. Nativism just so happens to be the more easily digestible dog whistle. It also mixes with authoritarian beliefs and perceptions that the system is broken, creating a highly combustible cocktail of political attitudes.

Central to the discussion is the interplay between nativism and White grievance. Racial resentment has long been a powerful force in American politics shaping attitudes toward welfare spending, party support, and political trust. While nativism and White grievance are conceptually distinct (see Chapter 2), there is considerable overlap. Nativist appeals work to cue White grievance through a more socially acceptable mechanism.

– Identity courses throughout our understanding of nativism. In Chapter 7, 'Who Are the Real Americans? How Americans Define Who Counts as an American,' we explore how nativism reflects and shapes public understandings of national identity. For nativists, national identity is deeply rooted in a nostalgic understanding of the past. In this reimagining, the American past (usually associated with their childhood) is Lake Woebegone with low crime, widespread economic prosperity, and political and social civility. Public life was guided by traditional morals and values. Nativists fear that we are either losing this America or that it is already lost.

Using empirical measures of national identity, we examine the relationship between nativism and the values that define American national identity. Nativist and non-nativist, we demonstrate, have very different ideas about what it means to be an American and what values an American should (must) embrace. In writing this chapter, we offer a corrective to what we see as a common misperception. Nativism does not simply reflect national identity; it also gives national identity its shape and meaning. The United States is a nativist nation.

We use original polling data to investigate who Americans believe is a 'real American,' to better understand the characteristics that individuals associate with being a 'real American' and how those characteristics differ for nativist (*versus* non-nativist) respondents. Overall, there are wide gaps between nativists and non-nativists, and Republicans and Democrats, in terms of who they believe is a real American. Specifically, we want to understand the contours of citizenship—who is and is not real American *and* how the nativist nation defines it.

– In Chapter 8, 'Not So Exceptional After All? Nativism Goes Global,' we explore the consequences of nativism throughout the world. How pervasive is nativism? In a word, it is everywhere. Even in the most unlikely places. Nativist sentiments have emerged throughout the world. In Brazil with Jair Bolsonaro, in Great Britain with Nigel Farage's Brexit Party/Reform UK, in France with Marine Le Pen, in Hungary with Viktor Orbán, even in Sweden. But nativism is more prevalent in some places than others. It takes different shapes and forms.

Why has nativism played a role in reshaping politics in some places but not others? In this chapter, we explore differences in nativist attitudes across 28 different countries with an eye toward explaining cross-national differences. We begin by mapping nativist attitudes across countries and identifying potential causal explanations for these spatial differences. Second, we model nativist attitudes considering both structural/contextual factors (populations shifts, macro-economic conditions, and political rhetoric) and individual-level predictors (age, pocketbook finances, economic perceptions, and party support). Our models reveal that nativist attitudes are a function of both the social and economic conditions within an individual country as well as individual demographics. Nativist appeals find greatest resonance when conditions are ripe and when political elites cue these attitudes so that they drive political evaluations. The specific shape and form of nativism is conditional on place, so we see nativism take different forms in Latin America, the United States, and Europe.

While our focus in the book is primarily on the United States, this comparative analysis helps to better understand the American context. Successful nativist movements require the right conditions to take hold, a leader who recognizes and is willing to make nativist appeals, and a public receptive to the message.

– Finally, in Chapter 9, 'Conclusions: The Future of Nativism' we explore why we think nativism will continue to play a prominent role in American politics. Nativism has been a powerful force throughout the history of American politics. Yet, if the presence of nativism is a constant, its political influence varies across time and space. In earlier chapters, we show that nativism remains a powerful force in American politics. But does this mean that nativism will remain a driver of politics into the future? In this concluding chapter, we give thought to the conditions that are necessary for a transition from nativist politics to whatever is next. For nativism to fade in importance, America must once again become a confident and cosmopolitan, willing to look outward to embrace an international role and to welcome immigrants seeking to embrace the American dream. The current state of American politics makes that seem unlikely but, even if nativism does fade in importance, it will likely reemerge in the future but with a different definition of what it means to be an American and who is (and who is not) included in that definition.

Chapter 2
What Nativism Is? (and What It Isn't): Conceptual Definitions and Origins Vignette: Pollster Insights

As pollsters, the more we delved into the data, the deeper we looked, the more we realized that American politics was nativist. Trump had figured that out. Mostly rural, mostly White Americans wanted to hit the pause button on the cultural changes that were (re)defining the world around them. They wanted to hold on to what it means to be an American, to live in the community they grew up in, to adhere to a set of traditional moral and cultural values. Immigration served as a useful explanation for why the world was changing around them, and nativism provided a simple solution for keeping larger cultural changes at bay. Build a wall, stop immigrants from illegally crossing into the US, and keep your local community and your country from losing its identity.

In this chapter, we provide a brief history of nativism in the United States and define nativism conceptually. In doing so, we differentiate nativism from other related concepts (nationalism, national identity, xenophobia, populism, authoritarianism, and racial resentment). In the next chapter, we outline our operational definition and demonstrate its reliably and validity. Here, our focus is on the conceptual. Our conceptual definition is, at first glance, relatively straightforward. Nativism refers to the general orientation that gives preference to native-born populations over foreign-born populations. But, in a nation of immigrants, who counts as 'native-born'? These definitional concerns are not trivial, but instead go to the core of contemporary politics. A politics rooted in nativism raises fundamental questions about national identity. Who counts as an American? Is it based on an ethnocultural understanding of identity, rooted in birthplace and ancestry (i.e., blood and soil)? Or is it rooted in civic understandings, based on embracing an American creed composed of individualism, economic and political freedom, equality before the law, and equality of opportunity? A politics rooted in nativism makes right-wing populist politics possible, it lays the foundation for authoritarian appeals (Trump made the comment "I alone can fix it" in his 2016 acceptance speech at the Republican National Convention),[10] and it cues racial resentment. As we show in Chapter 3, the concepts we outline here are not just conceptually related, they are also empirically linked in contemporary politics.

---

10 Politico Staff. (2016, July 21). Full text: Donald Trump 2016 RNC draft speech transcript. https://www.politico.com/story/2016/07/full-transcript-donald-trump-nomination-acceptance-speech-at-rnc-225974.

https://doi.org/10.1515/9783111384047-002

The origins of the American polity, as a nation of immigrants, confounds simple definitions. In the 1840s, nativist movements were decidedly anti-Catholic. Catholicism was seen as a threat to the American way of life when American national identity was largely defined as Protestant and Anglo-Saxon.[11] Nativist sentiments are hardly new to American politics, but who counts (and who doesn't count) as an American has shifted over time, as have the meanings of America's foundational beliefs in freedom, individualism, and self-governance. In this chapter, we connect nativist politics to the question of 'who counts' as an American, investigating the racial and ethnic implications of these definitions and the ideological foundations of American national identity. In doing so, we set the stage for subsequent chapters investigating the causes and consequences of nativism.

Nativist Politics and the Melting Pot

America as a melting pot, a loose collection of immigrants bound together by a common set of ideals, serves as a foundational myth in the telling of American political history (Gleason, 1964).[12] The Statue of Liberty physically embodies this myth with her call to bring "your tired, your poor, Your huddled mass yearning to breathe free."[13] The myth is embodied in the American creed, the commonly held belief that what makes someone an American is the embrace of American ideals—freedom, democracy, and individualism—and not who they are or where they came from. The American creed, in turn, serves as the foundation for American exceptionalism. The 'conservative' American revolution, the absence of a feudal past, and an expansive Western frontier made the United States unique in its history and its embrace of individual freedom, the rule of law, and equality of opportunity. To say that someone is 'American' imbues them with a set of beliefs rather than a racial or ethnic identity. To say that someone is un-American is similarly infused with meaning about what someone believes (or chooses not to believe). As a nation of immigrants, American identity has been rooted in ideology as much as it has been tethered to birthplace or ethnicity.

---

11 As late as 1960, it was unclear whether a Catholic could be elected president. As a Catholic, John F. Kennedy had to prove his electability in the West Virginia primary, a heavily Protestant state.

12 The specific phrase originated in Israel Zangwill's 1908 play *The Melting-Pot*. Zangwill, I. (1909). *The Melting-Pot: Drama in Four Acts*. New York: The Macmillan Company. Retrieved from https://www.loc.gov/item/09007333/.

13 Lazarus, Emma. *The New Colossus*. https://www.poetryfoundation.org/poems/46550/the-new-colossus.

Scholars of American identity distinguish between the ethnocultural origins of national identity, rooted in birth and ancestry (i.e., blood and soil), and the civic origins, rooted in ideas and institutions (Brubaker, 1990; Wright et al., 2012). Assignment to an ethnic national identity is ascriptive and objective, while assignment to a civic national identity is elective and based on the acceptance of core beliefs and political institutions. Germany and Japan reflect the ethnocultural ideal where birth and ancestry define whether one is (or is not) a member of the nation. France and the United States, in contrast, better reflect the civic ideal, where belonging is defined by acceptance of ideas and institutions. As Brubaker (1990) explains in a comparison of France and Germany, "the French citizenry is defined expansively, as a territorial community, the German citizenry restrictively, as a community of descent" (Brubaker, 1990). As a result, the French welcomed new immigrants allowing second-generation immigrants to become citizens. Germany provided no provisions for second-generation immigrants to become citizens.

The American mythology embraces the civic ideal of national identity. In practice, however, civic and ethnocultural understandings of national identity collide. Throughout the history of American politics—and not just in the contemporary era, the question of who counts as an American has often been the subject of fierce debate, reflecting fundamental differences over who should be allowed membership into the nation as a citizen. These debates reflect fundamental distinctions between exclusive definitions of citizenship based on 'blood and soil' and inclusive definitions based on one's willingness to subscribe to a core set of political beliefs. In comparative studies, ethnic definitions of national identity are associated with anti-immigration attitudes while ethnocultural definitions are associated with pro-immigration attitudes (Ceobanu & Escandell, 2008; Pehrson et al., 2009; Wright, 2011). Questions of national identity are intractably linked to immigration policy and attitudes.

Beyond questions of national identity, one of the myths embedded into the American political culture is that of the melting pot. Historically, the melting pot has had multiple meanings: (1) the blending together of distinct cultures into a single culture, or (2) the assimilation (or melting) of other cultures into an 'exceptional' American political culture (Gordon, 2010). If this seems like a trivial distinction, it is not. The melting pot as a blender of cultures yields a new and unique identity out of ethnic differences. New immigrants change the existing identity into a new and improved identity that takes the best from multiple cultural influences. Under this conception, our differences make us stronger. This is an oversimplification, but we might think of this in terms of food. Under this meaning, new immigrants bring new foods and flavors adding to the rich abundance of existing cuisines and fusing those flavors into something new and better.

In contrast, the melting pot as an assimilator takes these differences and forges them into an already well-defined and broadly accepted American identity. New immigrants, according to this view, must learn what it means to be an American, they must learn the language while embracing American values and conforming to existing social, political, and cultural norms. The melting pot forges them into an existing understanding of American national identity. Returning to our food analogy, new immigrants would leave their existing cuisines and learn to eat American foods. They would not add to or alter existing cuisines.

Despite the melting pot mythologies and the ethnocultural definition of national identity it assumes, the United States has long been hostile to immigrants and often viscerally opposed to new immigration, particularly immigrants who are seen as threatening the cultural heritage that defines American identity or who pose a threat to American political institutions (Anbinder, 2006; Gerber & Kraut, 2005; Higham, 1955; Young, 2017). Perhaps stated differently, if the mythology of American identity is based on acceptance of the American creed, the political reality has been much different. The meaning of American identity has been, and is, fiercely contested.

The Origins of America's Nativist Nation

If debates over national identity are as common as they are inevitable, is the US a nativist nation? Or is there a nativist nation within the United States? We contend that there is a nativist nation within the United States, Americans who believe that American national identity should be based on birth and ancestry rather than civic ideals. In this respect, they define what it means to be an American in ascriptive terms. These are the birthers, led by Donald Trump, who believed Barack Obama was not born in the United States, was subsequently not a 'real American,' and was not qualified to be president.[14] For America's nativist nation, identity is defined not by ideals, but by who is excluded based on birthplace and cultural heritage. In 2020, Trump raised similar questions about the birthplace of Vice President Kamala Harris. In 2024, he questioned the citizenship of his Republican primary opponent, former South Carolina Governor Nikki Haley. In questioning the citizenship of his political competitors, Trump

---

14 Fifty-eight percent of Republicans either believed Obama was not born in the United States (28 percent) or said they were unsure if he was born in the United States (30 percent). Thrush, G. (2009, July 31). 58 percent of GOP not sure/doubt Obama born in US. POLITICO. https://www.polit ico.com/blogs/glennthrush/0709/58_of_GOP_not_suredont_beleive_Obama_born_in_US_Page2.html.

appeals to voters who have a restrictive and exclusive understanding of what it means to be an American.

If the meaning of America's cultural heritage, and who is included in that heritage, has shifted over time, nativist reactions to these cultural threats have not (Schrag, 2010). During periods of increased immigration, when American identity has been threatened by cultural change, nativism has proven to be a powerful, recurring, and predictable force in American politics. It is often made more powerful when it is associated with conspiratorial beliefs that immigrants are infiltrating the political system to overthrow or undermine American democracy (Dickey, 2023; Higham, 1955). Under this logic, immigrants are seen not only as culturally different, they present a fundamental challenge to the political, economic, and social order. Periods when immigration has surged are often when nativist appeals have found traction, garnered public attention, and spurred political rhetoric aimed at protecting what nativist populations believe it means to be an American.

We are in such a period now. In raw numbers, there are more foreign-born residents in the United States than at any time in American history (See Figure 2.1). In relative terms, the percentage of foreign-born residents is higher than at any time since the late 1800s. As a result, foreign-born Americans now comprise a larger share of the American population than at any other point in American history. These are the conditions that give nativism resonance and give rise to a fierce nativist backlash. At times during our history, the backlash against nativism has included stripping immigrants of their citizenship or deporting naturally-born US citizens because of their ethnicity; or, in the case of women, because of their marriage to someone who was not a US citizen (Frost, 2021). During the Eisenhower Administration, under the auspices of Operation Wetback, approximately 1.3 million Mexican immigrants were deported.[15] Donald Trump's current call for "mass deportation now,"[16] which involves the deportation of between 15–20 million immigrants, fits within this broader political history. It is a difference in scale, partly because the scale is itself larger, rather than a difference in kind.

The relationship between waves of immigration and nativism is relatively straightforward. Nativism grows whenever foreign-born populations are large enough to be noticed and when they pose a political, cultural, or economic threat

15 Blakemore, E. (2018, March 23). The largest mass deportation in American history. History. com. https://www.history.com/news/operation-wetback-eisenhower-1954-deportation.
16 Rose, Joel. & Martínez-Beltrán, Sergio. (2024, August 14). Trump touts historic deportation plans, but his own record reveals big obstacle. https://www.npr.org/2024/08/14/nx-s1-5037992/ trump-immigrants-border-mass-deportation-presidential-race-migrants.

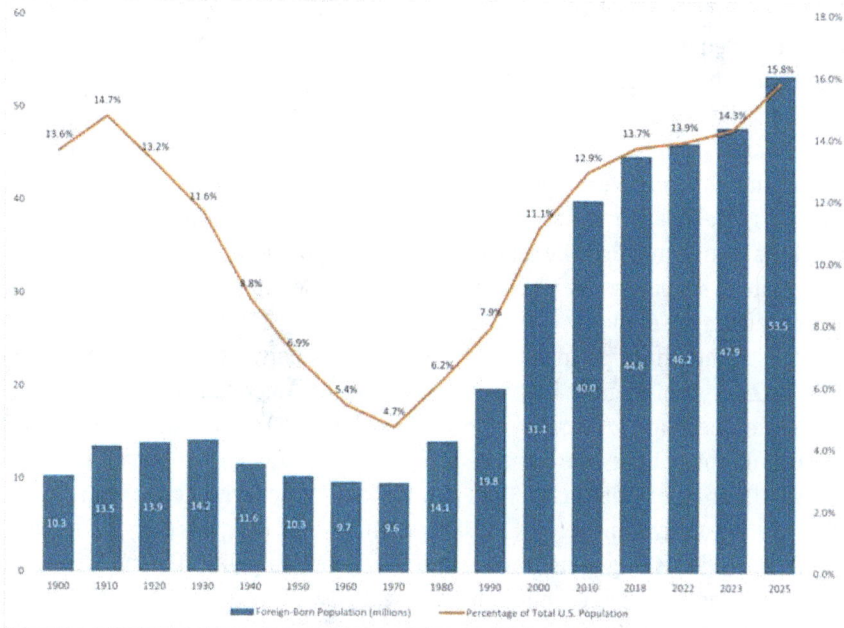

Figure 2.1: Percent and Number of Foreign-Born Immigrants in the United States (Source: Census Bureau & Center for Immigration Studies).

to native populations. Recognizing the importance of local context and stress on local infrastructure, Texas Governor Greg Abbott put immigrants on buses and sent them to pro-immigration cities. According to a January 2024 press release, under the auspices of Operation Lone Star, Texas had bused over 100,000 immigrants to cities across the country, including Chicago, New York, Washington DC, Philadelphia, and Denver. The goal was to spread the costs of immigration to communities not located on the border, and to move the immigration policy toward stricter border policies and more secure borders.[17] In February 2024, New York Mayor Eric Adams called for an end to New York's status as a sanctuary city.[18]

---

17 Goodman, J.D., Collins, K., Sandoval, E., and White, J. (2024, July 20). Abbott Texas migrant buses. The New York Times. https://www.nytimes.com/2024/07/20/us/abbott-texas-migrant-buses.html.
18 Ngo, E. (2024, February 27). Adams calls for change to New York City's sanctuary city laws in harshest statement yet. Politico. https://www.politico.com/news/2024/02/27/adams-sanctuary-city-laws-new-york-00143705.

Nativism waxes and wanes depending on the size of the foreign-born population and whether immigrant groups are seen as a threat to the American political culture, or the economic or political system. As note in our Nativist Activation Model in chapter 1, cultural threats matter much more than economic threats, though large economic shifts (e.g., industrialization in the 1890s, the transition to an information-based economy in the 1990s) influence perceptions of cultural threat. As a political force, nativism is most potent when it challenges native understandings of national identity and when native populations believe the American way of life is slipping away. These perceptions are tied to, but not determined, by broad shifts in the economy.

It is during these periods that the boundaries between civic and ethnocultural definitions of identity become less clear as the American creed becomes entangled in questions of ancestry and race (Smith, 1997). At various times, ethnic and racial groups have been seen as incapable of embracing American ideals because of their race or ethnicity. The Founders questioned whether Germans could embrace republican principles. Irish Catholics, with allegiance to the papacy, were seen as unwilling to assimilate into the American political culture. Nor, for various reasons, could one count on Chinese, Polish, Italian, or Jewish Americans to fully embrace the US Constitution or an American identity rooted in the core beliefs of freedom, individualism, and free markets (Goldstein, 2018). This is a common refrain throughout the history of nativism, including recent charges made against Hispanic immigrants (Huntington, 2004), that they are unwilling to learn the English language or assimilate into the American political culture.

The story of Springfield, Ohio in 2024 is instructive. Donald Trump made Springfield famous by falsely claiming that Haitian immigrants were eating dogs and cats. The claim was reinforced by his vice-presidential nominee, JD Vance. The reality in Springfield, however, was more complicated. Over the last several years, more than 12,000 Haitian immigrants moved to Springfield in search of jobs, straining schools, roads, and health care, creating a perception that the local community was being overrun, and increasing ethnic tensions.[19] The Haitians who moved to Springfield were legal immigrants provided Temporary Protected Status to immigrants from countries in political, social, or economic crisis. Their protected status allowed them to work legally and provided government benefits like food stamps. They gravitated to Springfield because Springfield was expanding and needed workers, but they also taxed local infrastructure, increased local housing costs, and

---

19 Jordan, M. (2024, September 14). Haitian migrants in Springfield, Ohio. The New York Times. https://www.nytimes.com/2024/09/14/us/haitian-migrants-springfield-ohio.html.

threatened to change the culture of the local community. These are the conditions that make a nativist backlash likely and that give political force to America's nativist nation. In Springfield, the ideals of the American melting pot and a civic definition of national identity met the pavement of political reality and ethnocultural definitions. Were immigrants who embraced the American dream real Americans? Or did their ancestry preclude them from a shared national identity?

As was the case in Springfield, immigration often becomes the foundation of conspiratorial beliefs (Dickey, 2023). Catholics, with allegiance to Rome, would overturn a democratic political system. Marxist radicals from Eastern Europe would use strikes and riots to disrupt the economic system. If such claims seem far removed from contemporary politics, Donald Trump, with support from Elon Musk, has claimed that Joe Biden and the Democratic Party allow illegal immigration as a concerted effort to increase Democratic vote shares.[20] QAnon alternatively (and more malignantly) claims that migrant children are being brought to the US as part of a sex-trafficking ring, feeding the larger conspiracy theory of pedophilia rings controlled by elite Democrats.[21] More broadly, immigration is commonly believed to be part of an elite effort to diversify culture and society at the expense of the native-born White population (Gaston & Uscinski, 2018). At the same time, Trump was claiming Haitian immigrants were abducting and eating cats and dogs, he was also claiming Venezuelan gangs had taken over the city of Aurora, Colorado. If elected president, he promised, militarized deportations would begin in Aurora and Springfield. In 2025, President Trump made deportations, often without due process, a reality.

The Varieties of Nativism

As this brief history reveals, nativism can take various forms, targeting different religious, political, or ethnic groups. The *religious nativism* directed at Catholic and Jewish populations is now frequently directed at Muslims (Payne, 2017). Speaking to Fox News' Sean Hannity in January 2016 while still a presidential candidate, Donald Trump commented that "Assimilation has been very hard. It's almost, I won't say nonexistent, but it gets to be pretty close. And I'm talking

---

20 Gold, M. (2024, March 2). Trump Makes Baseless Claims About Immigration and Voter Fraud. The New York Times. https://www.nytimes.com/2024/03/02/us/politics/trump-immigration-voter-fraud.html.

21 Jordan. M. (2022, March 9). QAnon Joins Vigilantes at the Southern Border. The New York Times. https://www.nytimes.com/2022/05/09/us/border-qanon-arizona.html.

about second and third generation — for some reason there's no real assimilation."[22] Islam, according to nativist logic, is incompatible with individual freedom and liberal democracy, thus it presents a threat beyond the mere presence of immigrant populations (Betz, 2017a; Hervik, 2015). A low-level nativist response is the fear that Muslim immigrants will not assimilate and threaten the culture as a result. A more conspiratorial nativist belief is that Muslim immigrants are coming to the US with the purpose of undermining (or attacking) the political or economic system, and to impose Sharia Law.[23]

More generally, *political nativism* is directed at ideological groups, communist and socialist, perceived as too radical and too incongruent with an American political ideology that valued individual freedom, capitalism, and self-governance. For example, after World War I, nativism was targeted at communists, socialists, and anarchists. *Ethnic or racial nativism* is directed at racial minorities, often targeted groups seen as unwilling (or unable) to assimilate. The lines between forms of nativism are often thin and overlapping. The common theme across nativist movements, whatever the target, is that groups are seen as outsiders and as cultural and political threats to the American way of life and to a democratic political system. Economics is part of the story, but nativism's economic origins are less important than cultural threats and fears that immigrants are undermining what it means to be an American (Bergquist, 1986; Betz, 2019; Higham, 1955; Mutz, 2018; Norris & Inglehart, 2019). Economic vulnerability is not, however, entirely disconnected from perceptions of cultural decline or status threat (Davis et al., 2019a; Goldstein & Peters, 2014). Regardless, in these moments, nativism becomes a blunt instrument for combatting social change and maintaining political control. As Colin Dickey concludes in *Under the Eye of Power* (Dickey, 2023):

> Conspiracy theories have also been a regular tool in maintaining and regulating how America will accept and integrate new populations, from religious to ethnic groups. Every time a traditionally marginalized segment of America has attempted to fight for equity, conspiracy theories have been used to suppress or curtail that fight.

We have made the case that nativism is hardly new, that the targets of nativism have shifted over time, but we have yet to define it. In his seminal account of the

---

22 DelReal, J. A. (2016, June 15). Trump claims assimilation among American Muslims is 'close' to 'non-existent.' The Washington Post. https://www.washingtonpost.com/news/post-politics/wp/2016/06/15/trump-claims-assimilation-among-american-muslims-is-close-to-non-existent/.

23 Hauslohner, A. (2016, November 5). How a series of fringe anti-Muslim conspiracy theories went mainstream — via Donald Trump. The Washington Post. https://www.washingtonpost.com/national/how-a-series-of-fringe-anti-muslim-conspiracy-theories-went-mainstream--via-donald-trump/2016/11/05/7c366af6-8bf0-11e6-bf8a-3d26847eeed4_story.html.

history of nativism, John Higham defines nativism as "intense opposition to an internal minority on the ground of its foreign (i.e., 'un-American') connections." We define it more simply as support for policies or actions that favor the rightful inhabitants of a country (Betz, 2017a); or in the case of the United States, 'real Americans.' This definition helps us to distinguish nativism from other related concepts (e.g., nationalism, xenophobia, populism, authoritarianism, and racism).

Nativism is not populism, though it often plays an accompanying role in right-wing populist movements. Nativism is not nationalism, though it often reflects differences in how individuals define what it means to be an American. Nativism is not racism. Though the targets of nativist impulses are often racially or ethnically distinct, nativism can also be directed at religion or ideology. We present simple definitions in Table 2.1. Below, we describe each of these concepts and distinguish them from nativism. It is important to note at the outset that there is considerable overlap across these definitions. If we imagine the terms as a series of Venn diagrams, we would see considerable overlap across terms. For example, nativism is an exclusionary form of nationalism (which can also be inclusive). Xenophobia, in contrast, is a pernicious and extreme form of nativism where favoritism toward in-groups is combined with 'fear of strangers.'

Table 2.1: Definitions of Nativism and Related Terms.

Term	Definition
Nativism	Support for policies or actions that favor the rightful inhabitants of a country or in the case of the United States, 'real Americans.' Nativism can take various forms. *Racial nativism* targets groups based on their race or ethnicity, *religious nativism* targets groups based on religious belief and/or affiliation (e.g., anti-Catholic or anti-Muslim), and *political nativism* is based on political ideology (e.g., anti-Communism).
Nationalism	The belief in national superiority, that one's nation of origin is superior to other nations. Patriotism is a positive form of nationalism marked by commitment and devotion to one's national identity.
National Identity	Individual sense of belonging and commitment to a nation, and identification with the culture, traditions, and symbols of a nation.
Xenophobia	Dislike or fear of people from other countries.
Populism	A 'thin' political ideology that views the world as conflict between ordinary people who are inherently good and a corrupt elite.
Racism	Dislike, fear, or prejudice against a group because of their race or ethnicity.
Authoritarianism	Preference for strong leaders who can ignore democratic political institutions and process, and who exercise power to maintain the status quo and punish non-conformists.

What Nativism Isn't! Nationalism, Xenophobia, Populism, Authoritarianism, or Racism

Nationalism is rooted in the belief in national superiority, that one's nation of origin is superior to other nations. Beliefs in national superiority may be rooted in foundational ideals (e.g., American exceptionalism), in one's racial or ethnic origins, or in economic and technological innovation. The connotations of nationalism are often negative, bringing to mind images of fascism. Yet, nationalism may also serve as the source of aspirational movements, such as Mahatma Ghandi in India and Nelson Mandela in South Africa (Mylonas & Tudor, 2021). Nationalism, or at least some perception of national unity, is also, arguably, critical to a functioning democracy (Dahl, 2008). Indeed, democratic backsliding is often attributed to growing tribalism and the fracturing of a shared national identity (Forgas & Crano, 2021; Kaufman & Haggard, 2019). Within the American context, nationalism might be expressed as support for the melting pot as a cultural myth (without requiring assimilation) or by first-generation immigrants who achieve the American dream and believe others should be afforded similar opportunities. Indeed, nationalists may even invite immigration because they believe in the superiority of the nation, and its ability to assimilate immigrant populations.

In nationalism, political boundaries often neatly (if imperfectly) map to cultural (or ethnic) boundaries creating a sense of shared national identity (Citrin et al., 2001; Mudde, 2007), including a sense of linked fate, the belief that the nation shares a common fate. *National identity* is an individual sense of belonging and commitment to a nation. By altering the ethnic makeup of the population, new waves of immigration challenge existing understandings of national identity while simultaneously increasing the salience of national identity. Often, the result calls for the exclusion of immigrant populations. Importantly, national identity is only one of any number of identities and, depending on context, may or may not be relevant to political evaluations. Nativist movements arise when questions of national identity are highly salient and politically charged. By our definition, nativists are nationalists but rather than simply expressing pride in their national identity, nativists seek to exclude or discriminate against foreign-born populations.

The distinction between Ronald Reagan, a nationalist, who believed America should serve as the "shining city on the hill,"[24] and Donald Trump, a nativist who wanted to build a wall to keep out immigrants, is instructive. Ronald Reagan was,

---

24 Reagan, Ronald. (1989, January 11). Farewell Address to the Nation. https://www.reaganlibrary. gov/archives/speech/farewell-address-nation#:~:text=That%20would%20be%20a%20very,describe% 20the%20America%20he%20imagined.

by most accounts, a nationalist but not a nativist.[25] Donald Trump, in contrast, is a nativist first and a nationalist second. Reagan's nationalism was expressed in the belief that the United States represented the best possible country and political system. Trump's nativism, in contrast, found expression in the belief that the United States should be an exclusive club, not open to just anyone. Nativism then can be seen as a malignancy, a distortion of nationalism, based on fear rather than pride. Rather than simply reflecting pride in one's country of origin, the nativist needs an internal enemy to target for not conforming to their idea of who counts as an American (Higham, 1955). For Trump, the result was a combustible mix of nativism and White Christian nationalism, rooted in evangelical beliefs, oriented toward the exclusion of other faith traditions, and the premise that America should be an explicitly Christian nation (Whitehead et al., 2018). America was defined, not by beliefs, but by who was excluded.

Because nativism is often rooted in a historical understanding of American national identity, it is often linked with *xenophobia*, an "antipathy toward 'internal' foreign groups" (Friedman, 1967) or, more simply stated, a "fear of strangers" (Hervik, 2015). Within the American context, these groups are thought of as hostile to American ideals. Nativism has been defined in similar terms, e.g., as intense opposition to foreign groups perceived as "un-American" (Higham, 1955). Nativism can exist, however, in a more benign form, without the antipathy toward foreign groups but with a preference for policies that favor native-born populations. It is possible, for example, to be open to outside groups provided they assimilate and adopt the values and norms of the American political culture while being opposed to groups that fail to assimilate.

Nativism, as we define it here, is based on policy preferences that advantage native populations and disadvantage foreign-born populations. For example, one could favor providing welfare benefits to native populations but not immigrants based, at least in theory, on financial concerns rather than outgroup antipathy. The combination of nativist policy preferences and outgroup hostility may be better described as xenophobia, though the conceptual lines here are exceedingly thin as nativism is typically associated with outgroup hostility and not mere policy preferences. In this respect, Mudde (2019) defines nativism as the combination of nationalism and xenophobia (Mudde, 2019). Our approach is slightly different, as we contend one can be nativist without being a xenophobe, that one need not fear strangers to prefer policies that disadvantage foreign-born populations. This

---

25 Despite his rhetoric, Reagan was criticized for his treatment of Cambodian refugees and his approach to immigration which involved detention. Sheehy, G. (1983, February 5). Cambodian Refugees: America's Double-Cross. https://www.washingtonpost.com/archive/opinions/1983/02/06/cambodian-refugees-americas-double-cross/98969c5f-9f8d-493d-8342-f0f764c343ef/.

includes favoring preferences in hiring Americans over foreign-born populations or restricting government services (access to public schools or welfare benefits).

Similarly, nativism is strongly correlated with racial attitudes, often defined in terms of *racial resentment or White grievance*. Nativist movements are, perhaps not surprisingly, most easily motivated and mobilized when the targets of nativist policy preferences are racially distinct from native populations. But one can be a nativist and not a racist, preferring policies that disadvantage racially or culturally similar populations for economic, religious, or political reasons (Mudde, 2019). Early nativist movements were often directed against European immigrants, including Germans, Irish, and Italians. Nativism was partly rooted in ethnicity during this period but was mostly rooted in religion. Having said that, it is also worth noting that at different periods in American history, neither the Irish nor Italians were considered 'White' (Ignatiev, 1994).

Nativism, in its more benevolent forms, can be supportive of assimilation for individuals from different ethnic and racial backgrounds. In its more malignant variety, the nativist believes that assimilation is impossible because of racial or ethnic background. Within the US case, nativism is mostly White, but there is no reason that this is necessarily the case, and there is ample evidence that Black Americans can be nativist or at least have antipathy toward immigrant populations (Hellwig, 1982; Lippard, 2011).[26] Nativism's political appeal, however, is, in no small part, based on its ability to activate White racial grievance without being explicitly racist because its target is often 'illegal immigrants' rather than immigrants more generally. The nativist net, however, catches lots of different groups, and the catch is rarely unintended.

Nativism and *populism* are similarly linked through anti-elite populist rhetoric. Like nativism, populism defines an 'us' (the common people against 'them' (an elite) (Betz, 2019; Mudde & Kaltwasser, 2017; Riedel, 2018). The elites in this telling are globalists, undermining local communities, local economies, and local cultures through international trade, globalization, and lax restrictions on immigration. Explicitly racist groups proffer that elites are looking to replace native-born White populations with immigrants who will demand less in wages and benefits. But populism may be less a set of beliefs than it is a political strategy, employed by an opportunistic political entrepreneur when the public faith in political institutions and processes has been shattered. In other words, public belief that 'the system is broken' allows populist political strategies to prove effective.

---

26 There is a question of whether this counts as nativism since Blacks have historically lacked the political power to act on these attitudes. Hellwig, D. J. (1982). Strangers in their own land: Patterns of Black nativism, 1830–1930. *American Studies*, *23*(1), 85–98.

While the two concepts are clearly linked and they fit neatly together, nativism is hardly synonymous with populism (Betz, 2017a; Iakhnis et al., 2018). First, one can attack establishment elites without coupling those attacks to immigrants or immigration. Immigrants are typically not elites and are not necessarily perceived as a tool of elite business interests. Second, one can be a nativist, but not a populist, particularly if preferred elites share one's anti-immigration views. Having said that, nativism is often used to distinguish left-wing populist movements (which are not necessarily nativist) from right-wing populist movements (where nativism is often the defining feature). Left-wing populists do, however, frequently point to immigration as a source for declining or stagnant wages, and Bernie Sanders (among others) has been criticized for his strong stances against immigration and, presumably, in support of US workers, but Sanders' populist appeals were never centrally about immigration. Recognizing shifts in the preferences of Democratic primary voters, Sanders moderated these stands in his 2020 presidential campaign. Regardless, historically, nativism and right-wing populism have coincided. Betz concludes, "In the current debate on populism, it is generally assumed that -with the notable exception of Latin America- populism and nativism go hand in hand" (Betz, 2017b). We might slightly refine this. Immigration provides a context in which populist political strategies find resonance among nativist populations.

With roots in populism, nativists often defend themselves as defenders of genuine democracy and in opposition to immigrants who either lack democratic values, who are intentionally opposed to those values, or who have immigrated to overturn the political and economic system (Betz, 2017a). The January 6th insurrectionists, for example, did not believe they were attacking the US Capital to overturn democracy, even if their purpose was to stop the certification of a democratic election. They believed instead that they were overturning an election, stolen, in part, by undocumented immigrants who voted illegally and pushed the election in favor of Joe Biden and the Democratic Party. Just prior to the 2024 Iowa Caucus, former president Donald Trump claimed that: "That's why they are allowing these people to come in — people that don't speak our language — they are signing them up to vote. And I believe that's why you are having millions of people pour into our country and it could very well affect the next election. That's why they are doing it."[27] Trump provided no evidence of his claim, but evidence was unnecessary for America's nativist nation. The claim itself was convincing enough.

---

27 Sherman, A. (2024, February 5) Fact check: Trump claims millions of immigrants are signing up to vote illegally. WRAL News. https://www.wral.com/story/fact-check-trump-claims-millions-of-immigrants-are-signing-up-to-vote-illegally/21269245/.

Ironically, self-proclaimed as guardians of democracy, populists are often *authoritarian* in outlook, preferring strong leaders to take the country back from immigrants, elites, and other forces designed to undermine American democracy. In this respect, populists often prefer strong leaders willing to ignore the rule of law as well as democratic political institutions and processes. Donald Trump expressed this impulse well when he said "I alone can fix it,"[28] referring to America's broken political system, and studies have found Trump's appeals resonated among authoritarian voters (MacWilliams, 2016; Norris & Inglehart, 2019). As noted previously, nativism is, at least in part, rooted in the perceived threat of immigrant groups and not just to their presence, though these two things are often correlated. Addressing the threats posed by immigrants requires a strong leader, unconstrained by elections, the legislative branch, or the courts. If authoritarianism is related to nativism, however, nativism appears to be more important and more proximate as a predictor of political choice. Young (2016), for example, found that authoritarianism did not significantly predict support for Donald Trump in models that included nativism (Young, 2016). Nativism was the stronger and more proximate cause.

More generally, authoritarian beliefs and attitudes are perhaps best summarized as a 'kiss up, kick down' orientation to authority. Authorities are revered, while out-groups are punished. Defining immigrants as outgroups provides an easy target for the public's authoritarian instincts and sets the stage for strong leaders who willfully ignore constitutional constraints. But one need not be an authoritarian to be a nativist, and one can be authoritarian without targeting immigrants as the central threat to the political system. While authoritarianism sits neatly beside nativism with its focus on outgroups, increasing polarization means that opposition partisans are also seen as a threat to democracy, though the threats posed to democracy by opposition partisans are often in the eye of the beholder. If Democrats see the threat to democracy as rooted in a January 6th style insurrection, Republicans perceive the threat in the criminal charges brought against Donald Trump.[29] Perhaps even more to the point, partisans tend to support unilateral executive action when their side is acting undemocratically. They oppose such actions primarily when the other side acts (Clayton et al., 2021;

---

28 Politico Staff. (2016, July 21). Full text: Donald Trump 2016 RNC draft speech transcript. https://www.politico.com/story/2016/07/full-transcript-donald-trump-nomination-acceptance-speech-at-rnc-225974.

29 Roth, Z. (2024, February 13). Are Americans really committed to democracy in the 2024 election? New Hampshire Bulletin. https://newhampshirebulletin.com/2024/02/13/are-americans-really-committed-to-democracy-in-the-2024-election/.

Kingzette et al., 2021).[30] As a final consideration, political scientist John Hibbing argues that Trump supporters are less authoritarian, they rejected COVID-19 mandates after all, and better described as securitarians (Hibbing, 2022). According to Hibbing, securitarians are guided by the perceived need to defend family, friends, and communities from outsiders (Hibbing, 2020). We would draw a similar distinction between authoritarians (focused on strictly adhering to authority) and nativists (concerned about protecting community and culture from outsiders).

Conclusions

In this chapter, we have provided a conceptual definition of nativism. Nativism is a predisposition to favor native-born people over foreign ones. Nativism has always been part of the American experience. At times, it has manifested itself more strongly. At other times, it has waited patiently in the background. The ebbs and flows of nativist expression have typically followed broader immigration patterns—when immigration was up, nativist expression was manifest in politics.

Nativism is conceptually distinct from a number of closely related concepts. Nativists are, by definition, nationalists, but nationalists need not be nativist. Nationalism might manifest in more positive sources of national pride. Similarly, nativism is often tied to right-wing populism. Indeed, it is often the defining distinction between right-wing and left-wing populist movements, but one can be anti-elite without necessarily being anti-immigrant. If populism pits a virtuous people against a corrupt elite, immigrants (especially second-generation immigrants) can identify as part of 'the people.' Nativism is similarly often linked to racism as nativist movements often target groups based on race and ethnicity, but nativist movements have also targeted groups based on religion and political ideology.

But if nativism is distinct from these other concepts, it is also closely linked. Nativist appeals often resonate with racists, authoritarians, and nationalists. Our argument is that nativism is the primary drive of contemporary politics because it serves to prime these other impulses. Nativism raises fundamental questions about national identity and who counts as an American. Nativist appeals to authoritarians who believe the only way back to simpler times is through a stronger leader willing to ignore democratic norms, institutions, and processes. And, nativ-

---

30 Goldman, J. Drutman, L., and Pocasangre, O. (2024, January 4). Democracy Hypocrisy: Examining America's Fragile Democratic Convictions. Democracy Fund. https://democracyfund.org/idea/democracy-hypocrisy/.

ism captures broader dissatisfaction with a broken political system overrun with corrupt elites.

In the US, Donald Trump exemplifies this nativist backlash. But this is only possible because the Republican party is largely nativist today. Trump is but a symptom, not the cause of our contemporary disfunction. Ironically, nativist attitudes are in decline as a percent of the adult population. This results from Democrats—not Republicans—becoming less nativist overtime. Strong nativists—or as we call them the 'nativist nation'—is only a plurality expression in 2024 America. That said, nativism has never been more relevant to politics—at least in the modern era. This seemingly counterintuitive trend is explained by the increasing ghettoization of nativism among Republicans. Most Republicans are nativist; most Democrats are not. Nativism, as such, has never been more important for understanding politics in America today. It drowns out other competing belief systems such as authoritarianism and populism. In the next chapter, we begin to explain how we know this by detailing how we measure nativism and what that measure reveals about the size and scope of America's nativist nation.

Chapter 3
Who is a Nativist? The Contours of a Nativist Nation

Vignette: Pollsters as Lay Scientists

It was June 2015. Trump was a political neophyte announcing his candidacy. But no baby steps for him. Trump immediately went where no other politician had gone before. His initial volley: "When Mexico sends its people, they're not sending us their best . . . [T]hey're sending people that have lots of problems . . . They're bringing drugs, they're bringing crime."[31] A bit later Trump would double down by warning that a "tremendous infectious disease is pouring across the border."[32]

The establishment was scandalized. Jeb Bush—a presidential hopeful and political scion quipped "To make these extraordinarily ugly kind of comments is not reflective of the Republican party."[33] Surely, all thought this would end Trump's chances as a presidential hopeful. Expectations were that his implosion was imminent.

But it didn't happen. Trump keep going up and up and up in the polls as 2015 progressed into 2016. He was a force of nature.

What was going on? What were all the analysts missing?

As pollsters, we were perplexed but curious. So, we listened, tested, and learned. Practically speaking, over the latter half of 2015, we lifted different words and passages from Trump's public engagements and tested them in our polling.

What did we learn?

That Trump resonated deeply with Americans and especially with Republicans. Yes, Trump was on to something. Jeb and the establishment were tone deaf.

Americans held strong views on the subject. At the time, we began to refer to them as 'nativist' beliefs. We wanted to separate such positions from anti-immigration attitudes. They

31 Gamboa, Suzanne. (2015, June 16). Donald Trump Announces Presidential Bid By Trashing Mexico, Mexicans. NBC News. https://www.nbcnews.com/news/latino/donald-trump-announces-presidential-bid-trashing-mexico-mexicans-n376521.
32 Dale, Daniel, Subramanian, Tara, Cohen, Marshall, and Steck, M. (2020, July 22). Fact check: Trump falsely suggests kids don't transmit coronavirus and that US case surge is due in part to protests and Mexican migration. CNN. https://www.cnn.com/2020/07/22/politics/fact-check-trump-coronavirus-briefing-july-22.
33 Meet the Press Transcript. (2015, July 5). https://www.nbcnews.com/meet-the-press/meet-press-transcript-july-5-2015-n386996.

https://doi.org/10.1515/9783111384047-003

were more visceral and, we believed, went directly to issues of American identity. There was something profound going on in our assessment.

In order to systematize our understanding of the moment, we developed a multiple item nativist index over the course of ten polls. In so doing, we deployed the scientific method. Iterating and testing. Iterating and testing. Iterating and testing.

Trump showed a political 'Spidey sense.' America was indeed nativist. Trump would proceed to vanquish all his political foes in 2016 through this nativist mantra. And nativism has been Trump's perpetual motion machine ever since, propelling him again to the White House in 2024.

Organization of Chapter

In this chapter, we ask three simple questions:
-   How do we measure nativism?
-   Is nativism a real thing?
-   And who is a nativist?

To answer these questions, this chapter will detail the step-by-step development of a multi-item index which we call the nativist index. What do we mean by this?

First, any good measure—whether it is a single question or multi-item index—must capture the underlying construct or concept in question. Practically speaking, the items of the index should fall along a nativist continuum—with some items being very nativist, others only moderately so, and still others not being nativist at all. Here, we want to discriminate people along the nativist continuum in question.

Second, we want to know if our measure—nativism—is reliable. This simply means that it is consistent over time and over multiple applications. Third, we want to determine if nativism is a valid measure. This means that nativism measures what it should be measuring. Finally, we profile nativists—who they are, how many of them there are, and so on. Here, we distinguish between nativists and non-nativists on a range of demographic, political, and policy indicators.

In a nutshell, our nativist index is a highly reliable and valid measure. Substantively, nativism shows itself to be a profoundly stable, ingrained belief system in the United States. There is nothing ephemeral or fleeting about what Trump ultimately tapped into. In that long ago day in June 2015, elites and analysts missed Trump's theory of the case. But public opinion did not. Why? The answer simply is—that America was already a nativist nation.

Measuring Nativism

One of the challenges of studying nativism is the diversity of definitions across studies, literatures, and disciplines. With no single accepted conceptual definition of nativism (see Chapter 2), it should come as no surprise that there is not a single widely accepted measure of it. Recall our conceptual definition of nativism, *a predisposition that favors native-born populations over foreign-born ones*. This is a policy-based definition that neither articulates a motive (racial, religious, or political) nor requires animosity toward, or fear of, foreign-born populations. Operationalizing this definition requires thinking carefully through the question of measurement as well as evaluating (and reevaluating) the performance of the measure both in terms of its internal properties and its relationship to other related concepts.

Our nativist index, developed in the waning days of 2015 (Young et al., 2019), was an attempt to understand Trump's success and was inspired by similar measures developed by the General Social Survey (Smith, 2018) and the World Values Survey (Inglehart, 2014). Specifically, we ask respondents their level of agreement on the following five statements:
- *Stop Immigration*: America would be stronger if we stopped immigration.
- *Allow Immigration*: America would be better off if we let in all immigrants who wanted to come here. (Reverse coded.)
- *Prioritize Hiring*: When jobs are scarce, employers should give priority to people of this country over immigrants.
- *Take Jobs*: Immigrants take jobs away from real Americans.
- *Take Services*: Immigrants take important social services away from real Americans.

Our objective was to develop a robust measure that would discriminate the population along varying intensities of nativism. In this spirit, some of the items were highly nativist, others somewhere in the middle, and finally still others less so.

Our analysis in this chapter combines data from various polls conducted between March 2023 and February 2025. Each poll is based on approximately 1000 Americans and the data were collected by Ipsos. The nativism index has been included in Ipsos polls from 2015 to 2025. After each poll, analyses are conducted to check the reliability and validity of the measures. The results are remarkably consistent over time. In Table 3.1, we provide a list of Ipsos polls that measured nativism from 2015 through 2025. In Figure 3.1, we present the distribution of these individual nativist items as well as the summated index.

We should expect some items to be universally acceptable, while others less so. We find such a trend in our five-item index as well. Take 'allow immigration

Table 3.1: List of Nativism Polls by Year.

Year	Name of Poll	# of Nativism Items	Other Questions
2015	Ipsos Nativism Poll 1	5	Nativist and System is broken items
2016	Ipsos Nativism Poll 2	5	Nativism, System is Broken, Authoritarianism, Social Issues, State Activism, Racial Resentment, Better off than Parents, Nostalgia, Policy Issues
2023	Ipsos Nativism Poll 3	5	Nativism, System is Broken, Authoritarianism, Racial Resentment
2025	Ipsos Nativism Poll 4	5	Nativism, System is Broken, Authoritarianism, Social Issues, State Activism, Racial Resentment, Better off than Parents, Nostalgia, Policy Issues, National Identity
2023	Ipsos National Identity Poll 1	5	Nativism, Real American, System is Broken
2023	Ipsos National Identity Poll 2	5	Nativism, National Identity (ISSP), System is Broken
2024	Ipsos National Identity Poll 3	5	Nativism, American Identity, System is Broken, Authoritarianism, Social Issues, State Activism, Racial Resentment, Better off than Parents, Nostalgia, Policy Issues
2016	Ipsos Global Populism Poll 1	5	Nativism, Populism, System is Broken, Authoritarianism, Optimism about Future
2019	Ipsos Global Populism Poll 2	3	Nativism, Populism, System is Broken, Spending
2023	Ipsos Global Populism Poll 3	3	Nativism, Populism, System is Broken, Spending
2025	Ipsos Global Populism Poll 4	3	Nativism, Populism, System is Broken, National Identity
2015–2016	5 Polls in the Development of the Index	5	Varied batteries and items
2016–2025	24 Nativist Battery included in other polls	5	Included as analytical control on other polls

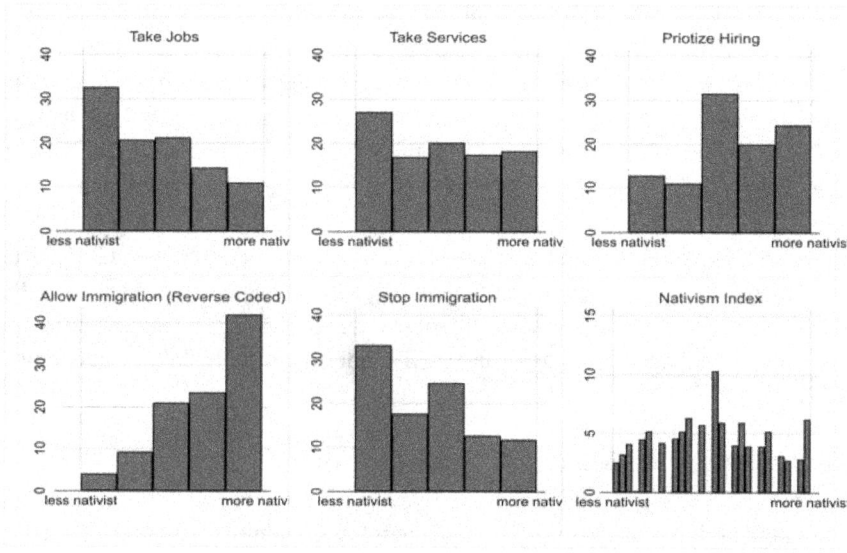

Figure 3.1: Distribution of Individual Measures of Nativism and Nativism Index
(Source: 2023 Ipsos Poll).

in all cases' as an example. A strong majority of Americans disagree with this (60% disagree strongly or agree somewhat). On the flip side, very few Americans think that 'immigration should be stopped outright' (34% agree strongly or somewhat agree). In the middle, a strong plurality believe that immigrants take 'social services away from real Americans' (49% strongly agree or agree). At first blush, the items seem to represent a reasonable spread along our construct of nativism.

Such nativist nuance is consistent in other studies as well. In *Immigration and the American Ethos*, Morris Levy and Matthew Wright argue that public opinion is less anti-immigrant than is commonly believed (Levy & Wright, 2020). There are many shades of gray when it comes to American attitudes toward immigration, as Levy and Wright contend. As we will show in Chapter 4, even as Americans have become less nativist, partisan divisions have grown, making it a defining issue in contemporary politics. Context matters.

Based on these items, we then build a summated index, which is the simple addition of each item to form an overall score. The higher the score the more nativist the predisposition of a given individual. Overall, the summated index in 2023 varied from 5 to 25 with an average of 15.1 and a standard deviation 5.1. We can depict a summated index as an equation:

$$S = \Sigma\, X_i,$$

where S is the summated score (total index score), X_i represents the score for the i-th item, and n is the total number of items in the index.

Summated indexes have two advantages. First, they better capture the variability of the underlying construct in question. Any one item might be unable to discriminate those clumped at the extremes or in the murky middle. Second, multiple items minimize potential biases or measurement problems of any given single item.

Think of a multi-item math test. Any one question might be poorly written or be too easy or too hard for a big swath of the population in question. Multiple item indexes also do a better job of discriminating people along our hypothetical math/verbal ability continuum by including some hard questions, some easy questions, and some in the moderate range. Our nativist index attempts to do the same thing.

Reliability: Is my Measure Consistent over Time?

The nativism index is also reliable. By reliability, we simply mean that the measure is consistent over time or over multiple draws, known as test-retest. Often, we assess such properties through the strength of the correlations among items in the index. So, what do we find?

Nativism has, in the past, shown itself to be consistent across countries and over time without losing its inherent meaning as a measure. Specifically, studies show the index to be reliable over time and across countries (Young et al., 2019) and, with few exceptions, metric invariant (Zhao, 2019).

Table 3.2: Matrix of Correlations for Nativism Indicators and Nativism Index.

Variables	(1)	(2)	(3)	(4)	(5)	(6)
(1) Take Jobs	1.000					
(2) Take Services	.761	1.000				
(3) Prioritize Hiring	.644	.612	1.000			
(4) Allow Immigration	.491	.569	.471	1.000		
(5) Stop Immigration	.709	.702	.556	.459	1.000	
(6) Nativism Index	.881	.892	.795	.709	.838	1.000

Source: Ipsos Survey 2023.

We find the same here. In Table 3.2, we present the correlations between the individual items we use to measure nativism. Values closer to 1.0 indicate stronger relationships while values closer to 0 indicate weaker ones. There are strong correlations among the items of the index. As can be seen above, each of the individual items is highly correlated with the other and with the overall index. The correlations range from .459 to .892. As further evidence, Cronbach's Alpha—a measure of the internal consistency of index items—is .92. We also find an average Cronbach's alpha of .878 based on thirty-seven polls administered between 2015 and 2025. What does this suggest?

Our nativist index exhibits strong measurement properties. The minimal acceptable Cronbach's alpha in the social sciences is around .65 (DeVellis, 2017). By this criterion, the nativism index clearly outpaces the industry standard reinforcing its reliability.

The nativism index also has strong test/retest properties. Test-retest gauges the degree of consistency in the measure over repeated draws or applications of it. In the case of the nativism index, we assess the rank order of the five items—is it consistent or not? We tested the rank order of four different indexes polled at different times. We took the average of the rank order correlations, which came to .88. For context, a test-retest correlation of .80 or better is considered strong. Again, our nativist index outperforms the industry standard (.88 vs. .80).

Table 3.3: Single Factor Solution for Nativism with Varimax Factor Rotation.

Items	Loadings
Immigrants take jobs away from real Americans	.876
Immigrants take important social services away from real Americans	.885
When jobs are scarce, employers should give priority to people of this country over immigrants	.785
America would be better off if we let in all immigrants who wanted to come here	.693
The United States would be stronger if we stopped immigration	.822

Extraction method: Principal component analysis.
**1 components extracted. Source Ipsos Survey 2023.*

Finally, we present the results of a factor analysis. Such analyses tell us whether the index in question measures the same underling construct. If it does, it will load on a single dimension. If not, a multi-dimensional solution, or factor, should appear.

Table 3.3 shows that each individual item loads strongly on a single factor, indicating they are measuring the same underlying latent construct. Yet another indicator that nativism is a simple but robust measure.

Validity: Is Nativism Capturing What It Should Be Capturing?

We want a valid nativist index as well. This practically means that our index measures what it should be measuring. Here, we assess three types of validity: convergent, divergent, and predictive. By convergent validity, we mean that nativism should correlated with conceptually congruent measures, such as authoritarianism, racial grievance, populism, or anti-immigration attitudes. Ultimately, we are looking for such measures to be positively correlated with nativism. However, the correlation should not be so strong as to make them indistinguishable from each other.

By divergent validity, we mean that nativism should be negatively correlated with conceptually incongruent measures, such as showing support for a path to citizenship. Such correlations reinforce the validity of our nativist index by suggesting that is measuring what it should be measuring.

Finally, by predictive validity, we mean that nativism predicts what it is expected to predict. Take voting in the 2024 presidential election. We should expect that nativist Americans were more likely to vote for Trump than non-nativists. Other outcome measures could include identification with the Republican party, vote in the 2016, or place of residents.

For the purposes of our analysis here, we examine the correlations between nativism and fifteen independent variables which we detail in the table below. Here, we have seven demographic questions, six summated indexes including nativism, two attitudinal questions, two media consumptions items, and finally stated voting intention for the 2024 presidential election. We analyze data from our 2023 and 2025 Ipsos Nativism polls.

We detail them in Table 3.4 below.

Table 3.4: Indicators Used in Assessing the Reliability and Validity of Nativism.

Concept	Year of Poll	Number of Items	Cronbach's Alpha	Dimensionality	Explanation
Nativism	2023	5	0.874	1 Factor Dimension	Battery capturing anti-immigrant attitudes. Developed by Ipsos 2016; some items borrowed from World Values Survey and General Social Survey
System is Broken	2023	6	0.732	1 Factor Dimension	Battery to capture anti-establishment predispositions. Developed by Ipsos and adapted from 'Caudillo battery' in Ipsos Populist Survey 2005

Table 3.4 (continued)

Concept	Year of Poll	Number of Items	Cronbach's Alpha	Dimensionality	Explanation
Authoritarianism	2023	4	0.506	1 Factor Dimension	Taken from Hetherington and Suhay (2011)
Better off than Parents	2025	5	0.905	1 Factor Dimension	Battery to capture gains/losses relative to parents; sense of loss of American Dream. Developed by Ipsos 2016; adapted from General Social Survey
Racial Resentment	2025	3	0.832	1 Factor Dimension	Battery adapted from past Ipsos studies. In particular, focuses on affimative action and fairness of race based programs
Government Intervention in the economy	2023	7	NA	Single Item	Question developed at Ipsos to gauge support for an activist government
Abortion	2025	1	NA	Single Item	More support/less support for varying permision for abortion
Stranger in own Land	2025	1	NA	Single Item	Agree/Disagree that feel that stranger in own land. Alternative item to capture nativist feelings of the 'other'

Source: 2023 and 2025 Ipsos Nativism Poll.

Our summated indexes include: Authoritarianism, Belief that the system is broken and White grievance. All attitudinal indexes have been shown to be strongly correlated with nativism (Young et. al. 2019).

So, what do all these measures mean for nativism?

Nativism: Convergent Validity, Divergent Validity, and Predictive Validity

First, we find strong convergent validity for nativism. Specifically, our attitudinal scales are strongly correlated with the nativism (see Table 3.5). A nativist is more authoritarian (.341), is more likely to believe the system as broken (.283), and is more racially resentful (.550). Nativists also are more likely to be Republican (.342), watch Fox news (.341), and more likely to live in a rural area (.161). Finally, nativists are more likely to support funding for the border (.644) and deportation of illegal immigrants (.539). Such relationships make sense given nativism's link to conservative politics.

Table 3.5: Statistically Significant Pearson's Correlations with Nativism: Convergent and Divergent Validity.

Convergent Validity	Divergent Validity
.283 System is Broken (2023)	−.283 Intervention in the Economy (2023)
.341 Authoritarianism (2023)	−.070 Better Off Than Parents (2023)
.550 Racial Resentment (2023)	
.078 Stranger in Own Land (2023)	−.677 Path to Citizenship (2025)
.644 Increased Funding for the Border (2023)	−.123 Income (2023)
.539 Deportation of Illegal Immigrants who committed a crime (2025)	−.239 Education (2023)
	−.068 Hispanic (2023)
.161 Rural (2023)	
.340 Watch Fox News (2023)	
.141 Age (2023)	

Source: 2023 and 2025 Ipsos Nativism Polls.

Second, we find strong divergent validity as well. Ethnicity (−.068), income (−.123), and education (−.239) are negatively associated with nativism—individuals who share such characteristics tend to be less nativist and have been shown to be consistently pro-immigration in their orientation. Attitudinally, nativists are also much less likely to agree with a path to citizenship for illegal immigrants (−.677). Simply put, our nativism index is behaving in a way that would be expected.

Finally, from a predictive validity perspective, nativists are much more likely to have voted for Trump in 2020 and 2024 (see Table 3.6). We detail this in Chapter 5 as well. Similarly, Republicans are more likely to be nativist than Democrats. Again, nativism predicts what it should predict when confronted with directionally incongruent measures.

Profiling Nativists: Who Is a Nativist? Univariate Analysis

In the final section of the chapter, we want to profile nativists—who they are, how many of them there are, and so on. We will do this in three ways. First, we determine how nativism varies by simple social, political, and demographic fac-

Table 3.6: Statistically Significant
Pearson's Correlations with
Nativism: Predictive Validity.

Predictive Validity

.638 Vote for Trump 2024 (2025)
.495 PartyID (Republican) (2025)

.446 Will Vote Trump 2024 (2023)
.361 Vote Trump 2020 (2023)
.395 Vote 2022 (Republican) (2023)

.342 PartyID (Republican) (2023)

Source: 2023 and 2025 Ipsos
Nativism Polls.

tors. Second, we will take these same variables and see how they behave in a multivariate context. Third, we will stand the analysis on its head and look at the percentage of Americans that are nativist and the percentage that are non-nativist. Of course, we will need to make some simplifying assumptions. But such an analysis will go far in gauging the pervasiveness of nativism in America.

Let's begin by examining mean differences in nativist attitudes by select demographics (see Figure 3.2). What do we learn from this analysis? Males are only slightly more likely to be nativist than females. But White, less educated, older, and rural Americans are more likely to be nativist. None of this is particularly surprising as this largely reflects the partisan differences displayed in Figure 3.3.

As can be seen in Figure 3.3, partisan affiliation is strongly correlated with whether someone expresses nativist attitudes. Republicans are more likely to hold nativist attitudes and opinions than Democrats or Independents. All of our understanding of the current political scenario validates this.

Who is Nativist? Multivariate Analysis

We can gain further insight into understanding nativists by employing multivariate regression models. In Figure 3.4, we present two sets of regressions. For ease of presentation, we present the results graphically. Variables that are statistically significant predictors of nativism do not touch the center-line (at the 0 point). Model 1 only includes demographic variables. Model 2 adds partisan affiliation. Model 1 largely confirms our early finding. Males, older, less well-educated, and rural Americans are more likely to hold nativist beliefs. Interestingly, income is also statistically significant with wealthier Americans expressing more nativist sentiments, though the effect is small.

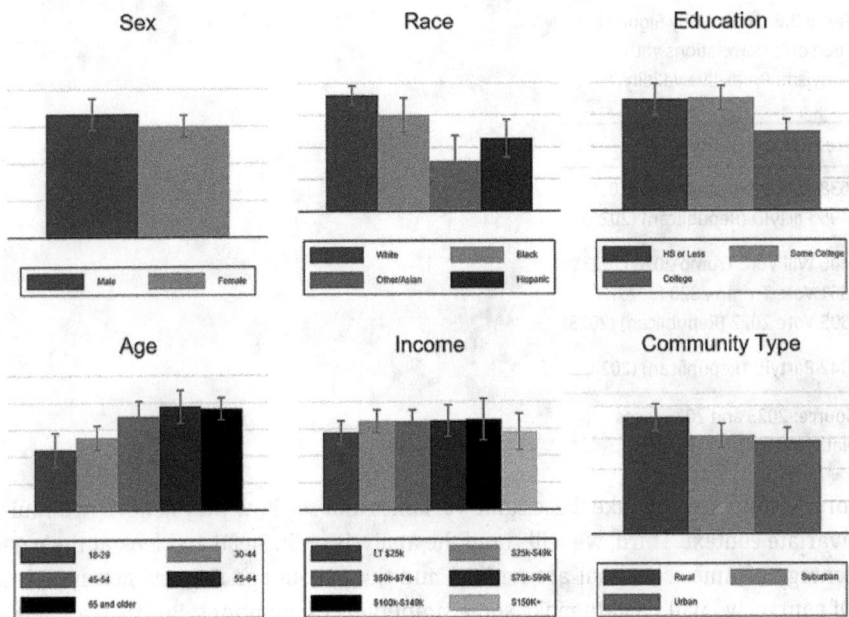

Figure 3.2: Mean Nativism Scores by Select Demographics.

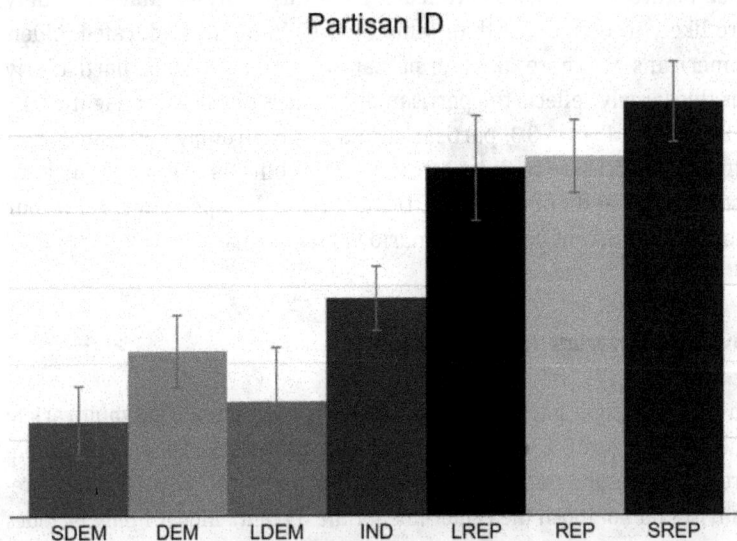

Figure 3.3: Mean Nativism by Partisan Identification.

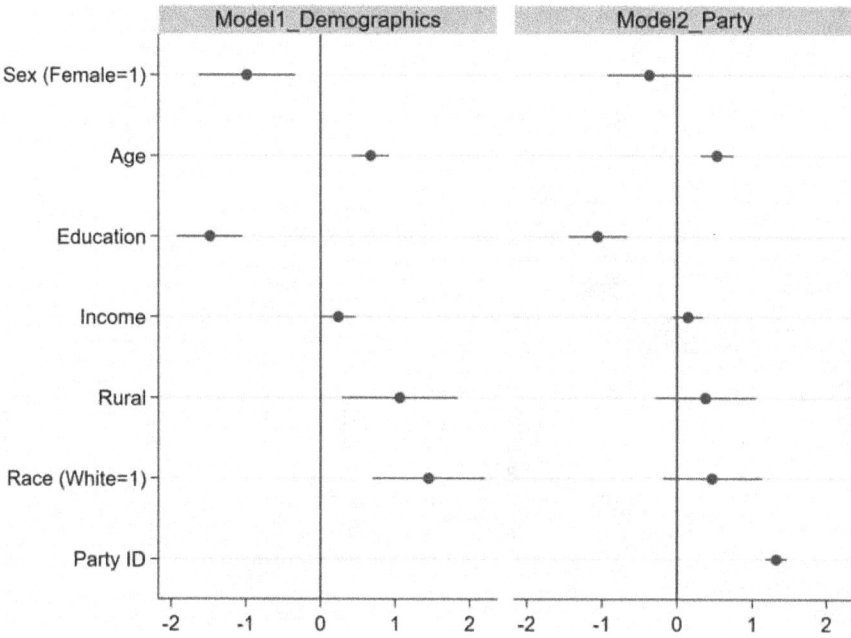

Figure 3.4: Regressions of Nativism on Select Demographics and Party Identification.

Once partisan identification is included in Model 2, only age and education are statistically significant. What does this mean? Sex, income, community type, and race influence nativism indirectly through partisan affiliation. Wealthier, White, rural males are more likely to be Republicans and, subsequently, are more likely to be nativists. Party affiliation ultimately accounts for most of who is and is not nativist.

Identifying the Nativist Nation

So, now that we know who is more likely to be nativist, how many of them are out there? To do this, let's identify their size and profile. By nativist nation, we mean individuals who are highly nativist.

We use our index to discriminate people by their nativist intensity. By our estimates, only a plurality of Americans—or about 33%—are highly nativist, which we refer to as nativist nation. We find that such levels are also highly consistent wave over wave.

Let's show our work. First, we create a summated index. The index varies from 5 to 25. We then re-code it into five approximately equal categories.[34] We then cross our recoded index against multiple questions including individual items of the index, demographics, and support for specific policies. What do we find?

Table 3.7: Five Category Nativism Variable by Specific Correlates.

Segment	Very High	High	Medium	Low	Very Low
(%)	14	19	24	21	21
College +	27	37	33	45	49
Hispanic	9	12	13	11	14
Rep	73	53	32	26	7
Dem	10	25	40	49	77
White	90	86	74	78	78
Black	7	9	18	14	10
19–39	19	33	44	40	42
40 +	81	67	56	60	58
Jobs Scarce	99	87	45	26	6
Jobs Real Americans	97	64	20	2	0
Stop Immigration	86	52	20	2	1
Strong Leader to fix	45	46	30	21	0

Source: 2023 Ipsos Nativism Poll.

In Table 3.7, we present the incidence rate for select demographic characteristics by nativism category. There is a clear pattern as noted earlier in the chapter. Republicans, White, and older Americans are more nativist. They also are more likely to believe in strong leaders, that the system is broken, and support restrictive immigration policies.

On these critical discriminatory variables, two distinct groups appear. Those Americans that fall into the two top categories 'very high' and 'high' have similar attitudinal profiles. In contrast, those who are low on the index—defined as 'low' and 'very low'—also look quite similar to each other. The medium level group olds a middling position.

Here, any definition of 'highly nativist' is arbitrary. But from the data, those individuals that fall into the 'very high' and 'high' categories appear to be Americans who strongly adhere to nativist principles. We will define this group as *the nativist nation*. They comprise 33% of the population.

---

34 Note our recoded nativist index include five categories. We define these categories as very high (5–8); high (9–12); medium (13–15); medium low (16–19); and low (20 +).

We classify the 'low' and 'very low' categories as non-nativist, while the medium category might be considered marginally nativist or nativist adjacent. Nativism is a plurality belief. And it is critical in organizing the Republican base as we will show in Chapter 5. But nativism should not be thought of as a political ceiling. The 2024 election showed this clearly. Nativism is malleable and can be reframed for broader appeal. Take, for instance, deportation of illegal immigrants who commit crimes. Such policies transcend the simple nativist plurality by tapping more universal concerns. Often, the nativist nation finds support from nativist adjacent Americans who can get on board if the message is right.

Bringing It All Together

What can we conclude from this chapter?

Our measure of nativism works well. It maps neatly to our conceptual definition giving it face validity. It is internally consistent, meaning the individual items that comprise the scale are strongly correlated and fit together. Nativism is also related, but not identical, to measures of authoritarianism and beliefs that the system is broken.

Examining who is a nativist also gives us greater confidence in our measure. Males, less educated, rural, and White Americans all score higher on our nativism index. These differences largely reflect partisanship. Compared to Democrats, Republicans are much more likely to say that immigration is the most important issue facing the nation, that immigration should be decreased, and that, when jobs are scarce, employers should prioritize hiring native-born Americans. In other words, the expression of nativist sentiments is very much a feature of contemporary politics.

Ultimately, we show that nativism is a profoundly stable, ingrained belief system in the United States. There is nothing ephemeral and fleeting about what Trump ultimately tapped into. From a measurement perspective, our nativist index is a highly robust, reliable, and valid measure. Nativist beliefs—a central component of our NAM framework discussed earlier—are not a fleeting fancy but a structurally ingrained orientation of modern American society. In mid-2015, elites and analysts might have missed Trump's theory of the case. But public opinion did not. Why? Because America was already a nativist nation.

Chapter 4
Why Now? The (Re)Emergence of Nativism

Vignette: A Task in Contradictions

You know, we didn't set out to uncover some deep historical pattern—we were just trying to understand what was happening in real time. It was early 2016, and for months, we had been tracking nativism, developing an index to measure it systematically. We knew it was fueling Trump's rise, but at some point, we started asking ourselves a bigger question: Had nativism always been this powerful? Or was something new happening?

So we turned to the *World Values Survey*, one of the longest-running studies of public opinion available. One (agree/disagree) statement, in particular, stood out:

"When jobs are scarce, employers should give priority to people of this country over immigrants."

It was straightforward, but it cut right to the heart of what we had been examining. If nativism was fundamentally about defining who belongs, this was a clean way to measure it across time. And when we looked at the data, we saw something surprising.

Nativism had always been with us. This wasn't something that suddenly appeared in 2016—it had shaped attitudes for decades. And at first glance, it actually looked like nativism was declining. Over time, fewer Americans overall agreed with the idea that native-born Americans should get hiring priority.

But when we broke it down by party, the picture changed.

Democrats had steadily moved away from nativism, but Republicans hadn't. In fact, the partisan gap on this question had been slowly but steadily widening since the mid-2000s. Twenty years before, there wasn't much difference between the two parties on this issue. But by 2016, the divide had grown into a chasm.

That was the moment we realized something important. Nativism wasn't fading—it was polarizing. Yes, fewer Americans held nativist beliefs overall, but those who did were increasingly concentrated in one party. And in 2016, a candidate had finally come along who spoke directly to them.

This raised an even bigger question. If nativism had always existed, why was it only now becoming such a dominant force in American politics? What had changed?

The answer, we soon realized, wasn't in 2016. It was in the election that came before it.

https://doi.org/10.1515/9783111384047-004

Barack Obama: Turning or Tipping Point?

Our analysis revealed that while nativist sentiments had been a consistent thread in America's social fabric, their political impact had intensified over time. This latent force found a focal point with the election of Barack Obama, whose presidency inadvertently magnified these sentiments, leading to unprecedented levels of political polarization and reshaping of the nation's political landscape.

The election of Barack Hussein Obama in 2008 appeared to be a turning point in American political history. The United States was entering a post-racial era where old-fashioned racism appeared to be quickly disappearing. Younger generations were racially more diverse, expressed greater political tolerance, and were increasingly aligned with the Democratic Party. Noting these trends, Democratic political consultant James Carville penned *40 More Years: How the Democrats Will Rule the Next Generation.* His argument was simple. The Republican Party had lost a generation of young voters and with it the ability to consistently win elections. Republicans might occasionally win office but it would be the exception in a period of Democratic dominance. Think of Woodrow Wilson winning as a Democrat when the Republican Party splintered in 1912 between Teddy Roosevelt's Bull Moose Party and William Howard Taft or Dwight Eisenhower winning in 1952 by rising above the partisan politics with the innocuous slogan 'I Like Ike.' In surveying the post-Obama landscape, Carville concluded, demographics was destiny and shifting demographics heavily favored the Democratic Party.

Carville was not alone in the projection. Recognizing the challenge confronting the Republican Party in the wake of Mitt Romney's failed 2012 presidential campaign, a Republican National Committee autopsy called for a more open and inclusive party and advocated for comprehensive immigration reform. As the report concluded:

> If Hispanic Americans hear that the GOP doesn't want them in the United States, they won't pay attention to our next sentence. It doesn't matter what we say about education, jobs or the economy; if Hispanics think that we do not want them here, they will close their ears to our policies. In essence, Hispanic voters tell us our Party's position on immigration has become a litmus test, measuring whether we are meeting them with a welcome mat or a closed door.[35]

With this as the backdrop, Trump's right-wing nativist appeals in 2016 seemed particularly ill-timed. The conventional wisdom was that the world was changing

---

35 Cillizza, C. (2013, March 18). The 10 things you need to know from the "Growth and Opportunity Project" report. The Washington Post. https://www.washingtonpost.com/news/the-fix/wp/2013/03/18/the-10-most-important-points-in-the-growth-and-opportunity-project/.

in ways that made nativist appeals ineffective at best and counterproductive at worst. So why did it work? Why did nativism emerge at this particular point in time? And why did it resonate with so many Republican voters?

The puzzle of 'why now?' grows more perplexing when one considers recent history. Running for the Republican nomination in 1992 in a speech that foreshadowed Donald Trump, Pat Buchanan proclaimed:

> I am calling attention to a national disgrace. The failure of the national government of the United States to protect the borders of the United States from an illegal invasion that involves at least a million aliens a year. As a consequence of that, we have social problems and economic problems. And drug problems.[36]

To fix the problem, Buchanan advocated fences (and other barricades), increases in the number of border patrol, and the use of the military. "[A]ny country that wants to call itself a nation," he declared, "has got to defend its borders." While Buchanan was able to mount a serious challenge to a sitting president, George H.W. Bush, unlike Trump, he ultimately fell short of securing the Republican nomination. In politics, timing is everything and the retrograde Buchanan was ahead of his time.

Nativism also flared, but failed to fully ignite in 1994 when California passed Proposition 187 by 59–41 margin. The 'Save Our State' referendum was designed to restrict undocumented immigrants from public services, including health care and education, and required state workers to report immigrants suspected of being undocumented to Immigration and Nationalization Services (INS). In his 1994 bid for re-election, unpopular California Governor Pete Wilson used his support of Prop 187 and his opposition to affirmative action as wedge issues to rally and win against Democrat Kathleen Brown. Despite his support, Wilson ran behind Prop 187 with 55 percent of the vote. The themes of the Wilson campaign would have fit neatly in Donald Trump's 2016 campaign. In a letter to President Bill Clinton, Wilson declared: "Our border is a sieve that makes a mockery of our laws, that cripples our ability to shape our own destiny and that places an intolerable burden on state taxpayers."[37] His ads explicitly linked his campaign to Prop 187, showed a border overrun by immigrants entering the country illegally, and

---

36 Rotella, S. (1992, May 13). Migrants hear Buchanan pitch a tighter border: Speech: The GOP candidate calls the 'invasion' of illegal immigrants 'a national disgrace' as border-jumpers wait for him to leave so they can cross. Los Angeles Times. https://www.latimes.com/archives/la-xpm-1992-05-13-me-1450-story.html.

37 California State Archives. (n.d.). Looking back at Proposition 187: Twenty-five years later. Google Arts & Culture. https://artsandculture.google.com/story/looking-back-at-proposition-187-twenty-five-years-later-california-state-archives/BwWRJ8CAUvmiLg?hl=en.

emphasized his use of the National Guard to control the border.[38] Despite finding political success in California as Governor, Wilson was unable to translate his nativist appeals into a successful run at the Republican nomination during the 1996 presidential campaign. Perhaps more importantly, the backlash against Prop 187 served as a turning point in California politics, mobilizing Latino voters, and realigning the state from purple to deep blue (Johnson, 2019; Monogan III & Doctor, 2017).

The politics of nativism had failed again. The lessons for the Republican Party were clear. Against shifting population demographics, anti-immigrant rhetoric (and policies) was a non-starter. The consequence was to align the fastest growing voting bloc with the Democratic Party. Jeb Bush articulated this view in 2014.

> The way I look at this is someone who comes to our country because they couldn't come legally . . . and they crossed the border because they had no other means to work, to be able to provide for their family, yes, they broke the law, but it's not a felony. It's an act of love, it's an act of commitment to your family.[39]

A widely shared conventional wisdom was that, to win elections, Republicans needed to expand their base beyond White voters. Population shifts and the growing progressivism of younger millennial voters socialized into politics during the Obama era demanded this. Nativist appeals would not accomplish this. Even so, Arizona provided an indicator that the politics of immigration might have shifted in favor of nativist appeals. In 2010, Arizona passed S.B. 1070, the *Support Our Law Enforcement and Safe Neighborhoods Act,* which required state and local law enforcement officials to check the immigration status of individuals stopped, detained, or arrested who might be suspected of being an illegal immigrant. The law also made it a crime to shelter, hire, or transport unauthorized immigrants. While the law was generally popular[40] and boosted Arizona Republican Governor Jan Brewer in the polls, several prominent Republicans spoke out against it, including 2016 presidential candidates Jeb Bush and Marco Rubio.[41]

---

38 Pete Wilson for Governor. (1994). Wilson's re-election ads on illegal immigration [Video]. YouTube. https://www.youtube.com/watch?v=o0f1PE8Kzng&t=51s.

39 Cooney, P. (2014, April 6). Jeb Bush says illegal immigration often an 'act of love.' Reuters. https://www.reuters.com/article/world/us-politics/jeb-bush-says-illegal-immigration-often-an-act-of-love-idUSBREA350P7/.

40 Wood, D. B. (2010, April 30). Opinion polls show broad support for tough Arizona immigration law. The Christian Science Monitor. https://www.csmonitor.com/USA/Society/2010/0430/Opinion-polls-show-broad-support-for-tough-Arizona-immigration-law.

41 Hunt, K. (2010, April 30). GOP frets Ariz. law could hurt party. Politico. https://www.politico.com/story/2010/04/gop-frets-ariz-law-could-hurt-party-036617.

Enter 2016 Donald Trump.

Trump defied the conventional wisdom, effectively used nativist appeals to separate himself from a gaggle of Republican career politicians (mostly governors or senators), and called upon Americans to build a big, beautiful wall that Mexico would pay for. An unqualified appeal to White grievance seemed poorly timed and likely to create the sort of backlash that would accelerate the Democratic Party's ascent to majority party status. Instead, Trump drew an inside straight in the Electoral College during the 2016 presidential election, winning just enough states in the Rust Belt to secure the presidency. The backlash against Trump's nativist rhetoric and policies never materialized at a level capable of transforming the Electoral College math in favor of Democrats. In this respect, Trump's loss in 2020 was mostly a story of retrospective voting, reflecting his failed leadership during the COVID-19 pandemic and the associated economic downturn (Neundorf & Pardos-Prado, 2022). Absent the pandemic, Trump likely wins re-election in 2020. Indeed, even as Trump lost the election, Trump ran stronger among Latino voters, especially in Miami-Dade County and the Texas Rio Grande Valley.[42]

Fast forward to 2024 and Donald Trump's return to power. The Californication of American politics never materialized. Trump improved his standing across most demographic groups, most notably with minority voters, including Hispanics, and young voters (18–29). Generation Z, it turns out, didn't share the progressive values of millennials. Demographics as destiny projections fell flat. The largest increase, however, was among Hispanic voters, especially Hispanic men.[43] Economic concerns, religion, and social conservative values trumped concerns about immigration, but Latino voters may not have been as reflexively pro-immigration as one might assume. A March 2024 Pew Survey, for example, found that 38 percent of Hispanics saw the border as a crisis and 74 percent believed the federal government was doing a bad job or somewhat bad job addressing the issue. Moreover, 47 percent of Hispanic respondents said the situation at the border was leading to more crime while one in three respondents (33 percent) said mass deportations would make the situation at the border better. Only 23 percent said increasing deportations would make the situation worse.

There was one indicator of how strongly the tide had turned. During 2024, 54 percent of Arizona Latino voters supported Proposition 314, the Secure the Bor-

---

42 Narea, N. (2021, May 19). New data helps explain Trump's gains among Latino voters in 2020. Vox. https://www.vox.com/policy-and-politics/22436307/catalist-equis-2020-latino-vote-trump-biden-florida-texas.

43 Lange, J., Erickson, B., & Heath, B. (2024, November 6). Trump's return to power fueled by Hispanic, working-class voter support. Reuters. https://www.reuters.com/world/us/trumps-return-power-fueled-by-hispanic-working-class-voter-support-2024-11-06/.

der act, designed to enhance state and local law enforcement of federal immigration laws. When S.B. 1070 passed in 2010, Latinos overwhelmingly (81 percent) opposed the measure. In 2024, only 23 percent of Latino voters opposed S.B. 314.[44] Overall, as Latino populations assimilate, they express less support for open borders (Knoll, 2012). Moreover, even where they perceive discrimination, they do not automatically or reflexively move into the Democratic Party camp.

Our point here is not to make a case for Latino support for Donald Trump, but instead to point out that the backlash against nativist politics that we witnessed after Prop 187 in California never materialized. More Latinos have voted, but they have moved away from the Democratic Party and toward the Republican Party despite Donald Trump's nativist appeals to build a wall or employ mass deportations. For Latino voters, other issues, especially the economy, have greater relevance. This means nativist appeals can reach their target audience without generating a backlash among minority voters.

Our thesis—as embodied by NAM—is that there is a strong current of nativism beneath the surface of American politics. Given the right conditions and a political actor who recognizes and takes advantage of the moment, nativism boils up to the surface and becomes an important political force. The year 2016 was such a moment and Donald took advantage of it.

Setting the Stage: The Necessary Conditions for Nativist Politics

Nativist politics do not just happen, they result from large contextual forces such as increases in immigration, population shifts, and perceptions of cultural threat. While economics plays a role—nativism does not necessarily spike during periods of economic disruption and dislocation (e.g., industrialization in late 1880s and globalization and automation today)—perceptions of cultural threat appear to matter more (Brader et al., 2008; Major et al., 2018; Mutz, 2018; Norris & Inglehart, 2019). When this occurs, this means that native-born populations believe that immigrants are undermining the political system or fundamentally changing the culture and American identity. We address each of these in turn.

Heighted immigration is a catalytic condition. In the United States, the percentage of the population that is foreign born has grown dramatically since its

44 Rouse, S., Pedraza, F., & Huizar-Hernandez. (2024, November 21). Why Latinos widely supported Arizona's tough, new immigration law. https://www.azcentral.com/story/opinion/op-ed/2024/11/21/arizona-latino-voter-immigration-prop-314-sb-1070/76451567007/.

nadir in 1970 when only 4.7 percent of the population was foreign born.[45] Not co-incidentally, the growth in immigration began after the US liberalized immigration laws in 1965. The Immigration and Nationality Act abolished the quota systems used to limit immigration based on country of origin, giving preference to immigrants with family ties in the United States and skills that could contribute most to the US economy.[46] Not only did immigration increase as a result, but America became more racially and ethnically diverse.

As an unintended consequence, the Immigration and Nationality Act of 1965 may have increased illegal immigration by ending the Bracero Program which allowed workers from Mexico to enter (and leave) the US on short-term employment contracts. Massey (2021) contends illegal immigration resulted as an unintended consequences of limiting circular migration, where workers routinely flowed back to Mexico. Limiting circular migration increased illegal and permanent immigration because immigrant workers were afraid to return home. Both parties contributed to an increasing militarized border which, in turn, contributed to an increase in illegal immigration (Massey, 2021). The media framed increases in illegal immigration as a palpable threat to Americans (Brader et al., 2008; Farris & Silber Mohamed, 2018; Kim et al., 2011; Massey & Pren, 2012).

By 2023, the foreign-born population had grown to 14.3 percent of the population (approximately 48 million residents). According to Pew Center estimates, 23 percent of the immigrant population was unauthorized (approximately 11 million residents).[47] The unauthorized population was also growing. According to the Migration Policy Institute, the unauthorized population grew by 3 million between 2019–2023 with much of this growth from Mexico and Central America. Over the past decade, the percentage (and number) of unauthorized immigrants from other Central American countries (Guatemala, El Salvador, Honduras, Cost Rico, and Venezuela) has increased as the percentage (and number) from Mexico has declined.

This wave of immigration, including illegal immigration, has coincided with demographic shifts as Hispanics have become the largest minority group in the United States and the majority non-Hispanic White population has declined as a percentage of the population (see Figure 4.1). According to current estimates, the

---

45 Moslimani, M. & Passel, J. (2024, September 27). Key findings about U.S. immigrants. Pew Research Center. https://www.pewresearch.org/short-reads/2024/09/27/key-findings-about-us-immigrants/.

46 Lyndon B. Johnson Presidential Library. (n.d.). Immigration and Nationality Act. https://www.lbjlibrary.org/news-and-press/media-kits/immigration-and-nationality-act.

47 Passel, J. and Krogstad, J.M. (2024, July 22). What we know about unauthorized immigrants living in the U.S. https://www.pewresearch.org/short-reads/2024/07/22/what-we-know-about-unauthorized-immigrants-living-in-the-us/.

non-Hispanic White population will become a minority by 2045 as population growth is driven primarily by immigration (and not fertility). Previous research has found that numerical decline alone may induce perceptions of status threat (Bai & Federico, 2021) and the fear that one's position in the social hierarchy is declining, but so too may signs of racial progress (Wilkins et al., 2017; Wilkins & Kaiser, 2014).

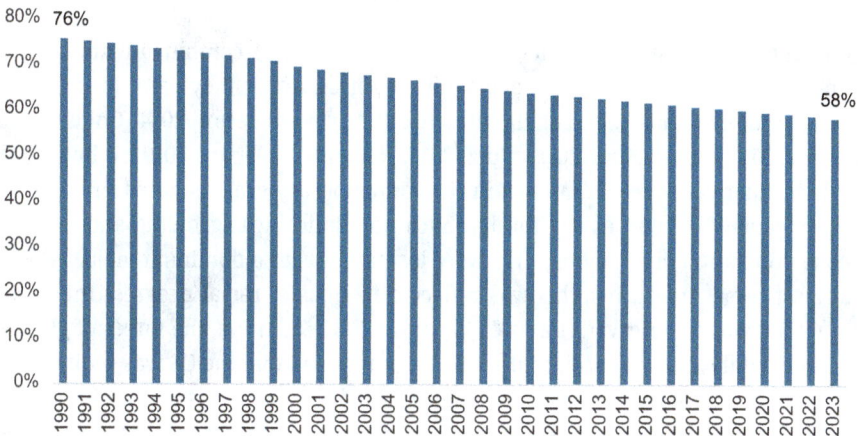

Figure 4.1: Non-Hispanic White Percentage of the Population.

Increases in immigration are often necessary, but not sufficient, to stirring nativism as a political force. Immigration must be combined with perceptions of cultural threat. Anti-Irish sentiment, for example, primarily reflected perceptions that, as Catholics, the Irish could not be real Americans. Similarly, anti-German sentiment existed prior to 1910s. Like the Irish, Germans were a target of the Know Nothing Party and the 100 Percent American movement,[48] but anti-German sentiment peaked with the start of WWI and the first 'America First' campaign because German immigrants were seen as a threat to American exceptionalism marked by a strong belief in individualism (Moench, 2018). As a result, German

---

48 The 100 Percent American movement arose out of concerns that European immigrants would not assimilate but would instead maintain European values and customs. The name reflects the rejection of hyphenated ethnicities (e.g., German-American). Americanism. https://www.loc.gov/exhibitions/world-war-i-american-experiences/about-this-exhibition/over-here/americanization/.

See also, An American and Nothing Else: The Great War and the Battle for National Belonging.

https://onlineexhibits.library.yale.edu/s/american-and-nothing-else/page/immigration-and-americanism.

language schools and newspapers common in the Midwest prior to WWI, were largely eliminated (Ramsey, 2002). As the writer Kurt Vonnegut observed (Vonnegut, 1981):

> the anti-Germanism in this country during the First World War so shamed and dismayed my parents that they resolved to raise me without acquainting me with the language or the literature or the music or the oral family histories which my ancestors had loved. They volunteered to make me ignorant and rootless as proof of their patriotism.

Current waves of immigration (as with those in the past), combined with population shifts, raised concerns among White Americans that they were losing their culture, their identity, and their influence (Craig & Richeson, 2014; Goldstein & Peters, 2014; Major et al., 2018; Mutz, 2018; Norris & Inglehart, 2019). Why would White Americans feel threatened in the contemporary era? As noted previously, they recognized that, as the foreign-born population was growing and the US-born population diversifying, they were losing status as a dominant majority. For at least some Americans, this was reflected in signs of racial progress that they often felt was undeserved (Davis & Wilson, 2022). In addition, the forces of globalization, while more general, confirmed the perception that the US was ceding control to foreign elites (Mutz, 2018). More broadly, and consistent with Donald Trump's political rhetoric, Americans perceived not only that globalization created a threat to American dominance in the world, but that international trade agreements were unfair to American workers (Mansfield & Mutz, 2009; Margalit, 2012; Mutz, 2018).

With this is as the backdrop, the stage was set for immigration to play a critical role in American politics.

Why Now? Nativism and Polarization in American Politics

While public opinion is not always anti-immigrant—context matters—nativist sentiments are ever-present. Prior to World War II, for example, Americans overwhelmingly opposed the admittance of German and Austrian refugees to immigrate to the US. According to a Roper Poll published in 1938, 67% of Americans wanted to keep German, Austrian, and other political refugees out of the country. Only 23% believed these European refugees should be allowed (5%) or encouraged (18%) to immigrate into the United States.[49] It is hardly surprising that anti-German sentiment grew prior to, during, and in the aftermath of World War I. This included legal restrictions on the use of the German language in public schools, as well as extra-legal political violence against German immigrations whose loyalty and patriotism were called into question (Moench, 2018). Rooted in fears that German social democratic thought challenged America's liberal traditions, this carried over into the 1930s, World War II, and beyond.

Other polling also revealed nativist sentiments. When asked specifically about voting 'yes' or 'no' to opening the doors to more European refugees in 1939, 83% of Americans said 'no thanks'.[50] Asked a similar question in the aftermath of World War II in 1947, 72% of Americans said 'no' to allowing immigration above and beyond existing quotas.[51] Much of the concern underlying this opposition was rooted in its potential for shifting the ethnic makeup of the country and, in turn, the individualistic and liberal political culture that defined American politics. Indeed, much of US immigration law has been based on this underlying logic. The Immigration Act of 1924 was explicitly designed to maintain the population's ethnic makeup, by setting quotas on immigration based on country of origin. Writing in the New York Times, Pennsylvania Senator David Reed, one of the co-sponsors of the Immigration Act, argued, that the new law would "mean a more homogenous nation, more self-reliant, more independent, and more closely knit in by common purpose and ideas."[52]

---

49 The specific question wording is as follows: "What is your attitude toward allowing German, Austrian, and other political refugees to come into the United States: ...We should encourage them to come, even if we have to raise immigration quotas...We should allow them to come, but not raise immigration quotas...With conditions as they are here we should try to keep them out?" Fortune Magazine. (1938). Roper Fortune # 1: General/Buying/Politics, Question 8 [USROPER.38–01.Q07]. The Roper Organization. Roper Center for Public Opinion Research.
50 "If you were a member of the incoming Congress would you vote yes or no on a bill to: Open the doors of the U.S. (United States) to a larger number of European refugees than now admitted under our immigration quotas." Citation: Fortune Magazine. Roper Fortune # 4: Politics and Government/General/Buying, Question 9. USROPER.39–004.R09B. The Roper Organization. Cornell University, Ithaca, NY: Roper Center for Public Opinion Research, 1939. Web. Jan-01-1939.
51 Specific question wording: "Would you vote yes or no on a bill in Congress to let 100,000 selected European refugees come to this country in each of the next four years, in addition to the 150,000 immigrants now permitted to enter every year under our present quotas?" Fortune Magazine. Roper Fortune # 59: Current Attitudes on Some Political and Economic Problems in US and on Possible Presidential Candidates, Question 11. USROPER.47–059.R09A. The Roper Organization. Cornell University, Ithaca, NY: Roper Center for Public Opinion Research, 1947. Web. Nov-30-1947.
52 Reed, D. (1924, April 27). America of the Melting Pot Comes to End. New York Times. https://www.nytimes.com/1924/04/27/archives/america-of-the-melting-pot-comes-to-end-effects-of-new-immigration.html.

In 1965, President Lyndon Johnson proposed unraveling the Immigration Act of 1924 by (1) increasing overall immigration; (2) ending the quota system which limited immigration based on country of origin; and (3) replacing it with a system based on skills. In a special message to Congress, Johnson argued:

> The fundamental, longtime American attitude has been to ask not where a person comes from but what are his personal qualities. On this basis men and women migrated from every quarter of the globe. By their hard work and their enormously varied talents they hewed a great nation out of a wilderness. By their dedication to liberty and equality, they created a society reflecting man's most cherished ideals . . .

> Violation of this tradition by the national origins quota system does incalculable harm. The procedures imply that men and women from some countries are, just because of where they come from, more desirable citizens than others. We have no right to disparage the ancestors of millions of our fellow Americans in this way. Relationships with a number of countries, and hence the success of our foreign policy, is needlessly impeded by this proposition.

> The quota system has other grave defects. Too often it arbitrarily denies us immigrants who have outstanding and sorely needed talents and skills. I do not believe this is either good government or good sense.[53]

Johnson signed The Immigration and Nationality Act into law in 1965. The American public, however, mostly disagreed (58%) with his proposal to increase immigration.[54] The public's verdict was more mixed when it came to changing from a quota-based system based on country of origin to a skills-based system, though the level of support depended on question wording. When asked simply about the tradeoff with no explanation, 70% of Americans preferred a skill-based system.[55] When provided with a more detailed explanation of the tradeoff, support fell to a

---

53 Johnson, L. B. (1965, January 13). Special message to the Congress on immigration. The American Presidency Project. https://www.presidency.ucsb.edu/documents/special-message-the-congress-immigration-0.

54 Question wording: "President (Lyndon) Johnson has proposed that the immigration laws of this country be changed to allow more people into the United States as immigrants. From what you know or have heard, do you favor or oppose letting more people come to the United States as immigrants?" Louis Harris & Associates (1965). Louis Harris & Associates Poll: May 1965, Question 7 [USHARRIS.053165.R1]. Louis Harris & Associates. Cornell University, Ithaca, NY: Roper Center for Public Opinion Research.

55 Question wording: "(Now I want to hand you a list of bills passed by this last Congress. For each, tell me if you approve or disapprove of that bill from what you know or have heard of it.) ... Immigration based on individual skill rather than country quota." Citation: Louis Harris & Associates. Louis Harris & Associates Poll: December 1965, Question 13. USHARRIS.010966.R2H. Louis Harris & Associates. Cornell University, Ithaca, NY: Roper Center for Public Opinion Research, 1965. Web. Dec-01-1965.

bare majority (51%) in a Gallup survey[56] and to a mere plurality (39%) in a Harris Survey.[57] Regardless, there was no strong embrace of immigration, even when it was directed at attracting highly skilled workers.

In the 1970s, in the aftermath of Vietnam War, Congress passed the Indochina Migration and Refugee Act, providing resources for 130,000 refugees from Vietnam, Laos, and Cambodia to immigrate to the United States. A plurality of Americans (49%) opposed the proposal.[58] Just two years later in 1977, 57% of Americans opposed a proposal from President Jimmy Carter to allow "15,000 more Indochinese refugees coming to live in this country."[59] In a review of the public opinion polls at the time, Lewis Stern concluded that the response to the Vietnamese immigrants was not unique, reflecting longstanding reluctance to immigrants from Europe in post-WWII era and from Hungary and Russia in the 1950s (Stern, 1981). Rather than widespread support for a tradition of open doors, Stern concluded that there was, at best, "a tentative and unstable minority favoring liberal immigration policies."

---

56 Question wording: "The current immigration law restricts the number of persons coming from some countries more than others. This is called the "quota" system. Would you favor or oppose changing this law so that people would be admitted on the basis of their occupational skills rather than on the basis of the country they come from?" Citation: Gallup Organization. Gallup Poll # 713, Question 21. USGALLUP.713.Q012. Gallup Organization. Cornell University, Ithaca, NY: Roper Center for Public Opinion Research, 1965. Web. Jun-24-1965.

57 Question wording: "One of the proposed changes in the immigration laws is to base quotas on the skills of people to be admitted to the United States rather than on the basis of their country of origin. Would you be in favor of such a change in the immigration laws or do you think a country quota system is right?" Citation: Louis Harris & Associates. Louis Harris & Associates Poll: May 1965, Question 8. USHARRIS.053165.R2. Louis Harris & Associates. Cornell University, Ithaca, NY: Roper Center for Public Opinion Research, 1965. Web. May-01-1965.

58 Question wording: "Do you favor or oppose allowing 130,000 Vietnam refugees to come to live in the United States?" Citation: Louis Harris & Associates. Louis Harris & Associates Poll: May 1975, Question 38. USHARRIS.062675.R1. Louis Harris & Associates. Cornell University, Ithaca, NY: Roper Center for Public Opinion Research, 1975. Web. May-23-1975.

59 Question wording: "There are still about 100,000 refugees who have fled communist governments in their home countries in Southeast Asia and do not have any country where they can go and resettle. Most of them, who are now in camps in Thailand and on boats without permission to resettle anywhere, would like to come to the U.S. to live. President Carter has proposed that 15,000 of these refugees be allowed to come here, in addition to the 15,000 already here. Do you tend to favor or oppose 15,000 more Indochinese refugees coming to live in this country?" Citation: Louis Harris & Associates. Louis Harris & Associates Poll: July 1977, Question 16. USHARRIS.082577.R1. Louis Harris & Associates. Cornell University, Ithaca, NY: Roper Center for Public Opinion Research, 1977. Web. Jul-23-1977.

Since its low point in the 1970s, immigration into the United States had increased. Due to the Immigration and Nationality Act of 1965, illegal immigration increased as circular immigration decreased and seasonal workers from Mexico feared returning home (Massey 2021). At the same time, the US population was growing noticeably more diverse as the non-Hispanic White population was shrinking as a percentage of the total population.

This was not only a context ripe for nativist politics, it was politics ripe for a politician more inclined to divide than to unite (Baker & Glasser, 2023). Nativism could be used as an issue to connect with those Americans who felt like they were losing their country to a rapidly changing world. Trump is important to our story because he takes advantage of the opportunity. But his success is, in no small part, due to timing. Hence, Trump was successful while Pat Buchanan in 1992 and Pete Wilson in 1996 were not.

News coverage of immigration likely amplified its political effects. First, news coverage of immigration increased significantly across news networks[60] and coverage was consistently negative, emphasizing the threats posed by illegal immigration.[61] The framing of immigration-related news differed across networks with Fox News viewers exposed to more negative coverage. As a result, Fox News viewers were more likely to have negative views of immigration, even controlling for ideological predispositions (Gil de Zúñiga et al., 2012; Hoewe et al., 2020). Consistent with Trump's rhetoric, Fox News framed immigration as a threat to personal security, emphasizing the distinction between illegal immigrants and immigrants "who did it the right way" (McDonald & Morgaine, 2016). MSNBC framed efforts to control immigration via S.B. 1070 as violations of personal freedom (McDonald & Morgaine, 2016). "Fox's underlying strategy on race," Berry, Glaser, and Schildkraut contend, "is to anger viewers by stoking their resentment of racial and ethnic minority groups in America and of non-White immigrants trying to get into America" (Berry et al., 2021). We can see some-evidence of this in Figure 4.2 based on Google searches (defined here as Google Interest).

In Figure 4.2, interest is measured on a 0–100 scale where 100 indicates peak interest. Figure 4.2 presents *average interest by year* from 2004 to 2023. Interest in nativism increased consistently from 2004 to 2016 when it began to decline. In 2020, when Donald Trump lost the presidency to Joe Biden, interest in nativism had declined significantly. In 2021, interest in nativism declined even further. The

---

60 Sides, J. (2017). Race, Religion, and Immigration in 2016. Democracy Fund Voter Study Group. https://www.voterstudygroup.org/publication/race-religion-immigration-2016.

61 Patterson, T. E. (2016). News Coverage of the 2016 General Election: How the Press Failed the Voters. Shorenstein Center on Media, Politics and Public Policy, Harvard Kennedy School. https://shorensteincenter.org/news-coverage-2016-general-election/.

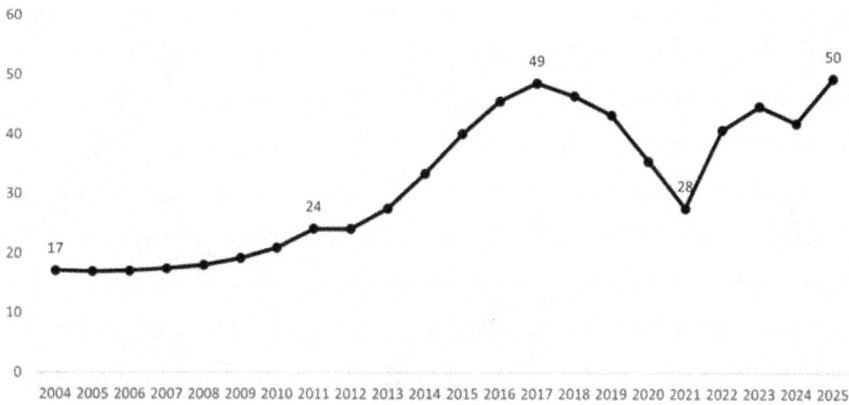

Figure 4.2: Google Interest Over Time for Nativism.[62]

level of interest expressed in nativism on Google Trends appears to correlate fairly strongly to Trump's rise and fall (and his rise again).

We can see a parallel trend if we examine cable television news coverage using the Stanford Cable News Analyzer.[63] As can be seen in Figure 4.3, cable news coverage of immigration increased through 2018 and then declined sharply during the pandemic and into the 2020 election. Fox News consistently gave more coverage to immigration than MSNBC or CNN. The fact that coverage of immigration peaked in 2018 should not be surprising. Facing a difficult midterm election year, Republican congressional candidates emphasized getting tough on immigration as means to mobilize their base. President Donald Trump, for his part, chimed in that "Democrats want to spend your money and give away your resources for the benefit of anyone but American citizens. If you don't want America to be overrun by masses of illegal immigrants and massive caravans, you better vote Republican."[64] In the midst of the election, news of a migrant caravan, carrying immigrants from Central America (mostly from Honduras), dominated the news and increased the salience of immigration. Trump reprised a familiar refrain: "That's an invasion. I don't care what they say. I don't care what the fake media says. That's an invasion of our country."[65]

---

62 https://trends.google.com/trends/.

63 https://tvnews.stanford.edu/.

64 Shear, M. D., & Davis, J. H. (2018, November 1). Trump sends troops to border, but his focus is on politics. The New York Times. https://www.nytimes.com/2018/11/01/us/politics/trump-immigra tion.html.

65 Scott, E. (2018, November 8). Before the midterms, Trump harped on the migrant caravan. Since then, he hasn't brought it up. The Washington Post. https://www.washingtonpost.com/poli

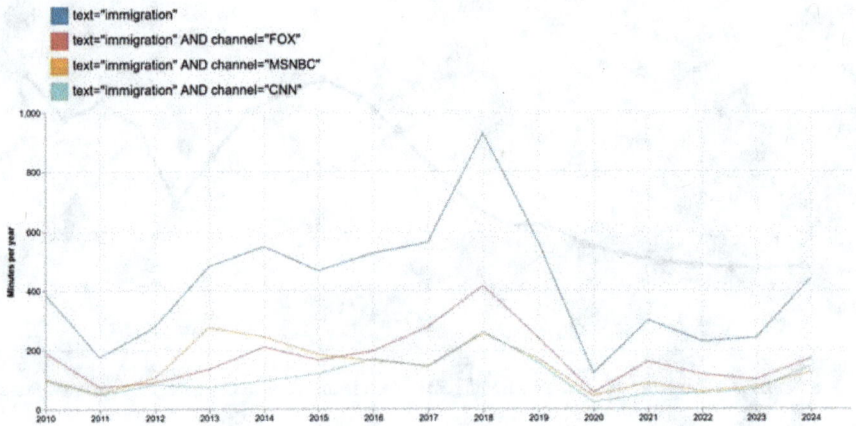

Figure 4.3: Cable News Coverage of Immigration by News Channel.

At least some analysts have claimed the 2018 midterm election results, in which Democrats picked up 41 House seats, reflected voter rejection of nativist, anti-immigration politics.[66] But, in our opinion, the results more reflected the weakness of Republican candidates, the limited efficacy of Trump endorsements, and Republican failed efforts to repeal the affordable care act (Obamacare).[67] A Kaiser Family Foundation poll, for example, found that health care was the most important issue for Democrats and Independents heading into the 2018 midterm elections, though immigration and the economy were more important for Republican voters.[68]

Even as Republicans were losing seats in Congress, the nativist impulse maintained a strong hold on the Republican base. More generally, immigration did not stop resonating with Republican voters and continued to play an important role in voting decisions after 2016. While the COVID-19 pandemic diverted cable news attention, news coverage of immigration picked up heading into the 2024 presidential

tics/2018/11/08/before-midterms-trump-harped-migrant-caravan-since-then-he-has-barely-men tioned-it/.

66 Muñoz Lopez, L. (2018, December 13). Anti-immigrant rhetoric was defeated in the 2018 midterm elections. Center for American Progress. https://www.americanprogress.org/article/anti-im migrant-rhetoric-defeated-2018-midterm-elections/.

67 Hall, C., & Tolbert, J. (2018, October 22). Health care and the candidates in the 2018 midterm elections: Key issues and races. Kaiser Family Foundation. https://www.kff.org/affordable-care-act/ issue-brief/health-care-and-the-candidates-in-the-2018-midterm-elections-key-issues-and-races/.

68 Muñoz Lopez, L. (2018, December 13). Anti-immigrant rhetoric was defeated in the 2018 midterm elections. Center for American Progress. https://www.americanprogress.org/article/anti-im migrant-rhetoric-defeated-2018-midterm-elections/.

election. This increase reflected both the reality on the ground—immigration decreased during the pandemic and then increased dramatically during the Biden Administration—and intentional efforts to highlight issues related to the waves of immigration crossing at the border after Biden's inauguration in January 2021. Texas
Governor Greg Abbott bussed more than 100,000 immigrants from the Texas border to Democratic-led cities (e.g., Chicago, New York, and Washington D.C.). At
Trump's behest, Republicans backed out of a deal with Democrats designed to enhance border security prior to the election. While this allowed Democrats to blame
Republicans for politicizing the issue, border politics continued to be a vulnerability for the Biden Administration. Subsequent efforts by Biden to act unilaterally
using executive authority were generally seen as too little, too late. All of this kept
nativism at the forefront of the minds of Republican voters and kept Trump firmly
in control of the Republican base.

Considerable evidence points to the importance of nativism in Trump winning the presidency in 2016 and carrying him through his first four years (Young
et al., 2019), and helping him to secure re-election in 2024. We discuss the importance of nativism in Chapter 5. Other research shows the role of nativism in shaping politics globally (Betz, 2019; Davis et al., 2019b; Iakhnis et al., 2018; Kešić &
Duyvendak, 2019). While Trump is unique, the importance of nativism as a driver
of politics is not. The flavor of nativism can (and does) vary from country to country. We will see this in Chapter 8. But such empirical consistency shows the prom-
inence of the concept in the face of large global population shifts and other existential threats (Young et al., 2019).

Trump's loss to Biden for re-election in 2020 appeared to mute the nativist cre-
scendo. Americans had spoken—voting multiculturalism over nativism. Americans,
it seemed, longed for a return to a less polarized and less nativist time. This was
short-lived. In 2022, congressional Republicans once again turned to nativist messaging in an effort to mobilize voters. According to America's Voice, a pro-immigration
advocacy group, more than 3200 paid Republican ads expressed nativist messages,
including messages criticizing Democrats for supporting open borders or connecting
immigrants to illegal drug trade. Foreshadowing the 2024 campaign, Republicans described the border as a 'crisis' and the influx of immigration as an 'invasion.' But in
2022, the messaging did not work, and the 'red wave' that many were anticipating
never materialized. Republicans lost a seat in the US Senate and, though they gained
control of the House of Representatives, they won far fewer seats than anticipated.[69]

---

69 Siders, D. (2022, November 9). The red wave that wasn't: 5 takeaways from a disappointing
night for the GOP. Politico. https://www.politico.com/news/2022/11/09/2022-election-results-analy
sis-and-takeaways-00065878.

The 2020 election deniers ran poorly during the 2022 midterms as did candidates who adopted anti-immigrant campaign messages. In an analysis of the election, America's Voice called the strategy a failure but noted that Republicans were 'doubling down' as they moved toward 2024. As the report concluded:

> The current leading forces in the GOP are running full speed towards the same nativist electoral strategy that has failed them repeatedly at the ballot box and repeatedly courted deadly political violence. Continuing this current trajectory is not inevitable, but the incentives inside the party make a course correction highly unlikely. Still, it should be clear that the GOP's investment in nativism is far from a silver bullet and may be a liability.[70]

Former President Donald Trump, for his part, never exited the stage, never relinquished the claim that he was the rightful winner of the 2020 campaign, and never strayed far from his nativist messaging. Despite concerns that he had been a liability in midterm campaigns and special elections since his victory in 2016, Trump emerged as the front runner for the 2024 Republican nomination. Challengers like Florida Governor Ron DeSantis, who tried to be a Donald Trump 2.0, a competent executive without the legal baggage, had to take a hard turn to nativism in an attempt to run to Trump's right.[71] Neither DeSantis nor South Carolina Governor Nikki Haley was willing to risk alienating Trump's nativist base.[72] Indeed, as long as they both remained in the race, they spent more time attacking each other than challenging their party's frontrunner. The calculation appeared to be that if they could end up in a one-on-one race with former President Trump, they could secure the nomination. With the benefit of hindsight, this was clearly a miscalculation.

Once he had secured the nomination, Trump upped the nativist ante from "building a big beautiful wall that Mexico would pay for" to the promise of "the largest mass deportation campaign in American history."[73] Nativism remained an important and powerful force in Republican Party politics.

---

70 New America's Voice. (2023, March 22). The GOP Investment in Nativism Failed to Deliver, Again: America's Voice Report on Nativist Political Messaging and Ads in the 2022 Midterms. https://americasvoice.org/wp-content/uploads/2023/03/22-REPORT_.pdf.

71 Kight, Stef. W. (2023, June 2). The GOP battle to show who's tougher on immigration. Axios. https://www.axios.com/2023/06/02/2024-gop-border-immigration (accessed June 8, 2025).

72 Haley did attack Trump once DeSantis was out of the race. When DeSantis was still in the race, they spent more time and effort attacking each other than the former president.

73 In 1954, the Eisenhower Administration launched Operation Wetback which deported over a million unauthorized immigrants. Ngai, M. M. (2014). *Impossible Subjects: Illegal Aliens and the Making of Modern America*. Princeton University Press.

Nativist Sentiment Over the Recent Past

As we have seen thus far in this chapter, nativism has persisted as a political force in America even with ebbs and flows over the last century and a half. But this analysis still leaves us with some unanswered questions about the more recent past. How have nativist attitudes trended over the last few decades? Is nativism increasing (or not) in political importance?

To answer these questions, we examine two separate nativism trends—we take one question from Pew and the other from the World Values Survey. Both trend lines span almost three decades (1995 to 2025), allowing us to validate one time series against the other.

The first (agree/disagree) statement, from the World Value Survey (WVS), reads: "When jobs are scarce, employers should give priority to people of this country over immigrants." We splice Ipsos data together with the WVS trend beginning in 2016. The WVS question has been validated against other attitudinal measures of nativism as well as objective behavioral items. It has been shown to have good measurement properties, and, as a result, serves as a robust measure of nativism (Young et al., 2019).

The second question trend comes from Pew. It reads: "Please tell me whether the first statement or the second statement comes closer to your own views–even if neither is exactly right . . . Immigrants today make our country stronger because of their work and talents, immigrants today are a burden on our country because they take our jobs and social benefits."[74] Like the WVS question, we combine the Pew time-series with more recent data from Ipsos.

For the Pew question, we analyze the "make country stronger" side of the scale. So, we expect the two trends to be divergent in direction if there is a trend at all. Both time-series run about 1994 to 2025. To gauge if we have a significant trend, we run a simple regression line through the aggregate data points.

We also conduct cohort analysis to determine the mechanism of change— *within versus between person change*. Here, we avoid the identification problem

---

74 This question is frequently used in surveys conducted by the Pew Research Center. For an example of the question and the specific question wording, see Pew Research Center. (2019, March 14). Topline Questionnaire: Spring 2018 Survey. https://www.pewresearch.org/global/wp-content/uploads/sites/2/2019/03/Pew-Research-Center_Global-Attitudes-Towards-Immigrants-Topline_2019-03-14.pdf.

in isolating age, cohort, and period effect (time).[75] Instead, we combine age and period effects and call it within person change.[76] We analyze this in two ways. First, we use simple tabular analysis. And second, we take a regression-based method developed by Firebaugh to parse out the relative effects of within and between person change (Curran & Bauer, 2011; Firebaugh, 1978; Yang, 2013). This allows us to estimate the proportion of each change component.

$$N = C + B1 + W2$$

Here, we define N as total change in nativism, C is a constant, $B1$ as between person change, and $W2$ as the within person change.

Nativism Trended: Attenuation and Strengthening

Is nativism on the decline? The answer is both yes and no. To show this, we look at the long-term trends in nativism using two separate questions as detailed below.

Attenuation of Nativism

Overall, the trend in nativism is downward. Americans are becoming less (not more) nativist. Take the first time series which employs a question from the World Value Survey (WVS) displayed in Figure 4.4. The trend is flat for part of the time with a sharp dip in the last few years. Specifically, the series starts out at 55 percent agreement that native born should be prioritized over foreigners. Agreement with the statement decreases to 48 percent in 2025—a 9-point drop.

The Pew series (see Figure 4.5) follows a similar trajectory. There is a slow yet steady increase then a stark jump in seeing "immigrants as beneficial." The numbers are striking: 40 percent of Americans said immigration was beneficial in 1995 compared to 61 percent in 2024—a 21-point bump. So, nativism has attenuated. Americans have become less nativist and more accepting of immigrants over the last quarter century. Why might this be the case? How could nativism have been a driver of contemporary politics if at the same time it is weakening?

---

75 By 'identification problem,' we mean the unique issue faced in cohort analysis where any two components are a linear combination of the third. As such, it is impossible to solve for all three.
76 Lau, A., & Kennedy, C. (2023, May 22). Assessing the effects of generation using age-period-cohort analysis. Pew Research Center. https://www.pewresearch.org/decoded/2023/05/22/assessing-the-effects-of-generation-using-age-period-cohort-analysis/#:~:text=For%20example%2C%20we%20can%20contrast,when%20the%20data%20was%20collected.

Nativist views among Americans has dropped since 2016

Q: When jobs are scarce, employers should prioritize hiring people of this country over immigrants. % Agree

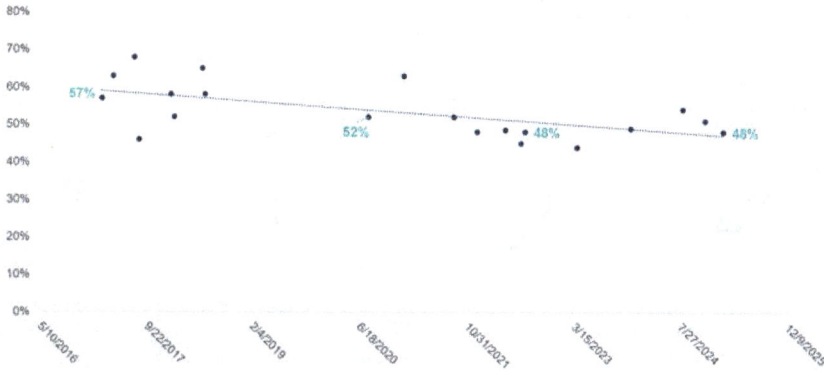

Figure 4.4: Percent Agreeing Employers Should Prioritize Hiring Natives, 1995–2025.
Source: World Value Survey and Ipsos

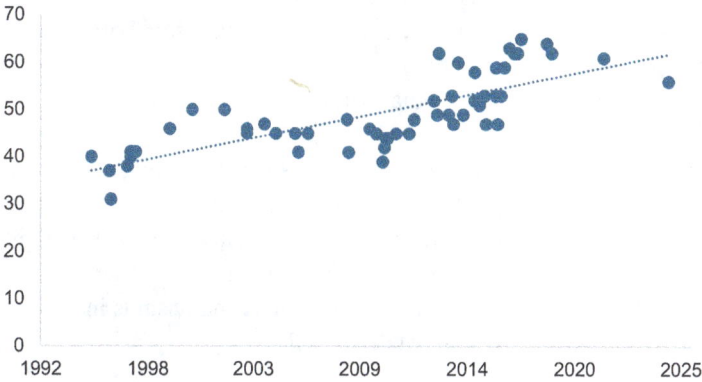

Figure 4.5: Rolling Average of Percent of Americans Saying Immigrants are a Benefit, 1995–2021.
(Source: Pew Center for Research, New York Times).

Here, we turn to cohort analysis to determine what kind of change are we seeing—are people changing their attitudes (within person change) or is the composition of the population changing with generational replacement (between person change)? To do this, we use two methods. First, we conduct a simple tabular generational analysis (see Table 4.1). To identify generations, we use standard cutoffs (Silent Generation 1928–1945; Baby Boomers 1946–1964; Generation X 1965–1980; Millennials 1980–1996; Generation Z 1997–2012). Second, we employ regression analysis to estimate *within* versus *between* person effects (Curran & Bauer, 2011; Firebaugh, 1978).

Table 4.1: Cohort Analysis: Percent Agreeing That Native-Born Americans Should Receive Preferential Treatment in Hiring.

	1995 (%)	2009 (%)	2023 (%)
Greatest Generation	73	64	**
Silent Generation	62	61	73
Boomers	59	55	53
Generation X	55	56	59
Millennials	**	42	40
Generation Z	**	**	40

Initially, we see that there is a strong generational component to the change in the WVS question. First, each successive generation is more tolerant towards immigrants than the previous generation. The Baby Boomers, for example, are less nativist than the Silent generation. In 2023, the Silent Generation (73 percent) is considerably more nativist than Millennials (40 percent), a remarkable 33-point difference between these generations. Overall, there are only weak within-person effects. This stability has been especially impressive during the Trump years when his gravitational pull was considerable, nativist appeals were a recurring part of political campaigns, and the media routinely covered immigration as a 'crisis at the border.'

To validate this, we estimate that 75% of the change is due to generational replacement, while only 25% results from within person change. Again, the slow march of history explains the trend towards greater tolerance and weaker nativist attitudes. Younger Americans are more tolerant of immigrants. That explains the trend but also raises more questions than it answers. If nativism is in relative decline, why is it so important as a political driver today?

The Paradox of Nativism: Fading but Rising

So, does this mean that nativism is increasingly less important for politics today? Here, the answer is unequivocally no. Indeed, it has never been stronger. How can this be? A quick look at the WVS question broken down by party identification (see Figure 4.6) shows an increasing bifurcation between Democrats and Republicans on nativism. The numbers are clear.

From 1995 to 2004, there was little difference between Democrats and Republicans on nativism. It wasn't until 2009 onwards that the difference becomes pronounced (Ollerenshaw & Jardina, 2023). Notably, this coincides with the election of Barack Obama and the growing 'birther' conspiracy that Obama was not born

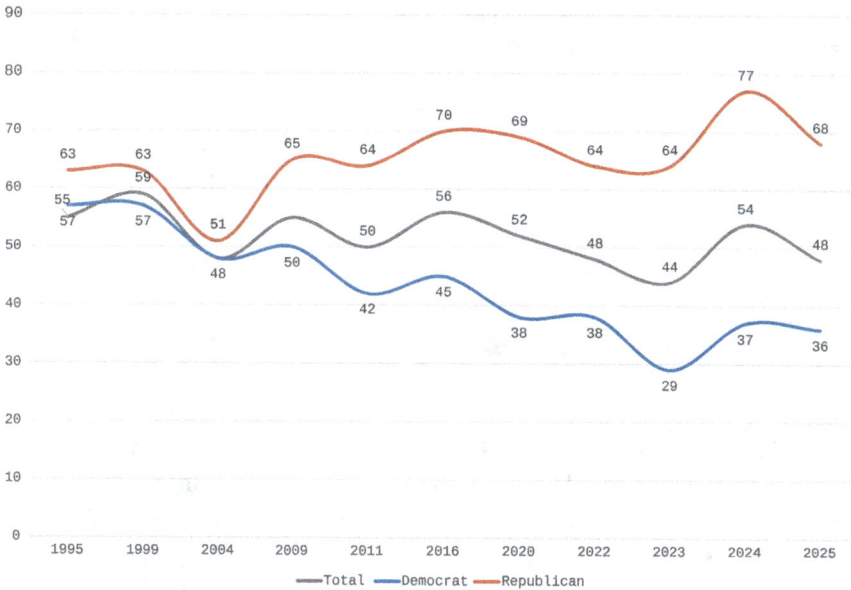

Figure 4.6: Nativism by Partisan Affiliation, 1995–2023.
(Source: World Values Survey & Ipsos Polls).

in the United States and therefore not eligible to be president (Kelley-Romano & Carew, 2017), and the Tea Party movement, motivated, in part, by beliefs that government policies were too favorable to illegal immigrants (Skocpol & Williamson, 2016; Williamson et al., 2011). By 2025, Democrats and Republicans are separated by a 32-point gulf. Interestingly, it is Democrats that decline significantly in their nativist bent from 57% in 1995 to 36% by 2025. Republicans, in contrast, hold steady in the mid- to high-60s.

We find similar trends in the Pew question on 'immigrants make us stronger.' The difference between Republicans and Democrats has grown overtime. Indeed, 32% of Democrats saw immigrants as beneficial in 1994, while 83% in 2022. Republicans, in turn, stayed relatively steady at 30% in 1995 and 36% in 2023.

What is driving the Democratic trend?

To understand this, let's look at Democrats specifically using a cohort table (see Table 4.2). Here, we find both strong generation effects and within person effects. Indeed, there is a 16-point difference between the 'Silent Generation' and 'Generation Z' in 2023. And there also a considerable within person change with the 'Silent Generation' becoming more tolerant overtime (63% versus 47%) and

Table 4.2: Age-Period-Cohort Analysis for Democrats: Percent Agreeing That Native-Born Americans Should Receive Preferential Treatment in Hiring.

	1995 (%)	2009 (%)	2023 (%)
Greatest Generation	76	54	**
Silent Generation	63	56	47
Boomers	55	51	42
Generation X	48	49	47
Millennials	**	44	30
Generation Z	**	**	31

Source: Ipsos; World Values Survey.

younger generations becoming more progressive on issues related to immigration.[77] Our regression method reinforces our tabular findings: 50% of the change is generationally driven, while 50% is due to within person change. Overall, Democrats are becoming less nativist—both from generation replacement as well as people changing their attitudes.

Conclusions

So, what did we learn?

Nativism has been a constant feature of American life since its conception. Nativist concerns peak during times of intense immigration and other forms of social and economic change. It has been different immigrant groups at different times that have challenged the body politic. Think of the Irish, the Chinese, the Italians and Eastern Europeans, Southeast Asians, and now Latin Americans. The reaction has been both political and legal. Early polling in the late 1930s even shows America's aversion to refugees from pre-war Europe. Nativism has always been an American staple.

Nativism has declined over the last quarter century. But this decline is primarily a result of Democrats becoming more tolerant, while Republicans have largely remained nativist. This partisan divergence began in the mid-to-late 2000s. Before that, Democrats and Republicans held relatively similar views on nativism. Today, the gap is striking—our most recent poll shows a 32-point differ-

---

77 We should note, however, that there is some evidence that Generation Z men are becoming more conservative even as Generation Z women are becoming more progressive. Miller, C. C. (2024, August 24). Many Gen Z men feel left behind. Some see Trump as an answer. The New York Times. https://www.nytimes.com/2024/08/24/upshot/trump-polls-young-men.html

ence between the parties. Sixty-eight percent of Republicans express nativist sentiment, compared to just 36 percent of Democrats. This shift is driven by generational replacement—each new cohort of younger, more diverse, and more tolerant voters further distances the Democratic Party from nativist beliefs.

Yet, despite this overall decline, nativism has not lost its political significance. In fact, the opposite is true—its importance has only grown. The Republican Party has become the political home of American nativism, in attitude, mood, and action. As a result, immigration and related issues became central in the 2024 election. The rhetoric has been unmistakably nativist, with candidates competing to prove their credibility on immigration. Take, for example, Ron DeSantis' decision to bus migrants to Martha's Vineyard—this was not merely a stunt to provoke liberals but a strategic attempt to establish nativist credentials within the Republican primary. Immigration was the number one issue for Republican voters in 2024, a direct result of this political alignment.

At the same time, nativism is no longer a majority opinion in America. Our most recent data show that only 48 percent of Americans agree with the statement "When jobs are scarce, employers should give priority to people of this country over immigrants." In 2017, that number was at its most recent high point—56 percent—driven by Trump's rhetoric and ability to keep immigration at the top of the national agenda. He repeatedly used symbolic events—like the so-called 'migrant caravan'—to prime nativist sentiment (Young 2019a). But eventually, other crises, such as impeachment and the Ukraine war, diverted attention.

The Democratic trend is equally important. Over time, generational replacement will likely continue to erode nativist attitudes, reshaping the political landscape. But in the medium term, the battle over immigration will remain a defining issue—a clash between two competing views of the world.

Looking ahead, if these long-term trends persist, many argue that the Republican Party risks becoming a nativist enclave—a party where nativism is dominant internally *but* increasingly disconnected from the broader electorate. We believe that this perspective is too simplistic. As our analysis has shown, there are many nativist-adjacent Americans that can be brought into the fold if the framing is done right. Trump won in 2024 by building a broader coalition of nativists and libertarians.[78] Here, the message was not just about fear of cultural change. Instead, Trump and the Republicans emphasized two nativist-adjacent themes: (1) the fundamental fairness of people jumping the queue by coming to the US illegally; and (2) strong borders to ensure national security.

---

78 Young, C. (2025). The Rise of 'Freedom First': A Political Realignment Reshaping America, in Substack, March 2025. https://substack.com/home/post/p-158997573.

As we detailed earlier in our Nativism Activation Model (NAM), Nativism needs catalytic conditions to make it active. It is a latent force that ebbs and flows, gaining power only when demographic, cultural, and political conditions align. The last thirty years of American politics are not just a story of changing demographics, but of how those changes have been interpreted, politicized, and mobilized. The widening partisan divide on nativism is not simply a reaction to immigration rates or economic stress—it is the result of political actors, media narratives, and shifting party coalitions.

What distinguishes the current era is not the existence of nativism but its partisan consolidation. Whereas past nativist movements cut across party lines, today's nativism is largely concentrated within the Republican Party, reinforced by the perception that demographic and cultural changes threaten the traditional American identity. The convergence of rising immigration, economic uncertainty, and media-driven narratives about national decline have created fertile ground for its resurgence. The long-term trajectory suggests that while nativism may continue to vary in intensity over time, its influence within the Republican coalition is likely to persist, shaping electoral politics and policy debates for years to come.

Ultimately, nativism is not merely a response to immigration—it is a political tool. And like all tools, its power depends on who wields it, and when.

Chapter 5
Why Nativism Matters: How Nativism Conditions Politics

Vignette: Watching a World View Take Shape

The summer of 2016. Convention season. Donald J. Trump had secured the Republican nomination with unsettling ease. What once seemed like a vanity project had become a political earthquake. He now stood as one of two contenders for the presidency.

To the establishment, Trump was a walking contradiction. An entertainer. A flimflam man. A reality TV star turned political wrecking ball. He had no governing experience, no coherent ideology, and no respect for decorum. And yet, there he was—towering over a fractured Republican Party.

Explanations flooded the op-ed pages and cable news panels. Some blamed globalization and the economic dislocation it wrought. Others saw racial resentment. Still others reached for authoritarianism. The 'Trump as authoritarian' narrative gained traction among media elites, aided by a study from political scientist Matthew MacWilliams.[79] Earlier in 2016, MacWilliams argued that the key to understanding Trump supporters wasn't demographics—it was authoritarianism.

It was a tidy narrative. It made sense. It fit the times.

But it wasn't right.

At Ipsos, we were seeing something different in the data—something deeper. Since late 2015, our polling had shown a consistent and powerful signal: the real driver wasn't authoritarianism, it was nativism.

We knew we had to test it head-on. So, we did what good pollsters do—we ran the numbers. We built models. We controlled not just for demographics, but for competing ideological explanations: populism, economic grievance, racial resentment, and, yes, authoritarianism.

The results came back. I remember staring at the screen. The relative importance of nativism wasn't just significant—it was dominant. Populism, economic dissatisfaction, even authoritarianism—they all registered, but none came close. Nativism was the signal; the rest was noise.

---

79 MacWilliams, Matthew. (2017, January 17). The One Weird Trait That Predicts Whether You're a Trump Supporter. And it's not gender, age, income, race or religion. Politico. https://www.politico.com/magazine/story/2016/01/donald-trump-2016-authoritarian-213533/.

https://doi.org/10.1515/9783111384047-005

In that moment, the story for us of 2016 shifted. While pundits warned of creeping authoritarianism, we saw something older, deeper, and more American. It wasn't the leader that mattered—it was the line. Who belongs. Who doesn't.

We published our findings in a white paper titled *It's Nativism* in September 2017 (Young, 2016). At the time, most thought Trump would lose. But we were already seeing the future.

We weren't just measuring public opinion. We were watching a worldview take shape before our eyes.

Nativism in Contemporary Politics

Over the past decade, nativism has defined contemporary politics. The origins of this shift began with the fight over Barack Obama's birth certificate. By questioning the legitimacy of President Obama's citizenship, Trump raised questions about whether Obama was a real American and, subsequently, whether his presidency was legitimate. If this mostly seemed like a curious and clownish sideshow, it helped set the stage for the nativist politics that followed. If a subset of voters was willing to question the legitimacy of a duly elected president, was it unreasonable to think that they would also question the legitimacy of their fellow citizens, of elections won by 'illegal votes', of an economy rigged against 'real Americans'?

Throughout American history, nativist politics has been closely linked to conspiracy theories proclaiming that dark forces were working to undermine the American republic and replace native-born Americans with newly arrived immigrants (Dickey, 2023; Gaston & Uscinski, 2018).[80] This is not unintentional but rather part of a political strategy designed to appeal to native-born voters. As Cas Mudde observes:

> With varying degrees of conspiracy theories — some more anti-Semitic, others more anti-capitalist — mass immigration is presented as a willing plot of (inter)national politicians, business leaders, and trade union leaders to strengthen their own position at the expense of the average citizen.[81]

---

80 Klofstad, C., & Uscinski, J. E. (2024, September 5). Why those who believe in "White Replacement" conspiracy theories may be even more dangerous than previously thought. LSE USAPP—American Politics and Policy. https://blogs.lse.ac.uk/usappblog/2024/09/05/why-those-who-believe-in-white-replacement-conspiracy-theories-may-be-even-more-dangerous-than-previously-thought/.

81 Mudde, C. (2012, May). The Relationship Between Immigration and Nativism in Europe and North America. Migration Policy Institute. https://www.migrationpolicy.org/sites/default/files/publications/Immigration-Nativism.pdf.

The most recent nativist iteration, led by Donald Trump, is no exception (Uscinski & Enders, 2023). Nativist appeals flowed seamlessly out of the conspiracy theories over President Barack Obama's birthplace and legitimacy as president, and they resonated among voters who feared 'hope and change,' preferring instead an America they remembered nostalgically from their childhood (Goidel et al., 2025; Goidel, Goidel, et al., 2024). Nativist appeals proved politically potent because they also connected to other themes of the Trump campaign. Returning America to a simpler time required a strong authoritarian president willing to break the rules (Knuckey & Hassan, 2022). Cueing in-group favoritism and out-group hostility did not just prime status threat and nativist sentiments, it also cued White racial grievance and modern sexism (Schaffner et al., 2018; Smith & Hanley, 2020; Tolbert et al., 2018).[82] And, the connection to conspiracy theories played into a worldview that saw the changes to American culture and society as the result of powerful and evil political elites working against the interests of working-class men and women (Norris & Inglehart, 2019; Oliver & Rahn, 2016; White, 2016).

Tucker Carlson, former Fox News Host and political commentator, played into these fears by articulating variations of the Great Replacement Theory, that non-White immigrants were being brought into the US to replace the White majority.[83] These themes were echoed by Donald Trump, first as a candidate and subsequently as a president and former president running to reclaim the office he lost in 2020. During his debate with Vice President Kamala Harris, Trump claimed of newly arrived immigrants: "They can't even speak English. They don't even know what country they're in, practically. And these people are trying to get them to vote, and that's why they're allowing them into our country."[84] Immigrants were not just being allowed into the country; they were being allowed into the country to vote illegally and to steal elections from native-born 'real' Americans.

Running as a US Senate candidate in 2022, J.D. Vance similarly claimed, without supporting evidence, that Democrats "have decided that they can't win reelection in

82 Lopez, G. (2017, December 15). The past year of research has made it very clear: Trump won because of racial resentment. Vox https://www.vox.com/identities/2017/12/15/16781222/trump-racism-economic-anxiety-study; Tesler, M. (2016, November 22). Views about race mattered more in electing Trump than in electing Obama. The Washington Post. https://www.washingtonpost.com/news/monkey-cage/wp/2016/11/22/peoples-views-about-race-mattered-more-in-electing-trump-than-in-electing-obama/.

83 Bond, S. (2023, April 25). How Tucker Carlson mainstreamed fringe conspiracy theories. NPR. https://www.npr.org/2023/04/25/1171800317/how-tucker-carlsons-extremist-narratives-shaped-fox-news-and-conservative-politi.

84 Joffe-Block, J. and Odette, Y. (2024, September 13). How Trump is relying on a racist conspiracy theory to question election results. NPR. https://www.npr.org/2024/09/13/g-s1-22583/trump-great-replacement-conspiracy-theory.

2022 unless they bring a large number of new voters to replace the voters that are already here."[85] Trump and Vance were hardly alone in connecting nativism to conspiracy theories aimed at cueing fears that immigrants were stealing jobs and elections. This was a recurring theme during the 2022 midterm elections. It resonated strongly with Republican voters and Fox News viewers.[86]

Nativist appeals, we contend, tied conspiracy theories, racial resentment, authoritarianism, and populism together in nicely wrapped package of discontent. This combustible mix of attitudes and orientations emerged during the 2016 campaign and has been in play ever since. Nativism proved to be the binding agent because of how it connected to and activated these other orientations.[87] Just to be clear, we are not claiming that racial grievance, authoritarianism, or populism were unimportant—only that nativism was the driving force of an emergent belief system.

Using original survey data, we show in this chapter the powerful effects nativism has had on voter turnout and voting behavior, mobilizing voters angry about a changing political culture, and aligning them with the Donald Trump-led Republican Party. Nativism was not just part of the story explaining Trump's hostile takeover of the Republican Party and ascendency to the US presidency, it was *the* story. Nor were the effects limited to Donald Trump, instead they influenced Republican voting in down-ballot races, including congressional and statewide elections. In short, nativism reset contemporary American politics.

How Nativism Conditions Politics

Perhaps no question has been more thoroughly researched than the how voters choose between competing candidates during an election campaign. Early research found that political campaigns had only 'minimal effects,' meaning that they mostly reinforced preexisting partisan attachments (Campbell, 1954; Campbell et al., 1960; Lazarsfeld et al., 1968). Except for a small group of unaffiliated and largely inattentive swing voters, partisan affiliation, rather than issues, drove individual voting decisions. To the extent that voters moved across party lines, they did so primarily

85 People, S. (2022, May 17). Republican Senate candidates promote 'replacement' theory. PBS. https://www.pbs.org/newshour/politics/republican-senate-candidates-promote-replacement-theory.

86 Bump, P. (2022, May 9). Nearly half of Republicans agree with the 'great replacement theory.' The Washington Post. https://www.washingtonpost.com/politics/2022/05/09/nearly-half-republicans-agree-with-great-replacement-theory/.

87 Young, C. (2016, September). It's Nativism: Explaining the Drivers of Trump's Popular Support. Ipsos Public Affairs. https://www.ipsos.com/sites/default/files/2016-09/Its_Nativism_Explaining_the_Drivers_of_Trumps_Popular_Support.pdf.

in response to short-term economic conditions. Moreover, because voters were poorly informed and lacked detailed knowledge about candidate policy stances, issues played a minor role except as they operated through partisan affiliation or as influenced through interpersonal discussions with opinion leaders. In short, Americans were not issue voters, they voted based on long-term partisan attachments formed during childhood that were resistant to change.

This early work called into question the assumptions of classic democratic theory where voters enthusiastically engaged in democratic political processes, became informed about political issues and candidates, and made rational calculations about which candidates best reflected their interests. Instead, voters proved to be poorly informed (perhaps rationally so), voted at low rates, and selected candidates (and parties) using cognitive shortcuts (or heuristics) to minimize the time and attention they needed to devote to politics. Much of the research that followed emphasized that, while voters fell short of the democratic ideal, they did pretty well with the limited information they had readily available. In the words of Herbert Simon, voters were 'satisficing' rather than optimizing when choosing between candidates (Simon, 1955). Partisan affiliation proved to be a useful guide to candidate issue-based preferences. And, as V.O. Key noted (Key, 1966), "the voters were not fools." They did not need detailed knowledge to know whether their lives were getting better or worse and to cast a vote retrospectively. In a 1980 presidential debate with Jimmy Carter, Ronald Reagan phrased the question this way:

> Next Tuesday is election day. Next Tuesday all of you will go to the polls; you'll stand there in the polling place and make a decision. I think when you make that decision, it might be well if you would ask yourself, are you better off than you were 4 years ago? Is it easier for you to go and buy things in the stores than it was 4 years ago? Is there more or less unemployment in the country than there was 4 years ago? Is America as respected throughout the world as it was? Do you feel that our security is as safe, that we're as strong as we were 4 years ago? And if you answer all of those questions yes, why then, I think your choice is very obvious as to who you'll vote for. If you don't agree, if you don't think that this course that we've been on for the last 4 years is what you would like to see us follow for the next 4, then I could suggest another choice that you have.[88]

Within this framework, issues mattered, even if the effect was not as direct or as powerful as might have been imagined under the tenets of classic liberal democratic theory. First, political candidates, believing that issues matter, strategically positioned themselves relative to other candidates in an effort to appeal to the median voter

---

88 Ronald Reagan Presidential Library. (1980, October 28). 1980 Ronald Reagan and Jimmy Carter presidential debate. https://www.reaganlibrary.gov/archives/speech/1980-ronald-reagan-and-jimmy-carter-presidential-debate.

(Downs, 1957; Enelow & Hinich, 1984). Under this framework, elections serve to moderate policy positions (assuming a normal 'single-peaked' distribution), as the most effective strategy is to appeal to the median voter rather than to the ideological extremes.

Much of American political history fits neatly within this Downsian framework. Running in 1968 under the label of the American Independent Party, George Wallace proclaimed: "There's not a dime's worth of difference between the Democrat and Republican parties,"[89] a refrain that reflected the conventional political strategy of appealing to the center of American politics. Candidates perceived as outside of the mainstream, too far to the right (Barry Goldwater) or too far to the left (George McGovern), suffered landslide defeats.

Yet, it was also possible to shift the ideological space. In 1980, Ronald Reagan not only won the presidency, he succeeded in shifting the center of political gravity to the right (Boot, 2024). The Republican Party, once the province of economic conservativism, increasingly appealed to socially conservative rural voters, working class Whites, and southerners. This was intentional and part of a long southern strategy (Maxwell & Shields, 2019). Liberal Republicans who resided mostly in the northeast and who helped secure the passage of the landmark Civil Rights Act of 1964 and the Voting Rights Act of 1965 were increasingly displaced (Abramowitz & Knotts, 2006; Schneider, 1982). Whether these shifts represented a realignment has been the subject of considerable dispute, including whether partisan realignments provide a useful theoretical framework for thinking about American party systems (Mayhew, 2008; Meffert et al., 2001; Petrocik, 1987; Shafer, 1991). We need not enter that dispute here but would simply note that Reagan transformed the American party system, moving the Republican Party toward socially conservative working class 'Reagan Democrats' while making it more difficult to successfully run for the presidency as a New Deal liberal. In 1988, George H.W. Bush won the presidency in no small part by portraying Michael Dukakis as a 'liberal' out of touch with mainstream politics (Lyons & Scheb, 1992).

In 1992, Bill Clinton emerged as the Democratic nominee out of the Democratic Leadership Conference, an organization designed to peel the Democratic Party away from its more progressive base and toward the center (Baer, 2000). Clinton's successful campaign was built on his appeal as a 'New Democrat,' targeting White working class 'Bubba' voters. In his early presidency, he veered left (including a failed effort to reform health care), but subsequently stayed mostly in the center of American politics (Zaller, 1998). After Democrats succumbed to the

---

89 Thomas, C. (2023, May 10). Democrats and Republicans — not a dime's worth of difference. TribLIVE. https://triblive.com/opinion/cal-thomas-democrats-and-republicans-not-a-dimes-worth-of-difference/.

Republican Revolution in 1994 and lost their majority in the House of Representatives for the first time in more than four decades, Bill Clinton engaged in a game of strategic positioning, triangulating between congressional Republicans on his right and congressional Democrats on his left.[90] As political consultant Dick Morris explained the strategy: "Triangulate, create a third position, not just in between the old positions of the two parties but above them as well. Identify a new course that accommodates the needs the Republicans address but do it in a way that is uniquely yours" (Morris, 1997).[91]

British Prime Minister Tony Blair adopted a similar strategy in leading the British Labour Party toward a 'Third Way,' embracing a middle ground between the false dichotomy offered between free markets or state intervention (Campbell & Rockman, 2001).[92] In the US, President Clinton would declare "the era of big government is over" during his 1996 State of the Union Address.[93] And, he would sign "The Personal Responsibility and Work Opportunity Reconciliation Act of 1996" making good on his 1992 campaign promise to end welfare as we know it.

Like Reagan before him, Bill Clinton reinvented his political party, successfully moving the Democratic Party to the center of American politics (Baer, 2000). Unlike Reagan, Clinton did not fundamentally reset American politics. Even his reinvention of the Democratic Party was only temporary, exposing the fault lines between progressive Democrats and centrists but not successfully alleviating them. As James Carville famously explained: "We didn't break the GOP electoral lock on the White House – we just picked it" (Ladd, 1993).

In 2000, in a campaign decided by just 537 votes in a Florida election marred by ballot irregularities, Al Gore ran as the continuation of the Clinton agenda (absent the accompanying scandals). George W. Bush, responding to the shifting landscape, ran as a 'compassionate conservative,'[94] an acknowledgement that Clinton had effectively occupied the middle ground of American politics and that the Republican Party needed to overcome the perception that it lacked empathy for average Americans. Indeed, in the 2000 election, one might be forgiven for

---

90 Smith, B., & Harris, J. F. (2010, December 10). The dirtiest word in politics. Politico. https://www.politico.com/story/2010/12/the-dirtiest-word-in-politics-046218.

91 Smith, B. and Harris, J. (2010, December 12). The dirtiest word in politics Politico. https://www.politico.com/story/2010/12/the-dirtiest-word-in-politics-046218.

92 Mellbye, A. (2003, February 10). A brief history of the third way. The Guardian. https://www.theguardian.com/politics/2003/feb/10/labour.uk1.

93 Clinton, W. J. (1996, January 23). State of the Union Address. The White House. https://clinton whitehouse4.archives.gov/WH/New/other/sotu.html.

94 Bush, G. W. (2018, Fall). President George W. Bush on compassionate conservatism. The Catalyst, George W. Bush Presidential Center. https://www.bushcenter.org/catalyst/opportunity-road/george-w-bush-on-compassionate-conservatism.

seeing "less than a dime's worth of difference" between Vice President Al Gore, running as a New Democrat, and George W. Bush, touting his record as a compassionate conservative. Both candidates were clearly hewing to the center of American politics.

The moderating forces of American politics that created the narrow choice between a New Democrat and a Compassionate Conservative in 2000, however, were beginning to falter. First, in 2000, due largely to shifts in campaign technology allowing for more precise microtargeting, politics began shifting from a politics of the median voter to a politics of the base (Abramowitz & Stone, 2006; Panagopoulos, 2016, 2020). Increasingly, the game was played by mobilizing base voters. Second, by 2004, evaluations of President George W. Bush had polarized due in part to the politics of 9/11, the Iraq War, and the war on terrorism. Rather than uniting the country after the 9/11 terrorist attacks, Republicans used the 2002 midterm elections to target centrist Democrats. The attacks on Georgia Senator Max Cleland, a Vietnam veteran and amputee, for being soft on terrorism, illustrate the dynamics of a larger campaign built around a politics of division. In the Georgia campaign, Republicans showed images of Ossama Bin Laden and Saddam Hussein while questioning Cleland's toughness in waging a war on terrorism.[95]

Absent the war on terrorism, Republicans might have lost control of the US House of Representatives and the US Senate (Gadarian, 2014; Jacobson, 2003; Sabato, 2003; Sides, 2006; Strach & Sapiro, 2011). Instead, defying historical patterns of presidential losses during midterm election years, Republicans picked up two Senate seats and eight House seats while widening (and deepening) a growing partisan divide. The 2002 midterms also created the playbook for the 2004 presidential campaign, the Swift boat attacks on John Kerry's Vietnam War record, and an increased emphasis on voter mobilization (Bergan et al., 2005). More generally, the increasing polarization of American politics made centrist-based appeals targeting swing voters less effective (Bartels, 2016; Panagopoulos, 2016, 2020).

Voter turnout in US elections has increased (see Figure 5.1), in no small part, because candidates and campaigns have increased their efforts at voter mobilization via targeted messaging and voter contact (Panagopoulos, 2016, 2020). This does not mean, however, that candidates are no longer attempting to persuade undecided voters or reaching across the aisle to persuade opposition partisans. They are doing so by taking positions on divisive issues that, at once, mobilize

---

95 Pierce, C. P. (2021, November 9). Max Cleland did not deserve what Rick Wilson did to him. Esquire. https://www.esquire.com/news-politics/politics/a38201636/max-cleland-obituary-attack-ad-republicans/.

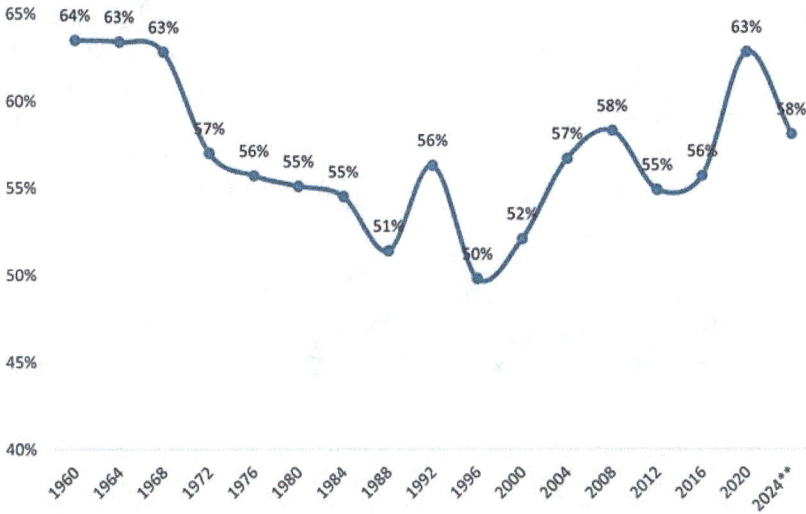

Figure 5.1: Voter Turnout in Presidential Election Years.
(Source: https://www.presidency.ucsb.edu/statistics/data/voter-turnout-in-presidential-elections).

base voters and persuade opposition voters (Hillygus & Shields, 2008). Immigration, we contend, is such an issue (Gimpel, 2019; Nteta & Rice, 2021).[96]

The underlying logic of the persuadable voter (Hillygus & Shields, 2008), and the use of wedge issues to appeal to opposition partisans, is similar to the logic, though more limited in scope, to realignment theory (Sundquist, 1973). New issues arise that cut across existing party cleavages altering the alignment of groups of voters to the political parties. This is the logic of immigration and the Republican Party's nativist platform. Nativism appeals not only to Republican Party voters but also to working class Democratic voters threatened by the economic, cultural, and political changes to their country. The result is that working class Democrats moved toward the Republican Party while more cosmopolitan college-educated voters increasingly moved into the Democratic camp. Nativism served as one of the impetuses for this movement.

Donald Trump's nativist appeals mobilized the Republican base *and* targeted cross-pressured White working-class voters (Sides et al., 2017). First, in 2016, Trump used nativist appeals to win the Republican nomination and capture the Republican

---

96 Though Gimpel notes that, after 2016, immigration may be less of a wedge issue because it increasingly reflects the partisan divide. Studies have even found anti-immigration rhetoric to be effective in creating a wedge between African-American voters and the Democratic Party (Nteta & Rice, 2021).

Party in what amounted to a hostile takeover. Using estimates from a logistic regression, Figure 5.2 shows the effects of nativism on Trump support during the 2016 Republican primaries among Republicans, among all voters, and on Republican Party identification (Young, 2016). For comparison purposes, we also show the effects of authoritarianism, belief that the system is broken, and abortion.[97] As can be seen in Figure 5.2, nativism dwarfs the other predictors of Trump's support during the 2016 primaries.

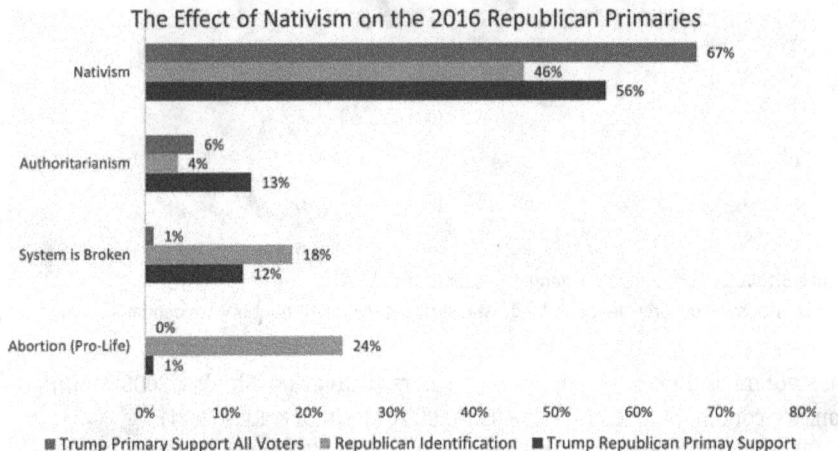

Figure 5.2: The Effect of Nativism on the 2016 Republican Primaries.
(Source: Ipsos).

Second, during the 2016 election, more White working-class voters turned out than in previous election years and the gap in turnout between the White working-class and other racial groups grew (Morgan & Lee, 2017; Whiteley et al., 2020). "[N]ativism plays an important role in populist mobilization," Hanz-Georg Betz argues (Betz, 2017a), "not least because it allows populist movements to transcend differences between social groups and gives them an opportunity to promote themselves as the champions of collective identity." Third, Trump ran stronger among the White working-class and, in doing so, attracted cross-pressured Democratic voters (Abramowitz & McCoy, 2019; Abramowitz, 2018). According to 2016 exit poll data, Trump ran 14 points stronger than Mitt Romney among White voters without a college de-

---

97 The model also included controls for standard demographics, economic perceptions, and beliefs about the American dream, these measures had fairly minimal effects on Trump's support. Unfortunately, the survey did not include a measure of White racial grievance but, in subsequent analyses, we show the effects of nativism hold even when controlling for partisan ID and White grievances.

gree and ran 16 points stronger among voters earning less than $30,000 per year. In 2016, he increased the Republican share of Democratic crossover voters by 5 points.[98] The mechanism driving increased voter turnout and Republican Party support connects to status threat and the anger that threat generates (Brader et al., 2008; Erisen & Vasilopoulou, 2022; MacKuen et al., 2010; Marcus et al., 2019).

Some caution is in order in interpreting these numbers. While Trump ran stronger among White working-class voters, this reflects a continuation of a larger trend of the White working-class moving into the Republican Party (Carnes & Lupu, 2021; Sides et al., 2017). Trump did not create the trend, he exploited and benefited from it. More important from our perspective is that at a time when the conventional wisdom that the Republicans needed to broaden their appeal, Trump doubled down on his appeal to the White working-class. He did so, in no small part, by employing nativist themes. These appeals worked to move anti-immigrant Obama voters into the Trump camp (Sides et al., 2017). This affected vote choice in the following ways (Enns & Jardina, 2021):[99]

1. As we have shown in previous chapters, nativists comprise approximately a third of the population. These are voters who express nativist sentiments and, absent some other compelling issue, are responsive to nativist appeals. Under this conception, nativist appeals serve primarily to activate existing nativist attitudes.
2. In addition to this core nativist group, there is a nativist adjacent population. These are individuals who have some nativist concerns but who we might not call nativists. They can, however, be influenced by nativist appeals when immigration is highly salient and top of mind. We can think of this trait versus state. Our first group of voters are 'trait' based nativist voters. For our second group of voters, support for nativism depends more on context.
3. As we show in the trends chapter (and has been documented elsewhere), nativist voters have increasing sorted into the Republican Party. This creates the paradox that while nativism has declined overall, it has simultaneously grown in importance as a predictor of vote choice.
4. Research by Enns & Jardina shows that racial White racial and anti-immigration attitudes not only influenced individual support for Donald Trump, but they also changed as a result of Trump's inflammatory rhetoric. Trump supporters become more nativist to better align with Trump's expressed issue positions (Enns & Jardina, 2021).

---

98 Huang, J., Jacoby, S., Strickland, M. & Lai, K. K. (2016, November 8). Election 2016: Exit polls. https://www.nytimes.com/interactive/2016/11/08/us/politics/election-exit-polls.html.
99 We borrow the framework developed by Enns & Jardina (2021) for racial attitudes because the same dynamics are in play here.

For our purposes, the mechanism is less important than the outcome. In contemporary politics, nativism is a key driver of voter turnout and vote choice. As we will show, the effects are not merely partisan affiliation by another name. Nor do the effects of nativism mirror the effects of racial resentment, authoritarianism, or populism. Though nativism is connected in important ways to each of these constructs, nativism has an effect above and beyond partisan affiliation, racial resentment, authoritarianism, and populism.

The Consequences of Nativism on Voter Turnout and Vote Choice

Who turns out to vote and who they vote for are questions central to the study of American politics. A considerable body of research has developed attempting to answer these questions. While we know these decisions are closely connected, much of this research implicitly assumes voter turnout and vote choice are independent decisions. That is, individuals first decide whether to vote and then decide who to vote for. Yet, we know well that politics and campaigns matter. Candidates and parties attempt to maximize turnout among likely voters and they do so in ways that mobilize and persuade potential voters (Rosenstone & Hansen, 1993). A candidate's issue-based appeals, for example, are not designed simply to attract independents or opposition partisans, they are also designed to motivate potential voters to show up on election day.

Estimating the effects of voter turnout on election outcomes has proven challenging, though the conventional wisdom has been that Democrats benefit from high voter turnout. This is largely a myth based on the idea that non-voters lean toward the Democratic Party (Shaw & Petrocik, 2020). Beto O'Rourke's failed campaign in the 2018 Texas Senate race serves as an illustrative example. O'Rourke based his campaign on mobilizing non-voters claiming "Texas isn't a red state. It's a nonvoting state."[100] Turnout during the midterm election year increased dramatically, by 18 percentage points,[101] and the increase helped make the Texas Senate race competitive; but the increase in turnout was not enough to upset incumbent Senator Ted Cruz. Why? Recognizing the threat, the Cruz campaign countermobilized. More generally, the short-term electoral forces that drive an increase in voter turnout do not necessarily provide a partisan advantage to the Democrats. Much

---

100 https://x.com/betoorourke/status/1301937692528316417?lang=es.
101 Wang, E. (2018, December 7). Texas saw the sixth-highest increase in voter turnout in 2018 midterms. The Texas Tribune. https://www.texastribune.org/2018/12/07/texas-voter-turnout-sixth-highest-increase-2018-midterms/.

depends on context. Infrequent (or low propensity) voters are less clearly partisan, less informed, and more likely to be influenced by short-term conditions.

Second, sometimes the level of turnout is less important than who turns out. In 2016, Hillary Clinton's campaign failed to inspire voters in critical rust belt swing states. She lost by 80,000 votes in three states. Part of this was a failed mobilization strategy, including decisions at the end of the campaign about where to devote resources (Devine, 2018).[102] It also reflected a lack of enthusiasm among key voter groups, especially among Black voters in rust belt cities (Sides et al., 2019).[103] In competitive races, small shifts matter a great deal. In 2016, Hillary Clinton and Donald Trump were the most unfavorably viewed candidates in the history of modern polling.[104] Trump voters, however, were more enthusiastic than Clinton voters.[105]

In 2020, the Biden campaign benefited from strong voter turnout and the relaxation of rules regarding mail-in ballots during the pandemic. Democrats were more likely to vote by mail or vote early than Republicans who were more likely to vote on election day (Herrnson & Stewart III, 2023; McDonald, 2022; McDonald et al., 2024). This relaxation of rules served as part of a foundation of Trump's claims of voter fraud (Persily & Stewart III, 2021). While Donald Trump's claims of voter fraud were unsupported by evidence, the increase in voter turnout clearly helped Joe Biden win the election (Shino et al., 2024). When it comes to voting laws, Republicans and Democrats act as though higher voter turnout helps the Democratic Party. Republicans may even 'pray for rain' on election day (Gomez et al., 2007). If this was true in the past (Nagel & McNulty, 1996, 2000), there is good reason to suspect this is no longer true (Goidel, Moreira, et al., 2024). Democrats benefit without Trump on

---

102 Dovere, E.-I. (2016, December 14). How Clinton lost Michigan—and blew the election. Politico. https://www.politico.com/story/2016/12/michigan-hillary-clinton-trump-232547.

103 McGreal, C. (2024, August 4). Hoping to avoid Clinton's 2016 mistakes, Harris courts three 'rust belt' states. The Guardian. https://www.theguardian.com/us-news/article/2024/aug/04/kamala-harris-blue-wall-rust-belt-states; Cohn, N. (2017, March 28). A 2016 review: Turnout wasn't the driver of Clinton's defeat. The New York Times.

https://www.nytimes.com/2017/03/28/upshot/a-2016-review-turnout-wasnt-the-driver-of-clintons-defeat.html?hp&action=click&pgtype=Homepage&clickSource=story-heading&module=first-column-region&region=top-news&WT.nav=top-news&_r=1;

https://www.washingtonpost.com/news/monkey-cage/wp/2017/05/08/why-did-trump-win-more-whites-and-fewer-blacks-than-normal-actually-voted/; Sides, J., Tesler, M., & Vavreck, L. (2019). *Identity Crisis: The 2016 Presidential Campaign and the Battle for the Meaning of America*. Princeton University Press.

104 Saad, L. (2016, November 9). Trump and Clinton finish with historically poor images. Gallup. https://news.gallup.com/poll/197231/trump-clinton-finish-historically-poor-images.aspx.

105 ABC News. (2016, November 1). Clinton, Trump all but tied as enthusiasm dips for Democratic candidate. https://abcnews.go.com/Politics/clinton-trump-tied-democratic-enthusiasm-dips/story?id=43199459.

the ballot, low propensity Republican voters stay home, and high propensity Democratic voters turn out to cast ballots during off-year elections.

Following the 2020 presidential election, Democrats won a series of special elections and outperformed expectations in the 2022 midterm elections because of turnout differentials. Flipping the script on long-held conventional wisdom, better educated Democratic voters, mobilized by the Supreme Court's decision to overturn *Roe v. Wade*, were more likely to turn out in off-year and off-cycle elections (Goidel, Moreira, et al., 2024). In 2024, with Trump on the ballot, Republicans benefited from higher voter turnout among low propensity voters. This increase was a function of Trump's personal appeal, Republican mobilization efforts targeting low propensity voters, especially young men,[106] and a campaign rooted in nativist appeals.

In Figure 5.3, we present evidence to this point by providing the results of an analysis of intent to vote during the Republican primary and general election. For the moment, we limit our analysis to 'intention to vote' prior to the election ranging from 0 capturing non-voters to 4 capturing certain voters. The data used in the analysis is from 2024. The models capture the effects of nativism controlling for the effects of partisan affiliation and White grievance as well as a standard set of demographics. One additional point bears mentioning: Our analysis of voter turnout and vote choice in the primaries includes Democratic and Independent voters (in addition to Republicans). This is intentional. While rules differ by states, in many states, voters can decide which primary to vote in. As such, Democrats or Independents might choose to vote in the Republican primaries. Our models capture the effect of voting in a Republican primary by partisan affiliation. Breaking out the results by partisan affiliation is revealing. First, when we limit to just Republicans, nativism is not significant but it is significant if we examine Independents *without Republican voters* or Independents *and* Republicans. Independents and Republicans who score higher on our measure of nativism reported they were more likely to vote in the 2024 Republican primary.

As can be seen in Figure 5.3, nativism and White grievance were strong drivers of voter turnout during the 2024 Republican primaries but not during the general election. Voter turnout helped Trump to capture the Republican nomination. If this seems like an obvious point, recall that Trump's renomination in 2024 was anything but obvious after the 2022 midterm elections. Trump's persistent election denial and his insistence other Republicans follow along hurt the GOP candidates during the midterms. Trump-selected Republicans performed poorly during

———
106 Riccardi, N. (2024, November 17). High voter turnout in the 2024 election benefited Republicans. AP News https://apnews.com/article/election-2024-voter-turnout-republicans-trump-harris-7ef18c115c8e1e76210820e0146bc3a5.

the midterms. Meanwhile, Florida Governor Ron DeSantis won reelection by 20 points and gained support in Democratic leaning areas like Miami-Dade County. In 2022, DeSantis was running ahead of Trump in the polls.[107] As a result, the door appeared to be open to a Republican challenger, like DeSantis or South Carolina Governor Nikki Haley, who could hold on to the Republican base while providing more competent and less mercurial governance. Missing from the analysis, however, was Trump's strong hold on his nativist base and his ability to elevate nativism as an issue. In short, Trump's hold on the Republican primary electorate was strong enough to not only secure the nomination but also to mute his opposition during a critical period of the campaign.

Trump was assisted by the inability (or unwillingness) of Democrats to secure the US southern border with Mexico. This played out in two ways during the campaign: Trump's nativist base turned out at a higher rate during the Republican primaries and, once mobilized, they were more likely to support Donald Trump during the primary and the general election. Perhaps recognizing this, DeSantis and Haley refrained from directly attacking Trump, even as he gained momentum and political support, and instead spent their time trying to dislodge the other candidate from the primaries.

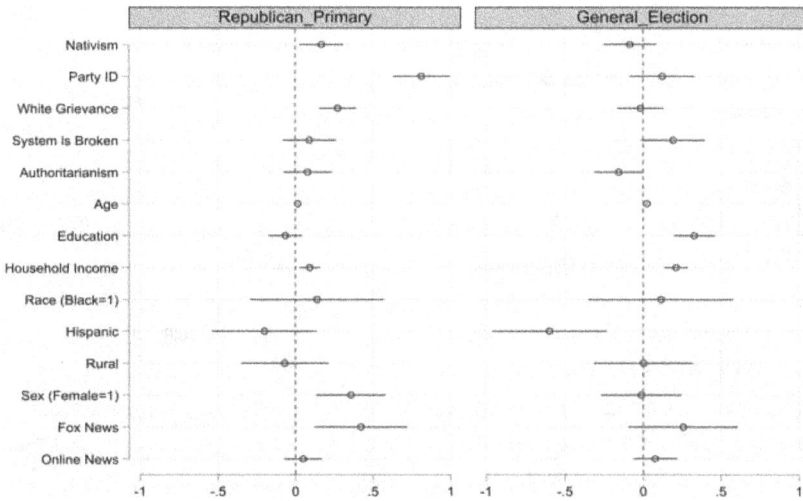

Figure 5.3: Ordinal Logit of Intended Voter Turnout in 2024 Republican Primary and General Election on Nativism.

---

107 Allen, J. (2022, December 15). Trump lashes out at polls showing Ron DeSantis with a big lead in the 2024 GOP primaries. NBC News. https://www.nbcnews.com/politics/2024-election/trump-lashes-polls-showing-ron-desantis-big-lead-rcna62000.

Nativism's Impact on Political Outcomes in Multivariate Context

We can see the effects of nativism on intended vote choice during the 2024 Republican primaries and the general election. Figure 5.4 presents the results from models of individual vote choice during the 2024 primary and general elections.[108] As in our previous models, we control for partisan affiliation, White grievances, and a standard set of demographics. What do we learn in this analysis? Nativism played a role in securing the Republican nomination for Trump though he also benefited from stronger support from Republican identifiers (as opposed to independents or opposition partisans) and from voters who expressed racial grievance.

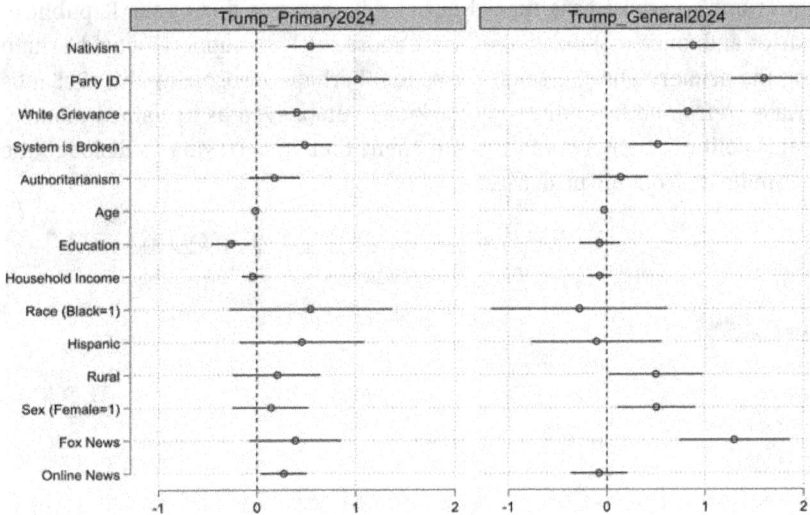

Figure 5.4: Logit of Trump Support in the 2024 Republican Primary and 2024 General Election.

Nativism also played an important role in the general election. Nativist voters were more likely to vote for Donald Trump even when we control for partisan affiliation and racial grievance. Put simply, without a strong nativist appeal, it is hard to imagine Trump winning the Republican nomination or the general election in 2024. One additional point, in Chapter 6, we make the case that nativism is conceptually and empirically distinct from White racial grievance. We see additional evidence of that here. Nativism has an effect on vote choice even after con-

---

108 The variables are coded 1 if the respondent reported voting for Donald Trump, 0 otherwise.

trolling for racial grievance and partisan affiliation, meaning that adding nativism to our models also helps us to better understand (and explain) vote choice during the 2024 presidential election.

The data presented to this point were collected prior to the 2024 primary elections and asked voters about their intended vote. To collaborate these findings, we collected additional data after the election in 2025 asking respondents about how they actually voted during the 2024 election. In doing so, we also included a richer set of controls, so we were able to account for whether individuals were better off than their parents as well as their views on abortion and government intervention into the economy. To measure whether individuals were better off than their parents, we asked them whether they were better off than their parents were at their age in terms of buying a house, saving for retirement, having a good job with benefits, and advancing professionally. Each of the individual items were strongly correlated (Cronbach's Alpha = .91). Abortion attitudes were measured on a 4-point scale gauging whether respondents thought abortion should be legal in most cases (1) or illegal in most cases (4). Finally, we gauge respondent beliefs about the appropriate role of government in the economy on an 11-point scale ranging from preferring no involvement (0) to complete involvement (10). In Figure 5.5, we present the results of this analysis.

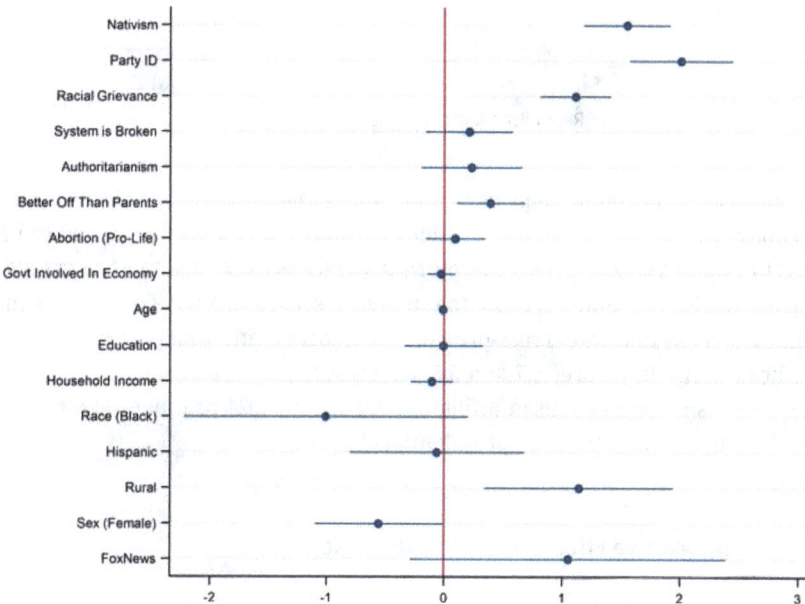

Figure 5.5: Logit Regression of Reported Vote for Donald Trump in 2024.

But this is not just a story about Donald Trump or 2024. Nativism has restructured politics even when Trump was not on the ballot. In Figure 5.6, we present the results from models predicting Republican support during the 2022 midterm elections. The patterns here are familiar. Nativism helps to explain Republican support during the 2022 midterm elections and Trump support during the 2020 presidential election.

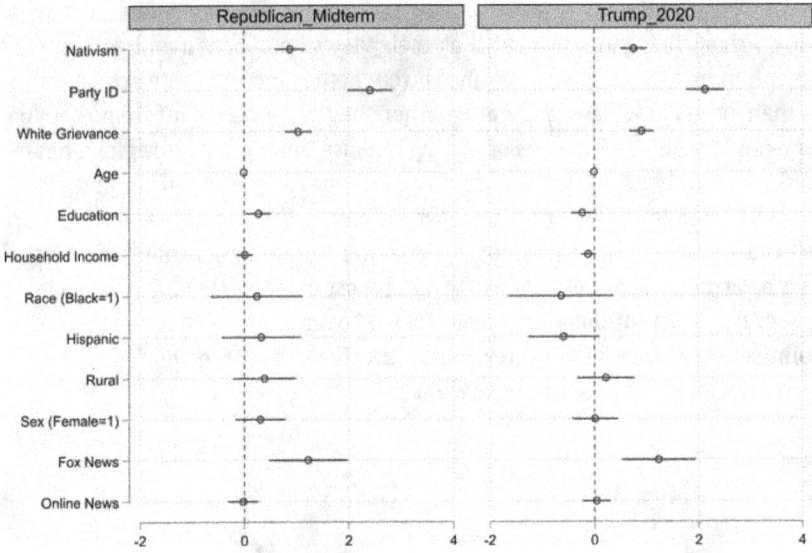

Figure 5.6: Logit Regression of Republican Midterm Vote and Trump Vote in 2020.

If our analysis to this point helps us to understand that nativism is a key driver of vote choice during recent elections, it does not fully explain why it proved to be critical to Trump's success. Here we return to the ideas expressed in *The Persuadable Voter* (Hillygus & Shields, 2008) that nativism served as a wedge issue, meaning that it helped to attract cross-pressured Democrats and Independents to the Republican Party. In Figures 5.7 and 5.8, we present this visually showing the effects of nativism across partisan affiliation during the 2024 presidential election, the 2022 midterms, and the 2020 presidential election.

Nativism's Interactive Effect: Like Attracting Like

Across models, the patterns are remarkably consistent. First, nativism increases support for Trump and the Republican Party across partisan affiliation. More nativists

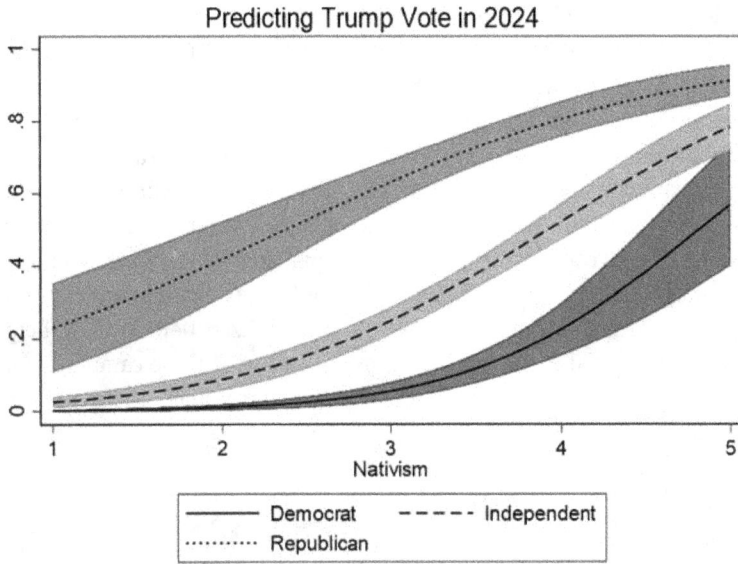

Figure 5.7: Interactive Effect of Nativism and Partisan Identification on Trump Vote.

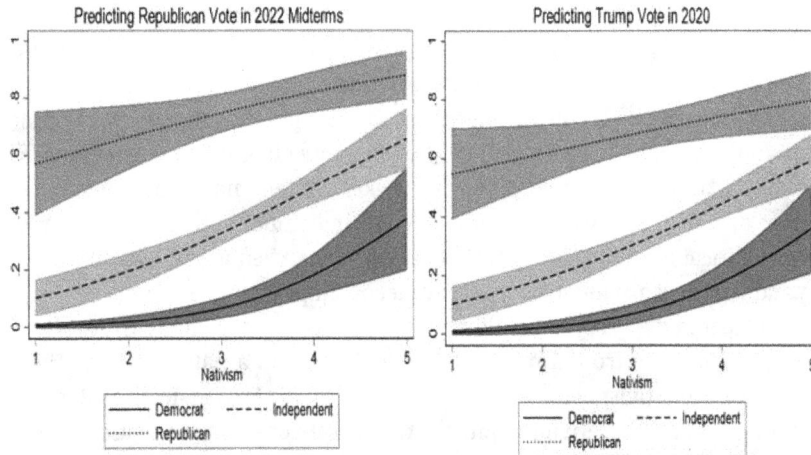

Figure 5.8: Interactive Effect of Nativism and Partisan Identification on Republican Midterm Vote and Trump Vote in 2020.

voters are more likely to support Trump regardless of partisan affiliation. Second, as Independent and Democratic voters become more nativist, the likelihood that they will support Trump increases. In short, nativism became a mechanism for pulling Independent and Democratic voters into the Republican Party.

Third, these patterns hold (with some minor variation) across election years. During the 2022 midterm elections, nativist Independent and Democratic voters were more likely to vote for Republican candidates. And, during the 2020 election, we see a similar pattern. Nativism pulled Independents and Democrats into the Republican fold.[109] Fourth, just because nativism defines contemporary politics, it does not mean nativism always wins. Instead, nativism divides the parties and structures vote choice. Other issues also matter. In 2020, Trump's nativist appeals were insufficient to overcoming the politics of the pandemic and Trump's largely ineffective management of the crisis. In 2022, Republicans ran aggressively on border issues, but the overturning of *Roe vs. Wade* mobilized Democrats to help prevent a red wave. Even if it was not a winning issue during these campaigns, it was there, playing a defining role in campaign messaging, voter mobilization, and vote choice.

Conclusions

Nativism is not just another variable in American political behavior—it is the most powerful predictor of politics today. Our analysis in this chapter reveals that nativism is not merely an attitude *but* a dynamic force that can be activated by changing conditions and mobilized by political leaders. Once activated, nativism predicts voter turnout, vote choice, and broader political attitudes. It is nativism, more than any other factor, that most reliably predicts support for Donald Trump and the Republican Party. Even when controlling for authoritarianism, economic anxiety, and perceptions of a broken system, nativism remains the strongest driver of political behavior. Beyond individual voting, it also shapes broader political attitudes, fostering distrust of elites, skepticism toward government, and a preference for strong, decisive leadership.

Our research also shows here that nativism has fundamentally transformed the Republican Party from a pro-business coalition into a nativist party. Those who hold strong nativist beliefs are overwhelmingly likely to identify as Republicans, more so than those who embrace traditional conservative values or economic beliefs. Even after Donald Trump's defeat in 2020, nativism has remained a defining feature of the Republican base, guiding voter preferences and driving support for Republican candidates in down-ballot races. The Republican Party is

---

109 We should note the interaction between nativism and partisan affiliation was not significant in the data collected after the 2024 election. This means that nativism had similar effects across partisans.

now a party defined by a vision of America that is culturally homogeneous, resistant to demographic change, and skeptical of global engagement.

Nativism Swamps Out Competing explanations for Trump

This transformation is not simply a matter of rhetoric or personality politics. Our analysis reveals that nativism consistently outperforms other commonly cited explanations for contemporary political behavior. While authoritarianism is often cited as a driver of Trump's appeal (MacWilliams, 2016), our data show that nativism has a stronger and more consistent effect. Even when authoritarianism is included in the models, nativism remains the dominant force. The popular narrative that Trump's rise was driven by economic anxiety and disillusionment with the future is similarly misleading (Norris, 2016).[110] Nativism is a far stronger predictor of political behavior, reflecting anxieties about cultural change rather than economic hardship alone. Nor is nativism simply another form of racial resentment. Our analysis in the next chapter will show that it has an independent and more substantial effect on political behavior. It is fundamentally about protecting a nostalgic vision of America, not just reacting to demographic diversity.

This chapter solidifies nativism as a highly ingrained belief system as well as the most important determinant of political behavior in America today. It is not just another factor—it is the central axis around which American politics is organized. As we have shown, nativism is a powerful, measurable force that shapes not only individual voter preferences but the broader ideological landscape of American politics. Understanding contemporary American politics means understanding nativism. In the chapters that follow, we will continue to explore how this defining force intersects with other dynamics, shaping the nation's political future.

---

110 Norris, Pippa. (2016) Trump, Brexit, and the Rise of Populism: Economic Have-Nots and Cultural Backlash. HKS Faculty Research Working Paper Series. HKS Working Paper No. RWP16-026.

Chapter 6
Racism by Another Name? The Politics of Nativism and White Grievance

Nativism and racial resentment are deeply intertwined. But they are not the same.[111] While both stem from a sense of status threat—the fear that a dominant group is losing its standing—nativism operates on a broader axis, encompassing concerns about language, culture, religion, and national belonging (see Figure 6.1). This distinction is crucial because it explains why nativism can be more politically potent: it allows for exclusionary rhetoric that avoids the social and political costs associated with explicit racial appeals. As we will see in later chapters, nativism's power lies in its ability to define the boundaries of national identity, shaping not only electoral politics but also the very meaning of who belongs in the nation.

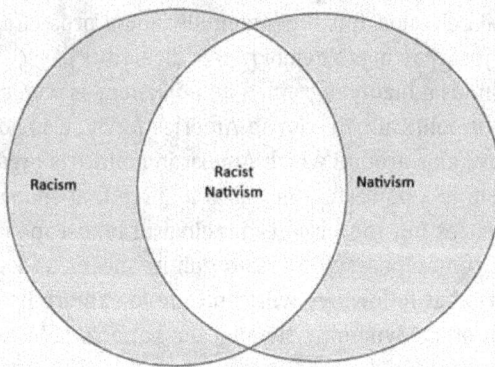

Figure 6.1: Nativism and Racism as Overlapping Constructs.

Understanding the relationship between nativism and racial resentment is critical to explaining its role in contemporary politics. While racial grievance has long shaped attitudes toward government, welfare spending, and party alignment, nativism's reach extends further, influencing views on populism, authoritarianism,

---

111 Prior to the Civil War, nativist (anti-Catholic) and anti-slavery beliefs were not seen as mutually exclusive in northern states. The Republican Party's ascension as a major party was, in part, due to its ability to attract nativists from the Know Nothing/American Party and abolitionists. (Gienapp 1985, 1987).

https://doi.org/10.1515/9783111384047-006

and even trust in democratic institutions. This distinction is particularly important in understanding Donald Trump's rise, where nativist appeals were more central to his coalition than explicitly racial ones. This chapter explores the link between nativism and racial grievance, while making clear that nativism is not merely racism by another name.

Vignette: The Birth of a Conspiracy

In the summer of 2011, Donald Trump, then a reality TV star and real estate mogul, seized on a long-running conspiracy theory: Barack Obama was not born in the United States. The so-called 'birther' movement had been percolating in the conservative fringe for years, but Trump amplified it into the mainstream. He repeatedly questioned Obama's birthplace, demanding to see his birth certificate, and implying that the president was not a 'real American.'

Trump's birther crusade was not just an attack on one politician—it was a broader statement about who belonged in America and who did not. If Obama was not born in the US, he was ineligible to be president, a usurper who had stolen the highest office in the land. But birtherism was never really about a legal technicality. It was a nativist reaction to the growing sense among many White Americans that their country was slipping away, that power was shifting to those who did not look like them, talk like them, or share their vision of American identity.

Ironically, Obama had always embodied a classic American success story. Born in Hawaii, raised by a single mother, he attended elite universities, climbed the political ranks, and spoke in soaring rhetoric about a United States that welcomed all. But for nativists, his story was not proof of America's openness—it was proof of an invasion. They saw him as foreign, a product of multiculturalism, an outsider who could never be fully American, no matter how many birth certificates he produced.

Trump's political rise, and later his presidential campaigns, can be traced back to this moment. He understood that nativist anxieties—about immigration, globalization, and cultural change—could be distilled into a simple, powerful question: Who is really an American? By questioning Obama's legitimacy, Trump was not just casting doubt on one man's citizenship. He was making an argument about national identity—an argument that would later form the bedrock of his political movement.

In reshaping contemporary politics, nativist attitudes do more than influence individual voting decisions, they activate a range of other attitudes and behaviors, including support for government spending, populist/anti-elite beliefs, and confidence in the political system. In this chapter, we explore these consequences to explain why nativism is a such a powerful force in contemporary politics. Central to the discussion is the interplay between nativism and racial grievance.

Racial resentment has long been a powerful force in American politics shaping attitudes toward welfare spending, party support, and political trust (Davis & Wilson, 2022; Kinder & Sears, 1981). While nativism and racial grievance are conceptually distinct (see Chapter 2), there is also considerable conceptual overlap (Lippard, 2011). Both nativism and racism are rooted in status threat, the fear that a majority group is losing standing to racial minorities and/or a new wave of immigrants (Hofstadter, 2011; Lippard, 2011; Parker, 2021) and both work to cue the in-group preferences and out-group hostility.

Racist appeals can cue racial nativists, increasing the salience of nativism and racial resentment in political judgments. Similarly, nativist appeals can work empirically to cue White grievance. Because they do so through a more socially acceptable mechanism, we contend, this a more effective strategy than overt or explicitly racist appeals which can backfire (Bonikowski & Zhang, 2023). Perhaps stated differently, there is little risk of backlash when targeting 'illegal immigrants.'

With Donald Trump's defeat in 2020, one might have expected nativism to recede as a political force. Such an interpretation, we contend, is a misreading of our current political environment. As we detailed in our Nativism Activation Model (NAM) earlier, the forces that gave rise to nativism—globalization, population shifts, and cultural change—have not receded. The shocks to the US political, economic, and social system remain unsettled and the future of the American polity remains uncertain and contested. Perhaps even more to the point, many Americans see their status and identity threatened by changing demographics. As a result, we should not expect nativism as a political current to fade soon. Moreover, nativism powerfully affects other attitudes and behaviors (populism, racial resentment, and authoritarianism) that define contemporary politics (Oliver & Rahn, 2016). Nativist nation is an aggrieved nation.

A Brief History of Race and Racial Backlash

Racism has played (and continues to play) a defining role in American politics. Racial inequalities were embedded in the US Constitution which not only recognized and protected slavery but defined slaves as 3/5ths of a person for the purposes of representation and taxation. Thomas Jefferson, who famously penned, "We hold these truths to be self-evident, that all men are created equal,"[112] was

---

112 U.S. National Archives and Records Administration. Declaration of Independence: A Transcription. America's Founding Documents. https://www.archives.gov/founding-docs/declaration-transcript.

also famously a slaveowner. The Union's victory in Civil War only temporarily empowered Black Americans to engage in conventional politics and assume political power. Reconstruction, a period of significant racial progress, ended with the contested election of Rutherford B. Hayes in 1876 and the Compromise of 1877. In exchange for the election of Hayes, Republicans agreed to pull remaining federal troops out of Louisiana and South Carolina and to return power to White southern Democratic majorities. The result was the Jim Crow Era, which legally recognized and allowed explicit racial discrimination by governments (especially state governments) and looked the other way when paramilitary groups defended White supremacy. Even before the Election of 1876 and the end of Reconstruction, paramilitary groups (e.g., the Red Shirts and the White League) were actively undermining Black political organization, Black elected officials, and Black voting rights through intimidation and political violence.

Much of the history of American politics follows this pattern. Racial progress is met with a racist backlash (Abrajano & Hajnal, 2015; Hewitt, 2005; Hughey, 2014; Klarman, 1994). While much of the backlash was channeled through federal and state government policy, the backlash was also expressed 'unofficially' through groups like the Klu Klux Klan. In this way, the history of racism in America parallels the history of nativism. The revival of the Klu Klux Klan in the 1920s maintained its origins in White supremacy but was fueled by anti-immigrant nativist sentiments and fears of immigrant political power, drunkenness, criminality, and corruption (Pegram, 2011). The threat to the power and status of White majorities has long been met with conventional political activity and legal discrimination as well as political intimidation and violence. Underlying nativist and racist perceptions are beliefs that the gains of racial minorities and immigrants arrive at the expense of White native-born Americans. Race, ethnicity, and national identity are conflated and difficult, if not impossible, to disentangle.

The Civil Rights Era further illustrates this point. The response to the 1954 *Brown v. Board* decision was the growth in private religious schools throughout the South.[113] Southern Whites voted with their feet to exit the public school system (Reber, 2011). The 1964 Civil Rights Act and the 1965 Voting Right Act were met with resistance, including a conservative backlash and a long southern strategy that began with Barry Goldwater, continued through and into the Reagan Revolution in 1980, and extended into the Republican Revolution of 1994 that

---

113 Southern Education Foundation. (n.d.). A history of private schools and race in the American South. https://southerneducation.org/publications/history-of-private-schools-and-race-in-the-american-south/#:~:text=From%20the%20mid%2D1960s%20to,North%20Carolina%2C%20and%20South%20Carolina.

transformed the US House of Representatives (Maxwell & Shields, 2019). Much of this backlash was directed at the growth of federal government power (hence, the conservative calls for returning power to the states). Much of that growth was necessary to enforce the provisions of the Civil Rights Act and the Voting Rights Act (Soss et al., 2008). The conservative movement to return power to the states (devolution) was, in no small part, a backlash against the growth of federal government to enforce civil rights and the demographic composition of the states (Soss et al., 2001).

Racial Resentment, Nativism, and Donald Trump

Donald Trump's ascendancy to the presidency was in no small part triggered by racial resentment and the racialization of politics that occurred as a result of the Barack Obama Presidency (Abramowitz & McCoy, 2019; Abramowitz, 2018; Fording & Schram, 2020; Tesler, 2016). If the hope was that an Obama Presidency would give way to a 'post-racial era,' the reality was that the Obama Presidency threatened the status of White voters and spurred a backlash against racial diversity (Arceneaux & Nicholson, 2012; Fording & Schram, 2020; Hughey, 2014; Parker & Barreto, 2014; Skinner & Cheadle, 2016; Valentino et al., 2018). At least in part, the 2016 Donald Trump presidential campaign reflected—and gave voice to—a politics of White grievance (Abramowitz & McCoy, 2019; Abramowitz, 2018).

Nativism was an important part of this story. Indeed, we argue that nativism, rather than racial resentment, was the primary driver of Donald Trump's ascendant 2016 presidential campaign and has played a central role in the realigning of American politics (Abrajano & Hajnal, 2015; Buyuker et al., 2021). This is not to suggest that racial resentment was unimportant, only that, relatively speaking, it was less central to Trump's support than nativism. Our logic is relatively straightforward. First, nativist appeals, especially those explicitly against 'illegal immigration,' impose smaller political costs than explicitly racial (or racist) appeals (Bloch et al., 2020; Bowler et al., 2006; Brown, 2013). As a result, nativist appeals can be made more openly and without concern about violating social norms, especially when the target of the appeal is 'illegal immigrants.' As a result, nativist appeals can trigger a more generalized out-group/in-group style of thinking that is activated across domains and values (Rooduijn et al., 2021). Donald Trump's 'birther' campaign questioning the legitimacy of Barack Obama's presidency was, at once, racist and nativist and deeply rooted in the status threat felt by White Americans. As Barack Obama explained in his memoir, "It was as if my very presence in the White House had triggered a deep-seated panic, a sense that the natural order had been disrupted" (Obama, 2020).

Second, to be delivered most effectively, conventional wisdom once held that racial appeals need to be implicit, cueing racial considerations without explicitly mentioning race (Hurwitz & Peffley, 2005; Kinder & Sanders, 1996; McIlwain & Caliendo, 2011; Mendelberg, 2001). This allows the messenger to claim they are being 'race neutral' or expressing some other value, e.g., deservedness or fairness (Davis & Wilson, 2022). Nativist appeals are not so constrained (Knoll, 2013). They can work as explicit or implicit appeals. For example, merely offering a Spanish language option has been shown to trigger nativist sentiments, but at least some appeals are more explicitly nativist. During his 2024 campaign, Donald Trump described immigration as an "invasion" that was "destroying the fabric of our country." Not to be outdone, his running mate, Ohio Senator JD Vance commented that "Our message to Kamala Harris is: Stop giving American homes to foreigners who shouldn't be in this country. Start giving them to American citizens who deserve to be here."[114] At least some research has argued that this opened the door to explicitly racial appeals, bringing back old-fashioned racism (Flores-González & Salgado, 2022; Fording & Schram, 2020; Tesler, 2013).

Third, and perhaps even more to the point, nativists are concerned with a core question of American identity. What does it mean to be an American? Should we define American identity using an exclusive definition, based on birthplace and citizenship, and intended to narrow the scope of who counts as an American? Or do we define American identity using an inclusive definition that defines an American on the basis of beliefs and ideals? To be an American is to believe in the ideals of freedom, self-determination, and equality before the law? Where one is born, or their race or ethnicity have no bearing on this definition. Just to be clear, our argument is not that racial resentment is unimportant to the conversations, only that it subsumed within these larger questions circling American national identity. Nativist appeals are typically strong enough to bring racially resentful voters on board (Tolbert et al., 2018). Racist appeals, however, don't extend as neatly or cleanly to include the broader swatch of America's nativist nation because nativism can be rooted in race and ethnicity, religion, or political beliefs.

Bernie Sanders and other progressives expressed nativist sentiments, for example, not for reasons of race but because they believed immigration undermined the wages of working Americans. This is not a position that appears to be supported by the empirical evidence (Butcher & Card, 1991; Card, 2009; Dustmann et al., 2013). More generally, nativism is primarily rooted in perceptions of cul-

---

114 Bender, M. (2024, September 22). On the Trail, Trump and Vance Sharpen a Nativist, Anti-Immigrant Tone. New York Times. https://www.nytimes.com/2024/09/22/us/politics/trump-vance-nativist.html.

tural threat rather than economic vulnerability. Nevertheless, according to Bernie Sanders in 2015,

> There is a reason why Wall Street and all of corporate America likes immigration reform, and it is not, in my view, that they're staying up nights worrying about undocumented workers in this country. What I think they are interested in is seeing a process by which we can bring low-wage labor of all levels into this country to depress wages for Americans, and I strongly disagree with that.[115]

The explicit connection of nativist politics to race (and racism) by Donald Trump has made such a position untenable in contemporary Democratic Party politics, but nativist preferences do not necessarily connect solely or primarily to racial resentment.

Finally, as with White grievance, nativism resonates because it captures an underlying anxiety that a way of life is being lost to demographic and cultural change. Scholars describe this as 'status threat' (Mutz, 2018), meaning that the White majority perceives its way of life is threatened by the growth of racially and ethnically diverse populations. Key to this notion is that the growth of minority populations threatens the prevailing social order including, but not limited to, the underlying values of the community. Within the context of contemporary American politics, status threat reflects the reality of demographic shifts that will result in the loss of a White majority. If the contemporary focus is on race and ethnicity, status threat also explains the nativism targeted at Irish and German Catholics during earlier historical periods. Status threat is activated by exposure to news stories about the numerical growth and political influence of minority populations. As a result, there is considerable overlap between racial resentment and nativism. Both concepts reflect perceived status threat.

Defining Racial Resentment

The concept of racial resentment is rooted in scholarly work on symbolic racism (Davis & Wilson, 2022). With changing social norms, White Americans increasingly resisted expressing explicitly racist sentiments. Racism had hardly disappeared, instead it had submerged, lurking just beneath the surface. It was expressed through seemingly race neutral values, e.g., individualism and the Protestant work ethic (Kinder, 1986; Kinder & Sears, 1981). This raised questions, however, about whether racial resentment reflected concealed racial prejudice or

---

115 Narea, N. (2020, February 25). Bernie Sanders's evolution on immigration, explained. Vox. https://www.vox.com/policy-and-politics/2020/2/25/21143931/bernie-sanders-immigration-record-explained.

ideological preferences (Feldman & Huddy, 2005; Sniderman, 1997). In recent work, Davis and Wilson (2022) argue that racial resentment, properly conceived, can include both anti-Black affect and/or ideological commitments to deservingness and fairness. In other words, one need not be explicitly racist to express racial resentment when one's values (e.g., fairness) are perceived as being violated. The transition from ideology to racial resentment happens because beliefs about deservingness are influenced by racial stereotypes. For example, individuals who subscribe to racist stereotypes that Black Americans lack a work ethic or are lazy, also perceive Black success as undeserving (Davis & Wilson, 2022). Successful Black politicians, like Barack Obama, stirred racial resentment because many White Americans believe their success was not merited. For Obama, the focal point of this resentment focused on questions of his ancestry, birth, and religion. Was Obama a legitimate president if he was, in fact, born in Kenya rather than Hawaii as the 'birthers' claimed? And was he secretly a Muslim rather than a Christian? In 2024, Kamala Harris was similarly described as a DEI candidate despite having won statewide office in California as Attorney General and as a US Senator, and her subsequent selection as Vice President.[116] By any standard, this was a strong resume for a presidential nominee, but the deservingness and fairness of the nomination were questioned.

For Wilson & Davis (2022), racial resentment might be rooted in racial prejudice, but it might also be rooted in beliefs that racial minorities have benefited because of their race and at the expense of White Americans. In other words, when Black Americans (or immigrants) succeed that success comes at the expense of White Americans (or native-born Americans). With Barack Obama as President, race not only affected vote choice, it also affected public opinion on a wide range of issues (Gilens, 1999). Even issues such as health care, that have little explicit racial overtones became racialized during this time (Tesler, 2015, 2019). By this, we mean that the issues were increasingly seen through the lens of race even if the primary beneficiaries of the programs were White, not Black, and were natives, rather than immigrants. Until recently, conventional wisdom held that racist appeals worked best when they were subtle and implicit rather than explicit. Barack Obama's ascension to the presidency, however, reignited "old fashioned" racism (Ford et al., 2010; Fording & Schram, 2020; Kam & Kinder, 2012; Knuckey & Kim, 2015; Lewis-Beck et al., 2010; Piston, 2010). Notably, the return of old-fashioned racism likely began before Trump's 2016 campaign (Tesler 2013).

---

116 The Heritage Foundation, for example, ran this story on its website—Gonzales, M. (2024, July 30). Yes, Kamala Is a DEI Hire. Shouldn't the Left Be Happy About That? The Heritage Foundation. https://www.heritage.org/progressivism/commentary/yes-kamala-dei-hire-shouldnt-the-left-be-happy-about.

Despite the fact that neither the 2008 nor the 2012 campaigns made explicitly (or implicitly) racist appeals, the transition from questioning Obama's legitimacy to Trump's nativist appeals was seamless. More importantly, nativism didn't carry the potential political costs that racism carried because nativism could be targeted at 'illegal immigrants,' rather than immigrants who followed the rules to become US citizens. This distinction was, of course, blurred but it provided an easy retreat for any pushback against the racial nativism employed by the Trump campaign.

Measuring Racial Grievance

Because we are not using standard measures of racial resentment (defined above), we refer instead to our measure as *racial grievance*. Our measures capture beliefs about reverse discrimination, institutional racism, and equality of opportunity. Previous work has noted the importance of recognizing that racism exists and the perceptions that the success of Black Americans comes at the expense of White Americans (Davis & Wilson, 2022). Specifically, respondents were asked their level of agreement with the following statements:

- Social policies, such as affirmative action, discriminate unfairly against White people.
- Black people do not have the same opportunities as White people in the US.
- Racism is built into the American economy, government, and educational system.

In Figure 6.2, we present the distribution for each variable and the overall racial grievance index. While we would not want to describe most White Americans as 'racially resentful' or as subscribing to White grievance, the percentage of White Americans who express at least some level of grievance is nontrivial.

- Just under 40 percent (39.7 percent) of White Americans agree (24.8 percent) or strongly agree (14.9 percent) that social policies, like affirmative action, discriminate against White Americans.
- A similar proportion of White Americans (38.1 percent) reject the claim that Black American have fewer opportunities than White Americans. Sixteen percent of White Americans disagreed, and 22 percent strongly disagreed that Black Americans lack opportunities.
- One in three White Americans (32.4 percent) reject the idea that racism is built into political, economic, and educational institutions. Fifteen percent disagreed, and 18 percent strongly disagreed that racism is built into American political institutions.

Looking across measures, a majority of White Americans (54.8) express some racial grievance, meaning they believe White Americans are being discriminated against by social policies, or they reject the idea that Black Americans lack equal opportunities, or they reject the idea that racism is built into America's political, economic, or educational institutions. Importantly, these statements better reflect more about deservingness and fairness than anti-Black affect and, as such, mirror the concepts of deservingness and fairness identified by Davis & Wilson (2022).

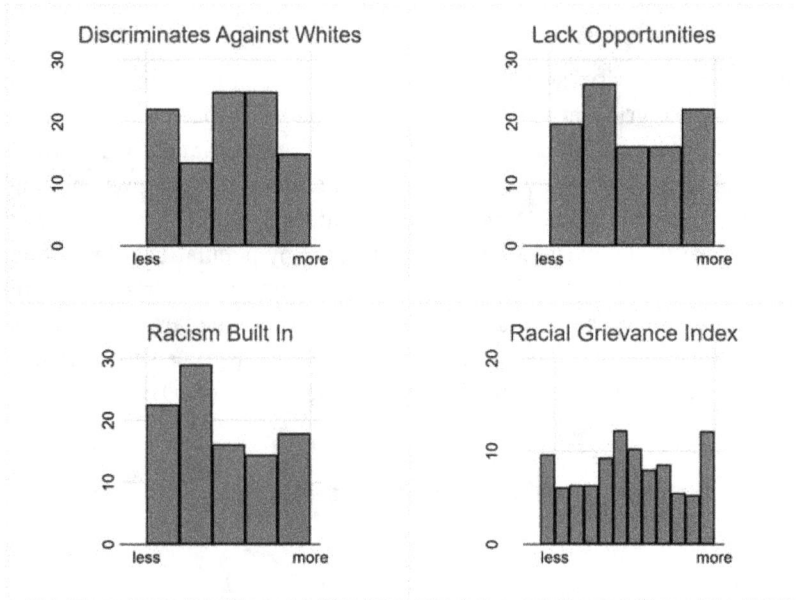

Figure 6.2: Distribution of Racial Grievance Measures.

Of course, this likely understates the overall level of racial grievance within the population. Concerned about expressing racially sensitive attitudes, at least some survey respondents will opt for the 'don't know' option or gravitate to the middle of the scale, electing to neither agree nor disagree with each of these statements (Alexander, 2018; Berinsky, 2002). As can be seen in Table 6.1, the measures are strongly correlated with each other, reflecting the strong reliability (α = .7956) of our racial grievance measure. But is racial grievance synonymous with nativism?

Table 6.1: Correlation Matrix for Racial Grievance Measures.

Variables	Discriminate	Opportunities	Built In	Index
(1) Discriminates	1.000			
(2) Opportunities	.596	1.000		
(3) Built In	.476	.613	1.000	
(4) Index	.817	.880	.827	1.000

Racial Grievance and Nativism

We have defined nativism as a preference for policies that privilege native-born populations. Racial grievance is instead based on the belief that racial minorities are being unfairly advantaged or that they are not taking advantage of opportunities available to all Americans. The psychological origins of racial grievance and nativism both reside in White Americans' perceptions of status threat, the belief that one's place in the world is being undermined by populations that do not share a core set of American values. But if there is conceptual overlap, there are also conceptual differences. Put simply, nativism need not be targeted based on racial distinction, though it often is. Race is also a social construct, such that over-time, the Irish (and the Italians) could become White (Ignatiev, 1994).

Figure 6.3: Correlations between Racial Grievance and Nativism.

Figure 6.3 presents the correlations between our nativism index and our measures of racial grievance. Belief that affirmative action discriminates against White Americans is strongly correlated with nativism, presumably because both capture perceptions that minorities, either Black Americans or immigrant populations, are gaining at the expense of White Americans. Beliefs about institutional racism, that racism is built into the economic, political, and educational system, are only moderately correlated with nativism. Perhaps more to the point, none of the racial grievance items are as strongly correlated with nativism as they are with each other. In a regression model, racial grievance explains about 30 percent of the variance in nativism suggesting strong overlap but also independence.[117]

We can demonstrate this further using Confirmatory Factor Analysis and comparing one model assuming that nativism and racism measure the same underlying latent construct to another model assuming that racism and nativism are distinct, meaning they measure different underlying latent constructs. We show the two models in Figures 6.4 and 6.5 and the goodness of fit measures for each model. Our second model, which assumes nativism and racial grievance measure distinct constructs, performs much better than our first model. How do we know this? The fit of the model is better when the Standardized Root Mean Squared Residual (SRMR) is lower, the Comparative Fit Index (CFI) and Tucker–Lewis Index (TLI) are higher, and when the Akaike Information Criterion (AIC) and Bayesian Information Criterion (BIC) are lower. By each of these metrics, our second model (assuming two factors) provides a better fit than our first model (assuming a single factor).

We can illustrate this further by examining individuals who score high on racial grievance with individuals who score high on nativism. Are they the same people? To explore this, we collapse our scales into three categories approximating a third of all survey respondents.[118] We illustrate this graphically in Figure 6.6. Knowing that someone scores low on our racial grievance measure is pretty good indicator that they are unlikely to be nativist. Two-thirds of survey respondents (67 percent) who score low on our measure of racial grievance also score low on our measure of nativism. Notably, however, a third of respondents who score low on racial grievance score at least moderately high on our nativism scale, meaning they do not express much racial resentment but they do express at least some

---

117 We aren't making a causal argument here. We aren't suggesting that racial resentment causes nativism (or *vice versa*) only that they are associated.

118 For our racial grievance measure, the 'low' grievance category represents individuals who score between 0–3 on our scale (32.5 percent of respondents), the moderate category represents individuals who score 4–7 (39.0 percent), and the high category represents individuals who score 8–12 (28.5 percent). For nativism, low scores represent individuals who score 0–7 (33.5 percent), moderate scores represent individuals who score 8–13 (38.5 percent), and high scores represent individuals who score 14–20 (28 percent). These are, admittedly, somewhat arbitrary cutoffs but the general conclusion here is robust to the decision of where to draw the line.

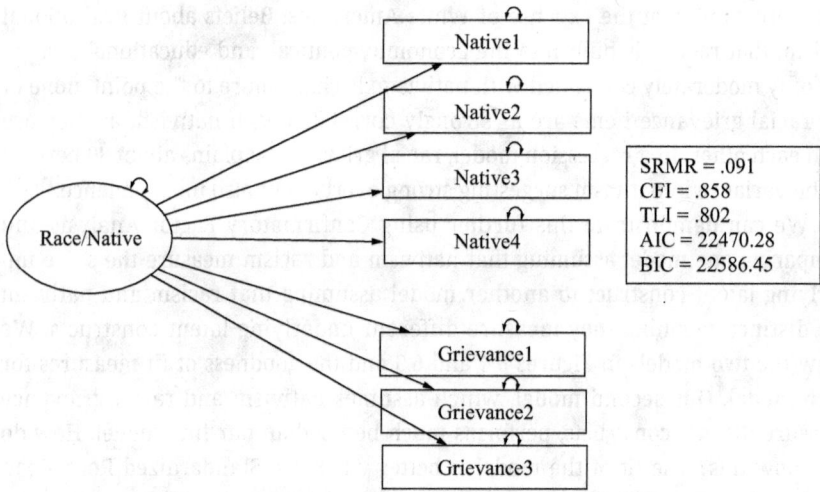

Figure 6.4: Measurement Model (Model 1) Assuming that Nativism and Racism Measure the Same Latent Construct.

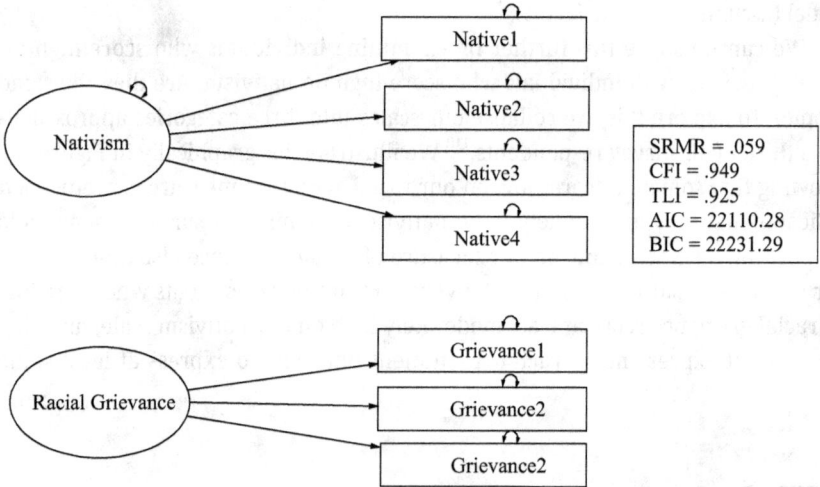

Figure 6.5: Measurement Model (Model 2) Assuming that Racism and Racial Grievance Measure Distinct Latent Constructs.

(moderate-level of) anti-immigration sentiments. Not surprisingly, as racial grievance increases, individuals are more likely to express nativist attitudes *but* the pattern is nearly as strong at the lower end of the scale. More than half of our respondents (53 percent) who score at the upper end of our racial grievance scale also score at the upper end of our nativism scale. meaning that they are both racially resentful and nativist, but this means that just less than half of our racially resentful respondents (47 percent) score lower on nativist scale.

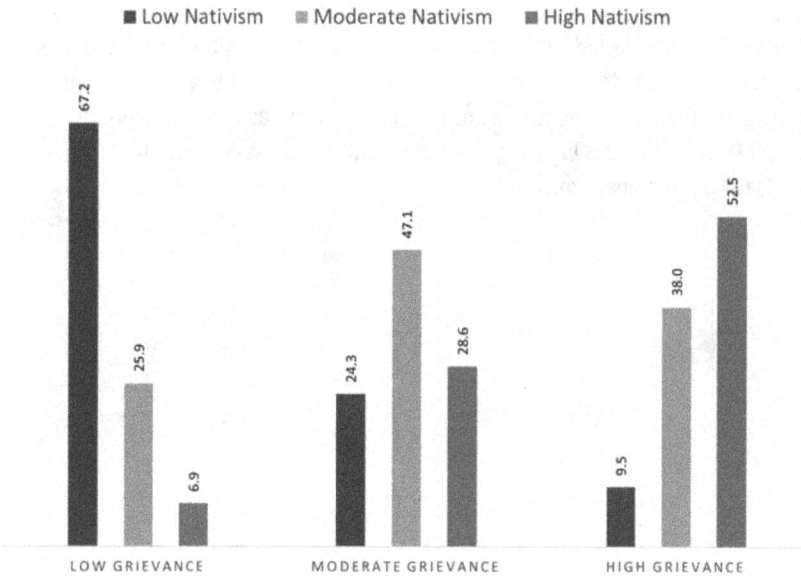

Figure 6.6: Nativism By Racial Grievance.

As a final consideration, we examine whether nativism has an independent effect on political outcomes *even after controlling for racial grievance.* To do this, we run a series of logit models predicting whether an individual recalled voting for Trump in 2020 and whether they intended to vote for Trump in 2024. We present the results graphically in Figure 6.7 as confidence intervals and point estimates for the effect of nativism and racial grievance on support for Donald Trump controlling for partisan affiliation. To make the results comparable, we recoded each of the scales from 0–1 so the coefficients represent the odds ratio of voting for Trump as an individual moves from scoring 0 on nativism (racial grievance) to the maximum value (recoded here to 1). As the results reveal, both nativism and racial grievance have a comparable effect on voting for Donald Trump in 2020 or intention to vote for Donald Trump in 2024. In 2020, the effects are roughly comparable but in 2024 nativism has the strongest effect. Substantively, this means that nativism has an effect even after controlling for racial resentment and the effect of nativism appears to be growing. We contend, however, that the effect of nativism is probably larger than demonstrated here because Trump uses nativist appeals to cue both nativist attitudes and racial resentment. When Trump says things like "We're the garbage can for the world,"[119] meaning the United States is the place where unwanted immigrants are dumped, he cues both racial grievance and nativism but he does so by using nativist rhetoric. This works because the social norms against nativism are not nearly as strong as against explicitly racist language. Even when the language has been called out as 'racist,' the consequences for Trump have been minimal.

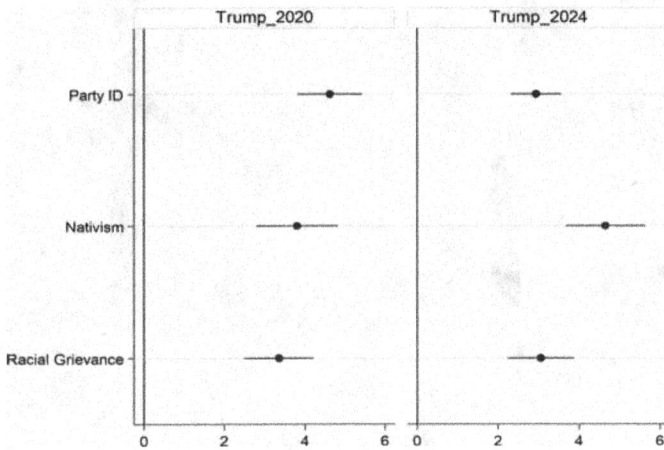

Figure 6.7: The Effect of Nativism on 2020 Trump Vote and 2024 Intended Vote in 2024.

Conclusion

Nativism and racial resentment are closely linked, but they are not identical. While both emerge from status threat—the fear that a dominant group is losing its standing—nativism extends beyond race. It is a broader belief system, encompassing concerns over culture, language, religion, and national belonging, whereas racial

---

119 Marcus, Josh. (2024, October 25). Trump comes up with new slur against US: "We're the garbage can for the world." The Independent. https://www.independent.co.uk/news/world/americas/us-politics/trump-us-immigration-slur-fascism-garbage-b2635333.html.

resentment is primarily focused on domestic racial hierarchies and perceived unfair advantages granted to minority groups.

Empirical evidence shows that nativism often takes on racialized expressions, particularly in a country like the United States, where race and national identity have historically been deeply intertwined. However, nativism is not reducible to racial resentment. It can be just as much about debates over language and cultural assimilation as it is about race. This distinction is crucial because it explains why nativism can persist—even flourish—in contexts where racial diversity is less pronounced and why it remains a defining force in American politics.

Politically, this distinction makes nativism a far more versatile and potent tool than explicit racial appeals. In the United States, direct racial appeals often provoke backlash due to existing social norms, but nativist rhetoric—framed around 'illegal immigration,' national security, or cultural preservation—offers a way to reinforce in-group/out-group thinking without violating mainstream taboos against overt racism. This is why nativism, rather than racial resentment, was the primary mobilizing force behind Trump's 2016 and 2024 campaigns and why it continues to structure American politics.

That said, the power of nativism is not just in its ability to mobilize—it is in how it shapes national identity. As we will explore in Chapter 7, nativism is fundamentally about defining who is truly part of the national tribe. While racial resentment focuses on who is receiving what within the nation, nativism focuses on who belongs to the nation in the first place. These are related, but distinct, forces—both influential, but nativism ultimately sets the terms of belonging itself.

Chapter 7
Who Are the Real Americans? How Americans Define Who Counts as an American

Vignette: A Tale of Two Americas

The debate about immigration is not really about immigration. It is about identity—who belongs to Tribe America and who does not.[120]

Nativism is not just an attitude toward immigration. It is a deeply ingrained, stable belief system that has shaped American identity for centuries. It ebbs and flows with the times but never disappears. More than just a preference for restricting immigration, nativism defines the boundaries of national identity—who is seen as a true American and who remains an outsider. It is one of the strongest predictors of political behavior today, shaping partisan alignment, policy preferences, and views on race and culture.

I saw this divide firsthand in 2016—not in a political rally or a policy debate, but in something as seemingly mundane as a high school wrestling match.

That year, my son was a senior and a competitive wrestler. Over the course of the season, I attended matches in two very different places—Potomac, Maryland, and Front Royal, Virginia. They were within 50 miles of each other, both filled with families passionate about the same sport.

But in those gyms, it felt like I had stepped into two entirely different Americas.

In Potomac, Maryland, the national anthem played before every match, but it was a formality, not a ritual. The crowd stood, but that was the sole expectation. Some placed their hands over their hearts, others didn't. A handful quietly mouthed the words, but most just waited for the match to start. There was respect, but no intensity. No social pressure. No grand display of patriotism.

Fifty miles away, in Front Royal, Virginia, it was a different story. A color guard marched in, flags raised high. Every person in the gym stood—no exceptions. Veterans saluted. And when the anthem played, it wasn't just background music—it was sung, loudly, by the entire crowd.

In Front Royal, you could feel it—the expectation, the unwritten rule. You stood. You placed your hand over your heart. You sang. And if you didn't? You stood out.

Same sport. Same moment. Two completely different relationships to American identity.

---

120 This vignette is based on Clifford Young's personal experiences.

https://doi.org/10.1515/9783111384047-007

At the time, I wasn't thinking about nativism. But as the 2016 election season heated up, I realized this wasn't just about patriotism—it was about belonging.

In Potomac, American identity was flexible, fluid, and civic. In Front Royal, American identity was sacred, restrictive, and tribal. These weren't just different communities. They were different definitions of what it means to be American. At the time, I had not made the connection between these displays and identity. But there was a clear one.

This chapter explores this connection—how nativists define American identity, how non-nativists differ, and why this battle over belonging has become one of the most powerful forces in American politics today. Nativism and identity are two sides to the same coin.

National Identity and Nativism

So, what did we witness in our wrestling example? This was perplexing as the 2016 electoral season reached a fever pitch. Here, let's note that the election that year was fundamentally one about what it meant to be an American—one definition is more restrictive; the other more diverse, diffuse, and inclusive. Trump's 2016 victory was a win for a more restrictive understanding of American national identity. Joe Biden's win in 2020 was a short-term victory for a more inclusive definition. But it failed to put the question to rest. Trump reemerged as candidate in 2024 in no small part because questions of national identity were left unanswered. In failing to secure the border, the Biden Administration left open the question of how newly arrived immigrants might be changing the social fabric of American culture, redefining who we are as Americans. As a result, immigration and 'make America great again' have been among the defining themes of our age.

At their core, those wrestling matches reflected how Americans in different places defined themselves differently. Critically, expectations of what was a real American in both places was determined by symbols and the relative adherence to them. In Front Royale, we saw a more intense and more restrictive relationship to all things American, while in Potomac less so. The observations made in 2016 continue to hold today. How Americans relate to symbols of national identity shift from place to place; such symbols are part of an ever-present undercurrent of American politics. Where demographic change occurs rapidly, they come to define politics. The cleavages that define American politics are neatly aligned around questions of immigration and identity.

By American symbols, we mean people, places, and things—such as the flag, the anthem, the founding fathers, veterans, mom, baseball, and apple pie—that are associated with being American. To have an idea of how such symbols play out, think of the difference between the wrestling matches. In Front Royale, the flag and strict ritual around the anthem were expected. To be part of the club, one felt obligated to have one's hand on heart, sing the words of *The Star-Spangled Banner,* and show the requisite reverence. In Potomac, all such rituals were optional; less restrictive. While never explicitly stated, the expectations in both places defined what it meant to be an American. But the definitions in each place were different.

How can we translate what we saw in Potomac and Front Royale to American identity? What do we know about American identity and its link to nativism?

American identity has varied across space and time. Higham (1955) details this in full. By identity, we mean a set of qualities, beliefs, personality traits, or expressions that characterize a person or group (Tajfel, 1981; Turner, 1975). American identity then is just that—the extent to which a person associates with those traits as quintessentially American. The answers are inevitably and inescapably political.

Who Counts as an American?

At the risk of overstatement, perhaps no question has loomed larger in the history of American politics than "Who counts as an American?" (Theiss-Morse, 2009). At first blush, the question seems simple, but it is deeply layered, reflecting America's historical experiences rooted in slavery, Jim Crow segregation, and gender discrimination. It is also intimately and intractably linked to periods of rapid immigration growth, shifting population demographics, and the backlash of nativist sentiments that these shifts have inspired (Higham, 1955; Ngai, 2014). One need not be an apologist to acknowledge that questions of who counts as an American are inevitable during periods of rapid population change. The growth of the Catholic population, for example, raised questions about the centrality of Protestant religious faiths to American identity. Waves of Irish, Italian, Eastern European, and Chinese immigration raised questions about ethnic heritage and the compatibility with liberalism. When culture and society are rapidly changing, questions of identity loom large, overshadowing much of the political process. Will newly arrived immigrants alter the civic values that define the American political creed? Or are they going to embrace the ideas and institutions that define America? Will they assimilate into the American political culture or will they redefine what it means to be an American?

The answers are never as easy or straightforward as they seem. Assimilation, Alba & Nee (2003) contend, is a two-way street where ethnic differences become less socially relevant over time but the mainstream also expands to include ethnic differences (Alba & Nee, 2003; Jiménez, 2017). In other words, immigrants do assimilate and adopt but they also alter the fabric of the American political culture.

These alterations, in turn, generate a backlash among rural, White, Protestant Americans who believe the culture should uniquely reflect their values. Residents, even legal citizens, who do not share their values are described by Trump as the "enemy within." As he stated at a 2024 rally in Wisconsin "The crazy lunatics that we have — the fascists, the Marxists, the communists, the people that we have that are actually running the country. Those people are more dangerous — the enemy from within — than Russia and China and other people."[121] They are, according to Trump, not real Americans. The desire to place rigid boundaries around what constitutes legal and illegal immigrants, further influences our understanding of who counts (and who does not count) when it comes to citizenship and the protection of individual rights (Ngai, 2014). Put simply, it is easier for certain ethnic, religious, and geopolitical backgrounds to become American. The first efforts to exclude immigrants were based on country of origin. The Chinese Exclusion Act of 1882 banned immigration from China (Lee, 2003). In the aftermath of World War I, quotas were established based on national origin, allowing more immigration from Northern and Western Europe and less immigration from Southern and Eastern Europe (as well as other regions of the world). The logic was straightforward: Immigrants from Northern and Western Europe were better suited based on genetics and culture to assimilate into the American political culture and to adopt the American political creed (Higham, 1955).

Immigration laws in the US changed as a result of the passage of the Immigration and Nationality Act of 1965, allowing immigration based on family status, work skills, and humanitarian considerations (refugee status). The result was a vast increase in immigration and a change in the ethnic makeup of the immigrant population (Gjelten, 2016). In short, the legal changes allowed for population shifts which, in turn, created a context ripe for a growing nativism backlash.

We noted in earlier chapters the competing definitions of national identity. In one version, what it means to be an American is narrowly defined by ethnicity and birthplace (Huntington, 2004). In the other, American national identity is based on a civic ideal, the embrace of American values—individualism, economic and political freedom, and laissez-faire economics—and an American mythology that individuals in the United States are limited only by their ambition, work ethic, and imagination. If these competing definitions appear, in the abstract, to be at opposite ends of a spectrum; in practice, they blend intractably into each other. Or rather, they contradict each other reflecting multiple traditions as op-

---

121 Cooper, J. J. (2024, October 26). Who does Trump see as 'enemies from within'? Associated Press. https://apnews.com/article/donald-trump-enemies-from-within-5c4a34776469a55e71d3ba4 d4e68cf62.

posed to a single ideological belief system rooted in classic liberalism (Smith, 1993, 1997). Schildkraut identifies three understandings of American identity based on previous literature: (1) an ethnocultural identity based on birth and ancestry; (2) an ideological identity based on the tenets of liberalism; and (3) a civic republican identity based on responsibilities to the community and active political engagement. While liberalism and civic republicanism are closely linked, liberalism emphasizes individualism and the protection of individual rights while civic republicanism emphasizes responsibilities and community. To this mix, she adds a fourth definition, incorporationism, based on the ideal of the assimilated immigrant and connected to the mythology of the melting pot (Schildkraut, 2013b). Under this definition, immigration and the diversity it brings to American culture is celebrated and defended. In this chapter, we explore these distinctions further, examining who Americans believe should count as 'American' and what characteristics define American national identity.

Measuring American National Identity

Much has been written on American identity and an equally large number of measures exist to capture it (Bui, 2024; Schildkraut, 2014). Roughly, the literature and corresponding empirical evidence shows that American identity can be broken down into two distinct clusters of values: (1) ethnocultural and (2) civic values which includes both liberalism and civic republicanism (Brubaker, 1990; Gerstle, 2017; Schildkraut, 2014).

By ethnocultural values, we mean more ascriptive attributes which are less malleable. Such values can include "speaking English," "being Christian," "being White European," "being born in the US," "defending the country at all costs," and so on (Wright et al., 2012). For Donald Trump and others who advocate ending the 14th Amendment's protection of birthright citizenship, being born in America is itself not sufficient to constitute citizenship. Citizenship, they contend, should be conferred by blood (meaning ancestry) rather than just place of birth. A core ethnocultural value has been 'being native born.' This remembers the definition of identity employed by nationalist movements in the past century. They often define citizenship as being born of a specific 'race' against the broader concept of *jus soli* which includes all those living in a given place (native born plus residents of foreign origin). In theory, America has aspired to be a *jus soli* republic. But the present immigration debate in the United States points to the tension concerning who is an American and, by consequence, who we are as a people.

By civic values, we mean those beliefs quintessentially thought of as "the American Creed", such as "equality before the law", "voting" and "those who work hard can get ahead", among others (Lipset, 1996; Schildkraut, 2013a, 2014; Smith, 1993; Theiss-Morse, 2009). Such values are often traced back to Alexis de Tocqueville and his keen observation about the emergence of a unique American culture. For many social scientists and political theorists, the civic conceptualization of "being an American" is wholly unique in human history because it is exclusively an ideological concept (Lipset, 1960). If you are here and believe in the 'American Creed,' you are an American. Only in America can someone be "Un-American" in contrast to countries where citizenship is viewed more as heredity. Indeed, it would be silly for us to think of someone being "un-British" or "Un-German." Not all Americans would agree with this solely civic understanding of Americanism. Indeed, at certain points of time and, including the present moment, ascriptive factors have taken on a special importance among certain demographic and political groups.

Ultimately, American group membership has depended on the relative mix of the two—ethnocultural and civic requirements. In broad brush strokes, the definition of who can be American has ebbed and flowed over time given the relative influx of immigrants. Historically, during nativist peaks, being American has taken on a more restrictive tone—'need to speak English,' 'be born in the US,' 'be Christian,' and so on. Take the 1840s and the Know Nothing Party, or the Chinese restriction acts of 1882, or the anti-immigration legislation after World War I. In contrast, civic values are the De Tocquevillian hallmark of what it means to be American. While always important, such values become even more so when the nativist fervor has waned.

Our wrestling example suggests that the definition of what it means to be American can vary from place to place and group to group at any given point of time. Potomac and Front Royale are perfect examples of this. Critically, we should expect a varied definition of what it means to be an American across demographic and political groups. For instance, the nativist should have a more restrictive set of requirements—one based on a strong combination of ethnocultural and civic values. Non-nativist, in contrast, should have a lower bar for being considered American—one stronger on civic values and weaker on ethnocultural ones. Such definitions might vary across demographics and political persuasions.

Connecting Nativism and National Identity

We have seen now that nativism is a stable belief system over time (Higham, 1955; Mudde, 2007). It is highly correlated with outcomes like voting and party identification (Abrajano & Hajnal, 2015; Sides et al., 2019). And it overlaps with other beliefs such as systemic distrust, nostalgia, and authoritarianism (Goidel,

Goidel, et al., 2024; Kešić et al., 2022; Stenner, 2005, 2008). Nativist beliefs resonate with a large swath of the population—about one third of Americans hold such beliefs strongly, while another 20 percent or so are nativist-leaning. Simply put, nativism as a belief system is a real phenomenon that conditions how many Americans see the world (Parker & Barreto, 2014). Nativism has political resonance because it is rooted in larger questions about national identity: Who is an American? And, by extension, who is not one?

We have discussed in passing the role of nativism in the debate around who is and is not American (Theiss-Morse, 2009). But thus far, we have not expanded specifically on its relationship with American identity. Indeed, to what extent do nativists define what it means to be American differently than other Americans? How might criteria for group membership—in this case membership as an American—be affected by nativist feelings? Much of the earlier literature makes the link between nativism and the definition of a real American (Huntington, 2004; Smith, 1997). But how does this play out empirically today?

One of the critical insights from this chapter will be that American identity is best understood as having two competing dimensions—one ethnocultural, one civic. While most Americans embrace the American creed as central to national identity, nativists insist on additional ascriptive characteristics such as being native born, speaking English, and having a particular cultural heritage. This divergence creates the fault line between nativists and non-nativists today.

Data and Method

To answer our questions, we analyze data from two national probability samples—one conducted in March 2023 and another conducted in 2024—both of approximately 1000 adults. They included measures of identity, nativism, and other related concepts. To capture national identity, we use a multi-item index of Americanism. By Americanism, we mean beliefs about what characteristics it takes to be an American. Such requirements can be ethnocultural or civic in nature. Citrin and colleagues define such a measure in their article *American identity and politics of ethnic change* (Citrin et al., 1990),[122] and we take from their work. The index in-

---

122 Citrin, et al. (1990) include the following: (1) believing in God, (2) voting in elections, (3) speaking and writing in English, (4) trying to get ahead on one's own effort, (5) treating people of all races and backgrounds equally, and (6) defending America when it is criticized. With the exception of 'treating people of all and backgrounds equally,' the items loaded on a single factor (though voting in elections loaded weakly on the first factor).

cludes seven items (displayed below in Figure 7.1) to determine the importance of different traits in defining an American (Cronbach's = .71).

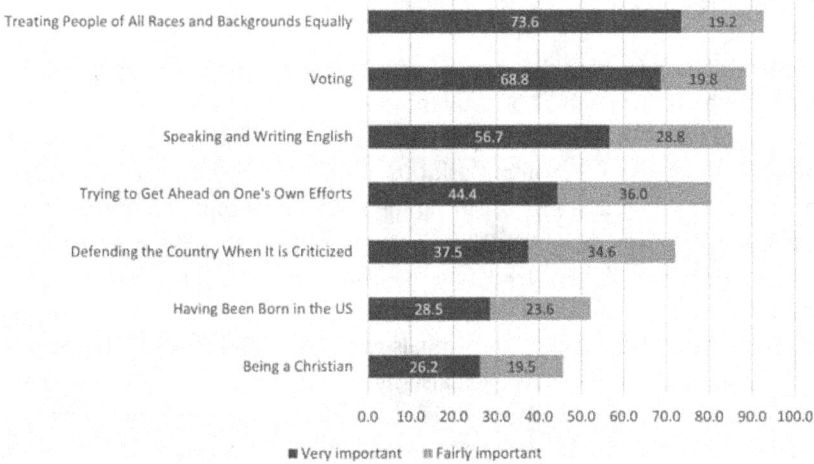

Figure 7.1: Importance of Characteristics to American Identity.

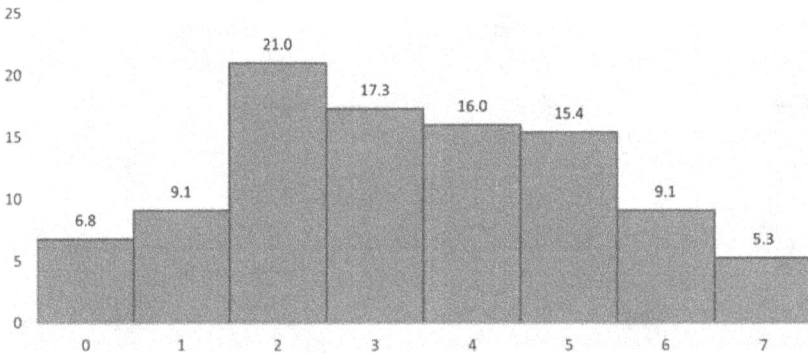

Figure 7.2: Number of Restrictions on American National Identity.

The individual items that make up this first measure of Americanism are displayed in Figure 7.1. Americans generally agree that treating everyone equally, voting, and speaking and writing in English are important characteristics of American national identity. They express considerably less agreement on religion (being a Christian) and birthplace (being born in the US). Bear in mind that part of the argument here is that certain individuals will adopt a more restrictive definition of what it means to be an American. We can see this in Figure 7.2, which shows the number of characteristics individuals identified as important to national identity. Very few Americans (6.8 percent) said none of these characteristics were 'very important' as part of American national identity. On average, respondents selected three characteristics ($M = 3.36$; $SD = 1.87$).

How do those characteristics cluster together across individuals? To better understand the underlying structure of beliefs about American identity, we employ a varimax factor analysis of the items. Factor analysis allows researchers to see if a set of variables reflect a single underlying dimension (or latent construct) or multiple dimensions. We might ask this a different way: Are the individual items that comprise our scale measuring the same underlying construct? Or are they measuring different constructs?

As can be seen in Table 7.1, we find that Americanism is a multi-dimensional concept with two factors which roughly fall along ethnocultural and civic dimensions. Substantively, this means individuals who are more likely to identify with one of the ethnocultural criteria are also more likely to select one of the other ones. For example, individuals who believe being born in the US is important are also likely to say being a Christian or being able to speak and write in English are important. Likewise, individuals identifying a civic criteria as important are more likely to identify other civic criteria. Individuals who believe treating people of all races and backgrounds equally is important are also more likely to believe voting is critical as well. In the analyses that follow, we examine our measure of Americanism using a single index, assuming all the items represent the same underlying construct, and two indicators, one capturing ethnocultural determinants of identity and the other capturing civic determinants.

Table 7.1: Factor Analysis of Americanism Index with Varimax Rotation.

	Ethnocultural (Factor 1)	Civic (Factor 2)
Having been born in the US	.79	
Being a Christian	.74	
Speaking and writing English	.71	
Defending the country when it is criticized	.64	
Treating people of all races and backgrounds equally		.80
Voting		.71
Trying to get ahead on one's own efforts		.51
% of variance explained (eigenvalue)	37.8 (2.64)	18.5 (1.29)

Source: Ipsos National Identity Poll 2024.

Being A Real American and American Exceptionalism

Let's cross-validate our findings. To do this, we analyze questions that ask "who is a real American?" Specifically, individual respondents were asked: From the list below, please indicate if you think a person like this is or is not a real American?

The options include characteristics ranging from being born in the United States to having extreme political views or a criminal background to being an undocumented immigrant. We don't employ this battery as an index, but it does have strong measurement properties. The thirteen-item battery has a strong Cronbach's alpha (alpha = .874) indicating that the individual items are strongly correlated. The percent of respondents agreeing that a particular trait constitutes a real American is presented graphically in Figure 7.3. As can be seen, there is generally wide agreement that being born in the US, having served in the military, being a naturalized citizen constitutes a 'real American.' Agreement declines somewhat but is still supportive of LGBQT populations and naturalized citizens who have not learned English. Americans express less support for individuals with a criminal background, political extremists, and undocumented immigrants. Employing this second definition of Americanism (below) increases our confidence that our findings are not due to measurement error.

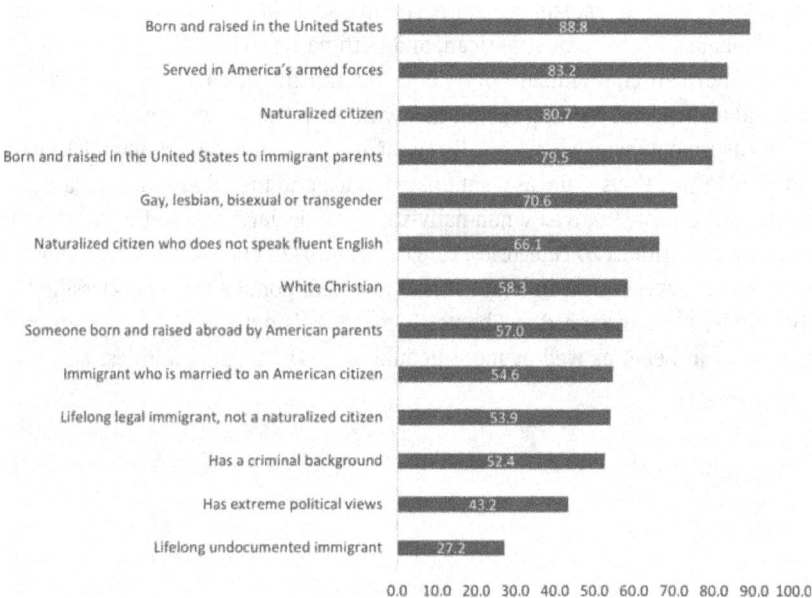

Born and raised in the United States	88.8
Served in America's armed forces	83.2
Naturalized citizen	80.7
Born and raised in the United States to immigrant parents	79.5
Gay, lesbian, bisexual or transgender	70.6
Naturalized citizen who does not speak fluent English	66.1
White Christian	58.3
Someone born and raised abroad by American parents	57.0
Immigrant who is married to an American citizen	54.6
Lifelong legal immigrant, not a naturalized citizen	53.9
Has a criminal background	52.4
Has extreme political views	43.2
Lifelong undocumented immigrant	27.2

0.0 10.0 20.0 30.0 40.0 50.0 60.0 70.0 80.0 90.0 100.0

Figure 7.3: Beliefs About Who Is a Real American (Source: Ipsos National Identity Poll 2024).

Closely linked to American values is the concept of American exceptionalism. By American exceptionalism, we mean believing that America is better or greater than other countries. Exceptionalism has been an important pillar of American foreign and domestic policy over the last century with a focus on that "shining beacon on a hill" (Lipset, 1979, 1996; Shafer, 1999). Exceptionalism is often spoken in the same breath as the American creed, but it is a distinct concept. Here, we measure exceptionalism using the following items (asked in an agree/disagree format):

- There are some things about America today that make me feel ashamed of America.
- I would rather be a citizen of the United States than of any other county in the world.
- Generally speaking, America is a better country than most other countries.
- The world would be a better place if people from other countries were more like the United States.
- People should support their country, even if the country is in the wrong.

Empirically, exceptionalism is a more restrictive and demanding notion of America. For our analyses, we include a five-item American exceptionalism index (Cronbach's = .59). Using factor analysis, we find that exceptionalism has one underlying construct, producing only one factor. Ultimately, we suspect that exceptionalism will be related to Americanism and nativism. In particular, nativism is a restrictive notion of what it means to be American, and both nativism and exceptionalism are forms of American chauvinism—one domestic and the other external. Here, we should find an especially strong correlation with American exceptionalism.

To measure nativism, we use our five-item scale as detailed in Chapter 3. Here, it is employed in two ways—one as a summated index and the other as a two-category segmentation variable (nativist v non-nativist). In particular, we sum five items—the resulting index includes 20 categories, ranging from 0–20 (M = 11.5; SD =5.5). Our cut point in both surveys results in about 33% of the adult population being classified as highly nativist.[123] As discussed in Chapter 3, this 33% is our nativist nation and are more nativist in belief as well as more Republican, White, rural, and less educated (see chart below).

---

123 We acknowledge the cut point here is somewhat arbitrary. The overall conclusions, however, remain largely the same regardless of the distinction, especially if we narrow who constitutes a nativist.

Analysis

So, what do we find? Americans have a diverse orientation toward what it means to be an American. Yes, an American is expected to 'vote,' 'speak English,' and 'believe that all should be treated equally.' Americans in turn are less likely to believe 'being Christian' or 'believing that working hard to get ahead' or stalwartly holding to 'my country right or wrong' is a critical value. In Table 7.2, we present differences between nativists and non-nativists across each of these items. For comparison purposes, we also present differences across education, race, and age.

Nativist Americans are much more restrictive in how they define being American. Indeed, a strong plurality to a super majority of nativists see each of these membership attributes as essential, compared to the average American. For instance, see how 77% of nativists believe "voting" is important; 85% "speaking English;" 61% "getting ahead on your own merit;" 66% "treated equally before the law;" 51% "being born in the US;" and 55% "defending the country when it is criticized." To be a nativist is to be restrictive or exclusionary in your definition of what it means to be an American. Group membership for nativists requires a mixture of both ethnocultural and civic values. In contrast, non-nativists place a premium on civic requirements. In

Table 7.2: Important Traits That an American Must Have by Demographics and Political Persuasion.

Group	Proud	Christians	Voting	English	Get Ahead	Treat Equally	Defending Country	Born in US
Total	71	25	69	57	44	74	38	29
Nativist	86	44	77	85	61	66	55	51
Non-Nativist	64	17	65	43	36	78	29	17
DELTA	15	18	12	28	17	-8	17	27
College+	73	22	74	50	46	78	32	18
White	74	27	71	57	46	74	40	28
Hispanic	54	16	58	53	38	74	25	23
18-29	49	16	61	49	37	71	24	20
30-44	60	21	60	49	42	73	26	24
45-54	79	30	68	60	47	70	32	30
55-64	80	31	82	64	51	72	41	32
65+	85	35	84	65	54	77	52	35
DELTA	37	19	15	22	17	-8	28	18
Republican	87	43	75	74	54	63	59	32
Democrat	33	20	77	44	37	81	32	24
DELTA	54	23	0	31	17	-18	27	17
Female	70	25	55	41	41	78	35	25

Source: Ipsos National Identity Poll 2024.

short, nativists and non-nativists express very different ideas about what is important when it comes to deciding who is (and who is not) an American.

Like nativism, party affiliation also shows significant variability in what it means to be an American. Republicans, for instance, see "being Christian," "speaking English," and "defending the country" as important criteria. Again, Republicans have a restrictive view of what it means to be American. Democrats, in turn, are much less rigid in their perspective. Only a majority require Americans to "vote" and "believe in being treated equally before the law." On all other requirements, only a plurality of Democrats think they are important. In summary, one side stresses the ethnocultural and civic aspects of Americanism, while the other mostly emphasizes the civic ones.

We also find significant variability in what it means to be American across age categories. For instance, Americans 65 years or older are much more restrictive in their definition than younger Americans between the ages of 18 and 29. If one looks at the data, it is striking. Only in the case of "treating all equally" do we find a majority of younger Americans in agreement with their older cohorts. Across all other values, only a plurality of the youngest age cohort holds them as important. Older Americans, in turn, are more likely to believe that both ethnocultural and civic values are critical in defining what is to be an American. For instance, take "voting" as a requirement. Only 49% of younger Americans believe it important, while 84% of older American think the same. Across all requirements, older Americans are more restrictive in their definition, whereas younger Americans have a much more diffuse sense of the same.

The definition of what it means to be an American varies across demographic group and political persuasion. And the patterning is clear—there are more restrictive and less restrictive notions of what it means to be an American. This differential understanding is linked to the relative mix of ethnocultural and civic requirements.

But are these results an anomaly? Let's validate our finding. To do so, we ask respondents to assess hypothetical descriptions of people and to determine if they are real Americans (see Table 7.3). So, what do we find?

All Americans—both nativists and non-nativists—believe that the "undocumented immigrants" should *not* be considered real Americans, though notably nativists are even more strongly averse to the "undocumented" than non-nativists. Only 5 percent of nativists agree that undocumented immigrants are real Americans compared to 37 percent of non-nativists. This consensus also goes for those with "extreme political views." Forty-three percent of nativists compared to 39 percent of non-nativists believe individuals with extreme political views are real Americans. It is no wonder that neither communism nor fascism found their roots in America. There is consensus at the extremes. In contrast, "White Christians," "a person born in the US," "a person born to immigrants but raised in the US," and "a naturalized citizen" are all seen as real Americans.

Table 7.3: Level of Agreement That a Given Set of Traits Is a Real American by Nativism.

	Non-Nativist	Nativist	Total
– Gay, lesbian, bisexual or transgender	72.7%	61.4%	68.9%
– Served in America's armed forces	79.5%	85.0%	81.3%
– Has a criminal background	55.4%	42.5%	51.1%
– Has extreme political views	43.1%	39.3%	41.8%
– Lifelong undocumented immigrant	37.0%	5.5%	26.4%
– Lifelong legal immigrant, not a naturalized citizen	58.4%	41.6%	52.8%
– Naturalized citizen	80.7%	75.4%	78.9%
– Naturalized citizen who does not speak fluent English	72.5%	49.4%	64.8%
– Immigrant who is married to an American citizen	57.8%	43.9%	53.2%
– Someone born and raised abroad by American parents	56.2%	54.9%	55.8%
– Born and raised in the United States to immigrant parents	81.1%	71.1%	77.8%
– Born and raised in the United States	86.1%	89.0%	87.1%
– White Christian	55.3%	60.3%	56.9%
TOTAL	84.1%	95.7%	87.9%

Source: Ipsos Nativism Poll 2023.

These results also reinforce our initial findings that nativists are more restrictive in their definition compared to non-nativists. Take, for instance, having a "criminal background," only a plurality of nativists sees such a person as a real American, while a majority of non-nativists see the same. Nativists and non-nativists diverge when "naturalization" and "language" are critical for determining who is a real American. Examples include "lifelong legal immigrant," "naturalized citizen who does not speak English," and "an immigrant married to an American." For the nativists, these mushy categories do not suffice. This shines light on the present DACA debate—without hard definitions, nativists will be against any path to citizenship for the children of undocumented immigrants (Davidson & Burson, 2017; Perea, 1997; Wright et al., 2012).

Here, the different world views are clear: Nativists are more restrictive, more legalistic, more demanding of group membership. Non-nativists are less so; their understanding of a real American is more fluid and less legalistic. For non-nativists, it only matters that a person resides in America for a time, or is married to an American, or has passed the citizenship test even if they speak broken English. In the case of non-nativists, being an American is a more diffuse concept analogous to our wresting match in Potomac where adherence to symbols was weak at best.

American Exceptionalism

We see very similar patterns when we look at attitudes toward American exceptionalism (Table 7.4). Like Americanism, we find a strong relationship between exceptionalism and nativism, party affiliation and age.

First, nativists are more likely than non-nativists to see America as exceptional. Take, for example, "I would rather be a citizen of the US than any other country." A supermajority of nativists (84%) agrees with this statement, while only 57% of non-nativists think the same. We find a similar trend on "thinking America is better than most other countries." Here, 79% of nativists believe this, while only 52% of non-nativists have similar views. This all said, a large majority of people of all political stripes still see America as a 'shining city on a hill'—just that some have a more intense view of it than others.

We see analogous trends for both party affiliation and age of respondent. Of note, age shows a similar pattern where younger Americans are much less likely to see America as special compared to their parents and grandparents. On the same question, only 48% of younger Americans would "rather be citizens of the US" compared to 87% of older Americans.

Table 7.4: Select Items on American Exceptionalism by Demographics and Political Persuasion.

Group	America better than most other countries	Rather be a citizen of the US	Ashamed of the US	Support country no matter what	Better if more like Americans
Total	64	69	12	27	26
Nativist	79	84	14	40	31
Non-Nativist	52	57	10	17	13
DELTA	27	27	4	23	18
College+	57	68	10	26	24
White	56	69	11	27	25
Hispanic	60	51	12	21	16
18-29	44	48	6	17	25
30-44	54	59	12	23	25
45-54	71	72	15	26	25
55-64	68	74	11	28	20
65+	79	87	13	29	31
DELTA (65+ - 18–29)	35	39	7	12	6
Republican	80	84	12	34	41
Democrat	63	66	12	26	23
DELTA (Rep - Dem)	17	18	0	8	18
Female	60	67	12	26	20

Source: Ipsos National Identity Poll 2024.

Critically, American exceptionalism and Americanism have similar correlates. It makes sense that a more restrictive view of being an American is strongly linked to a belief in American exceptionalism. Here, the only caveat is that exceptionalism has a broader popular appeal than the ethnocultural view of being American.

Americanism in Multivariate Context

So, what ultimately are the drivers of Americanism?

To answer this question, we look at the data in two phases. In the first, we examine the bivariate correlations between Americanism and other variables. In the second, we look at the same in multivariate context to assess the drivers of Americanism. Here, our simplifying assumption—based on the tabular data—is that there is a strong link between being American and nativism. That being nativist can also be understood as a restrictive way in defining national identity—who is and is not part of the group. Critically, once we consider other characteristics, is nativism still correlated with understanding of who counts as an American?

Bivariate Correlations

What do we find? A strong overlap of the key concepts (see Table 7.5). Here, Americanism and nativism are strongly correlated ($r = .497$). Americanism also shows a strong association with exceptionalism, age, and party affiliation. And we also find that Americanism is correlated in the expected direction with nostalgia, race, and ethnicity, as well as the belief that the system is broken. Most striking are the robust correlations between Americanism, exceptionalism, and nativism.[124] Each of these measures is also strongly related to "proud to be American." Simply put, Americans that are highly nativist or believe that the US is exceptional have demands on who can be considered an American.

Let's further peel away the onion on Americanism. This is where the story truly comes into relief. Here, we find, based on the factor analysis presented earlier in Table 7.1, that our index can be broken down into civic Americanism from ethnocultural Americanism.

We then combine four items into our ethnocultural index and three items into our civic index. Specifically, the ethnocultural index captures the importance

---

124 In Chapter 3, we make the case that, while these concepts are related, they measure distinct concepts.

Table 7.5: Bivariate Correlations Among Select Measures.

	Americanism	Americanism – Ethnocultural	Americanism – Civic	Nativism
Americanism	–	.954**	.535**	.497**
Americanism -Ethnocultural	.954**	–	.256**	.593**
Americanism-Civic	.535**	.256**	–	.070*
Nativism	.497**	.593**	.070*	–
Proud	–.480**	–.466**	–.234**	–.327**
Nostalgia	–.133**	–.150**	–.007	–.263**
American Exceptionalism	.482**	.536**	.042	.488**
System is Broken	.131**	.153**	.095**	.143**
College	.063*	.121**	–.140**	.188**
White	–.057*	.047	.051	–.123**
Hispanic	.090**	.081**	.062	.143**
Age	–.312**	–.291**	–.186**	–.208**
Female	.073*	.107**	–.065*	.088**
Rep	–.328**	–.363**	–.032	–.459**
Dem	.110**	.176**	–.142**	.398**

Source: Ipsos National Identity Poll 2024.

of being "born in the US, Christians," being "Christian," "speaking and writing English," and "not criticizing the US" (M = 10.5; SD = 3.6; α = .72). The civic index measures importance of "equal treatment," "voting," and "getting ahead on your own merit" (M = 2.8; SD = 3.6; α = .50).[125]

From a bivariate perspective, nativism (r = .593) and exceptionalism (r = .536) are highly correlated with ethnocultural traits as expected. In a multivariate context, it is nativism that explains the largest share of the variance in ethnocultural Americanism (51% in total). This makes sense. Nativism is a more restrictive belief system which aligns in part with the chauvinistic veneer of exceptionalism. Practically, nativism sets a bar high on who can be considered an American.

Civic Americanism, in turn, does not depend on the more restrictive belief systems of nativism or exceptionalism. Instead, belief in a functioning political and economic system (the system is broken) and being proud to be American are the key pillars of civicism. The "American Creed" as noted by Alexis de Tocqueville

---

125 We should note that, based on reliability scores, the civic index does not 'work' as well as the ethnocultural index. Given Schildkraut's distinction between a liberal understanding of American identity and a civic republican understanding, this is not unsurprising. While the individual items in our civic index are correlated, the correlations are not as strong as in our ethnocultural index.

depends on virtuous self-regulation and belief in the system (de Tocqueville, 2000). The data bear this out; those that are civic minded think civically.

Multivariate Context

How do the bivariate correlations hold up in a multivariate context? In Table 7.6, we present the results of a regression model predicting Americanism. In Figure 7.4, we graphically illustrate the relative importance of each of the individual predictors. Here, we find similar patterns to those in our bivariate analysis. Nostalgia, exceptionalism, age, gender, party affiliation, and race all have significant and independent effects on Americanism.

Both nativism and exceptionalism are key drivers of Americanism. To get at the relative effect, we take their beta weight, and turn it into a percentage of total explained variance. Here, we find that American exceptionalism, pride in being an American, and nativism are the most important drivers of Americanism. A result that is consistent with our bivariate analysis above. Critically, nativism is a unique world view which conditions how we define who is and who is not an American.

Table 7.6: Regression of Americanism Index on Nativism.

	Americanism Index		
	B	SE	Beta
Political Orientations			
Nativism	.195	.025	.261
System is Broken	.22	.047	.122
Proud	−2.27	.266	−.249
Nostalgia	−.257	.217	−.031
Exceptionalism	.178	.034	.173
Demographics			
College	.084	.211	.01
Race (White)	.471	.259	.047
Ethnicity (Hispanic)	−.518	.337	−.039
Age (Categorical)	−.444	.08	−.149
Gender (Female)	.126	.202	.015
Partisan Affiliation			
Republican	−1.152	.264	−.128
Democratic	−.831	.251	−.094
Constant	10.144	.746	
R-Squared	**.38**		

Source: Ipsos National Identity Poll 2024.

Drivers of Americanism

Driver	Percent
Nativism	30%
Proud	27%
Exceptionalism	13%
Age (Categorical)	10%
Republican	7%
System is Broken	7%
Democrat	4%
Race (White)	1%
Ethnicity (Hispanic)	1%
Nostalgia	0%
Gender (Female)	0%
College	0%

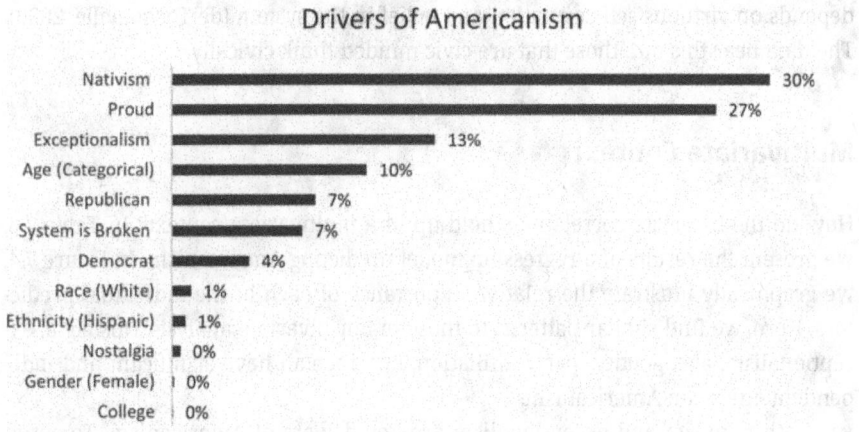

Figure 7.4: Key Drivers of Americanism as Defined by Percent Variance Explained.
Source: 2024 National Identity Survey.

Table 7.7: Bivariate Correlations of Select Variables Including Ethnocultural and Civic.

	Americanism Ethnocultural			Americanism Civic		
	B	SE	Beta	B	SE	Beta
Political Orientations						
Nativism	.24**	.021	.361	−.04**	.009	−.174
System is Broken	.11*	.038	.07	.109**	.017	.194
Proud	−1.57**	.218	−.197	−.70**	.1	−.246
Nostalgia	−.26	.178	−.036	.002	.081	.001
Exceptionalism	.19**	.028	.207	−.008	.013	−.025
Demographics						
College	.33*	.173	.045	−.24**	.079	−.093
Race (White)	.45*	.213	.051	.017	.097	.005
Ethnicity (Hispanic)	−.50*	.277	−.042	−.019	.127	−.005
Age (Categorical)	−.30^	.065	−.114	−.145**	.03	−.156
Gender (Female)	.25*	.166	.035	−.13^	.076	−.049
Partisan Affiliation						
Republican	−.86**	.217	−.11	−.29**	.099	−.103
Democratic	−.49**	.206	−.064	−.34**	.094	−.124
Constant	6.00**	.613		4.14**	.28	
R-Squared	.49			.16		

Source: 2024 National Identity Survey.

Ultimately, our multivariate model shows that Americanism is largely defined by a restrictive understanding of what it means to be American. We find that nativism and exceptionalism have strong impacts on Americanism. We saw this in our tabular analysis and it is only re-confirmed here.

What happens if we break out our Americanism index into its consistent parts (see Table 7.7)? Ethnocultural *versus* civic values? We see that nativism and exceptionalism are important predictors of an ethnocultural understanding of American identity *but* are less important as predictors of a civic understanding of American identity (see Figure 7.5). Nativism alone accounts for more than 50 percent of the explained variance while exceptionalism accounts for 31 percent. None of the other variables do much to explain an ethnocultural understanding of American identity. Consistent with our bivariate findings, civic understandings of Americanism are more closely associated with perceptions that the system is broken and pride in being American. Nativism is important, but considerably less important here. Our model also performs more poorly when we try to explain civic understandings of Americanism. Notably, age is important across models, but is more important as a predictor of civically-based Americanism.[126]

Drivers of Ethnocultural and Civic Americanism

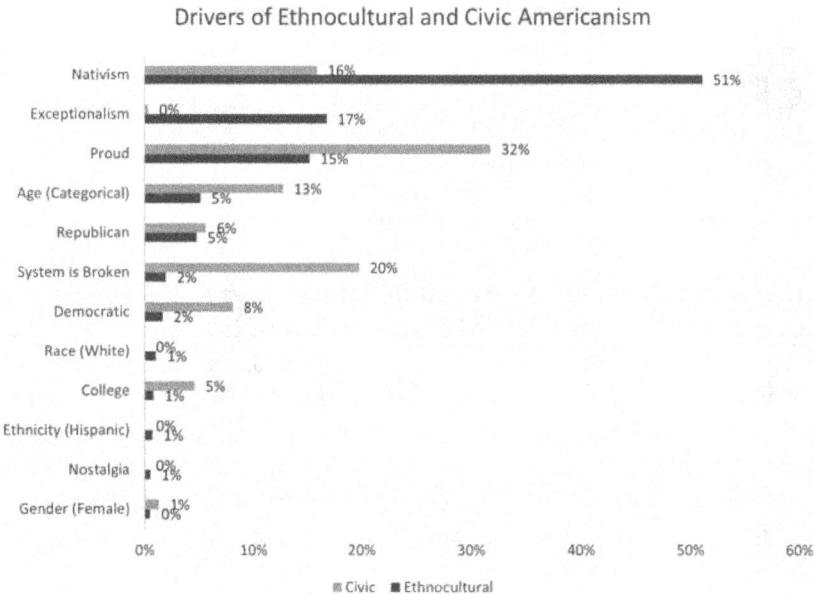

Figure 7.5: Drivers of Ethnocultural and Civic Americanism.

---

126 Many of our demographic variables (age, race, and education) influence Americanism through our attitudinal measures. The same is true of partisan affiliation. It is a more powerful

Americanism, Nativism and Policy Attitudes

As a final consideration, we examine the effect of nativism and Americanism on support for immigration policies. Specifically, we examine support for providing a pathway to citizenship (a liberal policy) and support for building a wall (a conservative policy). We present the frequencies of these measures by nativism in Figures 7.6 and 7.7. As can be seen, nativism is a strong predictor of opposition to a pathway to citizenship and support for building a wall. How do the effects of nativism compare to Americanism? We show this in Table 7.8, which includes our American index, and Table 7.9, which includes the constituent parts of Americanism.

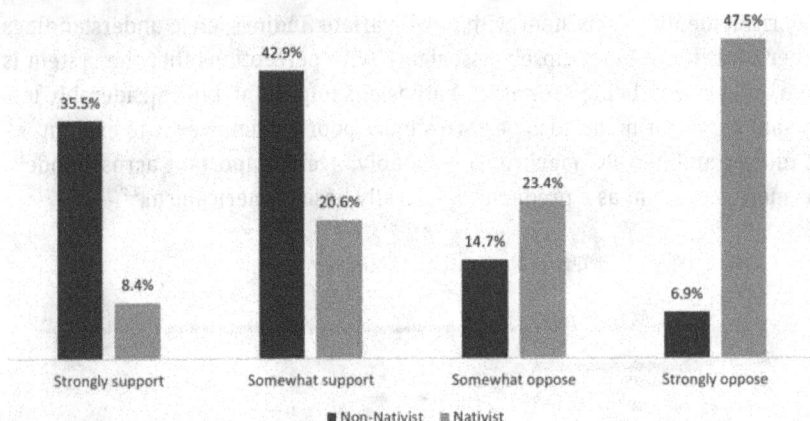

Figure 7.6: Support for Providing a Pathway for Citizenship.

As can be seen in Table 7.8, if we examine the effect of Americanism and nativism on policy support—controlling for other attitudinal variables, demographics, and partisan affiliation—we find that nativism is a strong driver of opposition to a pathway to citizenship and support for building a wall. Additionally, Americans who believe the system is broken are less likely to support a pathway to citizenship. Note that partisanship is also significant here but the effects are not particularly strong. The Republican coefficient is only marginally significant. This isn't to suggest that partisanship is unimportant, but rather that it operates through nativism.

---

predictor in models without the attitudinal measures. That model, however, also explains a much lower percentage of the variance (19 percent vs. 38 percent).

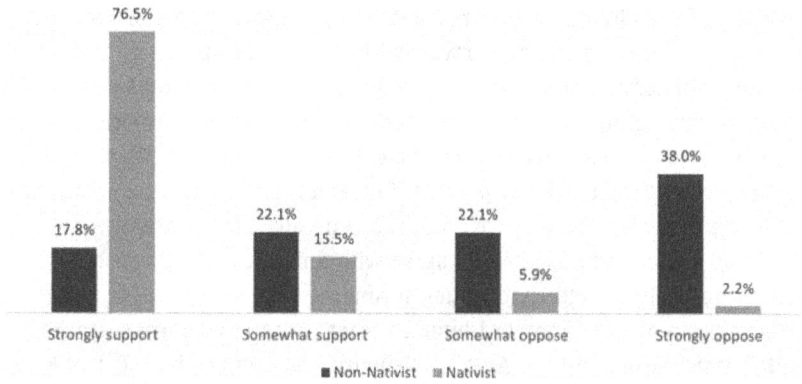

Figure 7.7: Support for Building a Wall.

Table 7.8: Regressions of Policy Support on Americanism and Nativism.

	Pathway to Citizenship			Build a Wall		
	B	**SE**	**Beta**	**B**	**SE**	**Beta**
Political Orientations						
Americanism	.01	.01	.047	.02^	.009	.055
Nativism	−.11**	.01	−.572	.12**	.007	.56
System is Broken	.04**	.01	.078	−.01	.012	−.015
Proud	−.11	.077	−.045	.09	.074	.032
Nostalgia	.10	.06	.045	−.02	.057	−.008
Exceptionalism	−.001	.009	−.004	.041**	.009	.137
Demographics						
College	−.03	.059	−.015	.001	.056	0
Race (White)	.03	.073	.01	−.03	.07	−.01
Ethnicity (Hispanic)	−.12	.096	−.033	.08	.091	.021
Age (Categorical)	.05*	.023	.063	.001	.022	.001
Gender (Female)	−.03	.056	−.012	.06	.054	.025
Partisan Affiliation						
Republican	.13^	.074	.057	−.28**	.07	−.106
Democratic	−.15*	.071	−.067	.21**	.067	.081
Constant	3.34	.226		−.16	.215	
R-Squared	.40			.58		

When it comes to building a wall, Americans who are more likely to see America as exceptional also express greater support for building a wall. This is consistent with the notion that fear of cultural dilution and change drive opposition. Ultimately, it is about the belief that immigrants won't assimilate. None of the demographic variables matter substantively once we account for nativism. Not surprisingly, support for building a wall is more strongly rooted in partisanship. Republicans predictably support building a wall, while Democrats oppose it.

We can gain additional insight by breaking Americanism into its two constituent parts—ethnocultural and civic conceptualizations of being American. Overall, our conclusion remains largely the same. Nativism is the principal driver of support for immigration-related policies. But Americanism plays a differential role. On this, those who hold more ethnocultural values are more likely to support building a wall *and* less likely to agree with a pathway to citizenship. Those who are more likely to hold civic values of Americanism also support a pathway to citizenship *but* are tepid toward building a wall. The results are clear. Ethnocultural Americanism and civic Americanism are two completely different world views that envision two very different Americas.

Table 7.9: Regressions of Policy Support on Americanism and Nativism.

	Pathway to Citizens			Build a Wall		
	B	SE	Beta	B	SE	Beta
Political Orientations						
Ethnocultural	−.011	.011	−.037	.032*	.011	.094
Civic	.113**	.026	.123	−.037	.024	−.037
Nativism	−.099**	.008	−.517	.115**	.007	.532
System is Broken	.031*	.013	.065	−.004	.012	−.008
Proud				.081	.074	.03
Nostalgia	.092	.06	.042	−.011	.057	−.005
Exceptionalism	.008	.009	.03	.038**	.009	.127
Demographics						
College	−.009	.059	−.004	−.017	.056	−.007
Race (White)	.035	.073	.013	−.037	.07	−.012
Ethnicity (Hispanic)	−.126	.095	−.035	.093	.09	.023
Age (Categorical)	.053*	.023	.068	−.003	.022	−.003
Gender (Female)	−.005	.056	.001	.046	.054	.019
Partisan Affiliation						
Republican	.127^	.073	.054	−.276**	.07	−.105
Democratic	−.147*	.07	−.064	.206**	.067	.079
Constant	2.965**	.197		−.041	.221	
R-Squared	.41			.58		

If nativism is fundamentally about defining who belongs, then it is no surprise that it has become one of the most powerful predictors of politics today. In the previous chapters, we explored in greater depth how nativism, more than economic status or traditional ideological beliefs, explains voting behavior and party loyalty in contemporary America. The alignment between nativists and the Republican Party is not just a matter of political strategy but reflects a deeper divide over what it means to be an American.

Identity vs. Economy: The H-1B Debate

The debate over H-1B visas has become a flashpoint in the broader struggle between economic pragmatism and cultural protectionism, exposing the tension between economic and identity-based nativism. While proponents argue that high-skilled immigration fuels innovation and economic growth, critics contend that it erodes national identity and undercuts American workers.

Vivek Ramaswamy, a biotech entrepreneur and 2024 Republican presidential candidate, ignited controversy when he called for a drastic reduction of the H-1B visa program despite having previously employed visa holders at his own company. His stance, which many saw as hypocritical, was emblematic of the broader Republican shift from an economic growth-based immigration perspective to a more nativist, identity-driven approach. Ramaswamy argued that "The lottery system needs to be replaced by actual meritocratic admission. It's a form of indentured servitude that only accrues to the benefit of the company that sponsored an H-1B immigrant. I'll gut it," a position that resonated with populist conservatives who view high-skilled immigration as an extension of corporate globalism.[127]

Steve Bannon has long framed the issue in cultural terms, claiming that H-1B visas represent an elite-driven "scam" that suppresses wages and weakens national cohesion.[128] He has positioned the fight against high-skilled immigration as part of a larger war to reclaim American sovereignty, arguing that economic justifications for the program amount to "a scam by the oligarchs in Silicon Valley." This rhetoric aligns with the broader nationalist critique that sees immigration—whether high- or low-skilled—as a mechanism for diluting American identity.

Donald Trump, despite initially advocating for a skills-based immigration system, capitalized on anti-H-1B sentiment during his presidency by imposing stricter regulations and suspending new visa issuances in 2020. His stance reflected a broader shift in Republican politics, where economic arguments for immigration increasingly took a backseat to concerns about cultural and national

---

127 Ward, Myah. (2023, September 16). Ramaswamy wants to end the H-1B visa program he used 29 times. Politico. https://www.politico.com/news/2023/09/16/ramaswamy-h1b-visa-gop-visa-00116383.

128 Rashid, H. (2024, December 27). Steve Bannon Joins War Against Elon Musk as MAGA implodes. The New Republic. https://newrepublic.com/post/189694/steve-bannon-maga-war-elon-musk-immigration.

integrity. "We have a moral duty to create an immigration system that protects the lives and jobs of our citizens,"[129] Trump said in 2020, reinforcing the idea that even high-skilled immigration could be framed as a threat.

These debates illustrate a crucial shift: nativism is no longer solely about low-wage, undocumented immigration but has expanded to encompass high-skilled immigration as well. The transformation of H-1B opposition from an economic critique into a cultural and identity-based grievance demonstrates the growing salience of national identity in American politics. As Davis et al. (2019b) notes, economic vulnerability alone does not predict nativist attitudes; rather, "perceptions of cultural decline and identity threat" are the key drivers.

The H-1B debate ultimately reflects the broader themes of our book—nativism is not merely an economic phenomenon but a deeply cultural one. While traditional conservative arguments once framed high-skilled immigration as an economic necessity, today's populist movement sees it as an existential challenge to American identity.

Figures like Ramaswamy, Bannon, and Trump illustrate the evolution of the Republican Party's stance, shifting from a business-friendly approach to a nativist one that prioritizes cultural cohesion over economic efficiency. The battle between economic pragmatism and identity protectionism will likely define future debates over immigration policy, reinforcing the central argument that nativism is fundamentally about who belongs to the American tribe.

Bringing It All Together

So, what does all this mean?

Nativism first must be understood through the lens of American identity. Nativists employ a more restrictive definition of what it means to be an American. This is a critical point. Too often, the debate reduces nativism to racism by another name, or authoritarianism, or economic anxiety. At its core, nativism is a belief system that defines national belonging—who is and is not American. The political and cultural debate unfolding in the US today is about this fundamental fulcrum.

We have also seen that American identity is best understood as a two-dimensional concept—one ethnocultural, the other civic. Most Americans broadly embrace civic ideals like the American creed as essential to national identity. In

---

129 Trump, D. (2020, June 2022). President Donald J. Trump Is Putting American Workers First as We Restore Our Economy to Greatness. https://trumpwhitehouse.archives.gov/briefings-statements/president-donald-j-trump-putting-american-workers-first-restore-economy-greatness/.

contrast, nativists—and adjacent groups such as Republicans—see ascriptive, ethnocultural traits as equally or even more important. For a nativist, being American requires more than just embracing democracy and freedom; it also means speaking English, being born in the US, and sharing a particular cultural and historical lineage.

This divide is the fault line of American identity today: nativists *versus* nonnativists. As earlier chapters have shown, nativism is one of the most powerful explanatory forces behind electoral outcomes and party affiliation. It is a defining feature of contemporary politics, shaping not just policy preferences but also deeper perceptions of belonging. Nativism reflects the anxiety with a changing America. While some Americans welcome these changes as a natural evolution of the country, others see them as a fundamental threat to American culture and the American way of life. More than anything, these changes challenge deeply held beliefs about what it means to be American.

While today's debate over American identity feels unique, it is not without precedent. From the Know Nothing Party of the 19th century to the restrictive immigration policies of the early 20th century, the tension between inclusive and exclusive definitions of Americanism has shaped the nation's political landscape for generations. Understanding this history helps put our current moment into perspective.

Donald Trump and the politics of our era reflect and amplify these tensions. Our Potomac and Front Royal examples illustrate the divide—two Americas, each with its own definition of belonging. One more restrictive, the other more inclusive. One more nativist, the other more civic. Both see themselves as authentically American, even if they struggle to see the other as such.

To return to our central point, nativism is ultimately a belief system about group membership—who is and is not part of the national tribe. While its intensity rises and falls with levels of immigration, nativism remains a persistent force in shaping American identity. Whether active or latent, it has played a crucial role in defining who Americans believe they are as a people. Our examples of Potomac and Front Royal bring this divide into sharp relief—one holding onto a more restrictive definition of American identity, the other embracing a broader, more diffuse one.

Again, this is a tale of two Americas.

While this chapter focuses on the nativism-identity link in the American context, the broader question of national identity is not confined to the United States. In the next chapter we examine how similar debates are playing out across the world, from the rise of nationalist parties in Europe to identity conflicts in Asia and Latin America. The American experience is part of a larger global struggle over who belongs and who does not.

Chapter 8
Not So Exceptional After All? Nativism Goes Global

Vignette: Brexit's Foreboding

I had just gotten off a red-eye flight from Washington DC. It was early morning in London, February 2016.[130] I caught a black cab to our offices on Borough Road in Southwark, London. I always had to stop and think about how to pronounce Borough—"Buh-ruh Rohd"—otherwise, I'd be misunderstood with my slight American Midwestern twang, "Bur-row Rowd."

The cabbie was listening to the radio—all the talk was about the upcoming Brexit vote later that year. After a few minutes, I asked what he thought. Emphatically, he was a 'yes' for Brexit.

"See," he said, pointing toward West London, just off the Westway (A40) over-ramp. "I grew up over there. Too expensive now. Damned Russians bought up all the flats. I have to live way past Heathrow now."

His words had conviction—a grievance rooted in economics, place, and belonging. Something was going on here.

A few days later, on my way back to Heathrow, I caught another black cab.

Different driver, but eerily similar reasoning. He too was a 'yes' on Brexit.

"It's a race to the bottom," he said. "The Poles are driving illegal taxis and undercutting our prices. Something has to be done for native-born Brits."

Two different cabbies, two almost identical justifications. The message was clear: Brexit had strong legs. And sure enough, when the vote came that June, Brexit won 51.89% to 48.11%.

At the time, I made note of the similarities between Brexit and Trump. I saw them as parallel phenomena—both riding waves of grievance and national pride, but distinct in their origins. It wasn't until late 2016, when we conducted our first global populism poll—just before Trump's surprise victory—that I saw the deeper connection.

What had seemed like a collection of isolated populist uprisings was actually a singular global force. The same themes—displacement, cultural anxiety, and national identity—were reshaping politics across the Western world. Brexit was not just about the UK, just as Trump was not just about the US.

---

130 This vignette is based on Clifford Young's personal experience.

https://doi.org/10.1515/9783111384047-008

The same underlying sentiment—the belief that one's nation was slipping away, that outsiders were changing it beyond recognition, that something fundamental needed to be reclaimed—was fueling a new political order.

Nativism from US to Global Context

We have learned many things in the preceding chapters about nativism. First, it is a stable, deeply ingrained belief system in the US. It ebbs and flows—as it responds to contextual changes like heightened immigration—but it has always been there with us. Pound for pound, nativism is the most important political driver in America today. This does not mean that it determines every election. But rather that it shapes the logic of political coalitions. Our multivariate modeling has shown just this—that nativism soaks up a large part of the variance explained, independent of party identification and other factors.

The analysis clearly shows here that nativism is not just about economic deprivation or want—it is an enduring cultural feature of the American experience. A critical variable that cannot be ignored when trying to understand America today.

We also learned that nativism is not simply racism by another name. While racial resentment and nativism do overlap—a nativist is more likely to be White and aggrieved by policies like affirmative action or DEI-like programs. But nativism is more than that. Indeed, at its core, nativism is about identity—it speaks to the definition of who is and is not American. A nativist has a more restrictive notion of American identity: White, Christian, and born in the US, compared to non-nativists who have a more diffuse and inclusive conception. Remember Front Royal, Virginia *versus* Potomac, Maryland in Chapter 7.

Global Polling Evidence: Methodology and Reliability

This all begs the obvious question: Is nativism just a US phenomenon, or does it have broader global reach? While the American nativist experience is rooted in its unique historical context, the core drivers—demographic change, cultural anxiety, and a perceived loss of national identity—are not unique to the United States.

To answer our question, we will examine multiple global polls that span almost a decade (see Table 8.1 below). In the first of the five global surveys, we use the full five-item nativism battery outlined in Chapter 3. In other waves, we employ a reduced nativist battery of three items focused on the core themes of national threat, cultural belonging, and exclusion. These items include:

1. Immigrants take important social services away from real [nationals].
2. When jobs are scarce, employers should give priority to people of this country over immigrants.
3. [Country] would be better off if we let in all immigrants who wanted to come here.

We specify which data are used in each analysis—but overall, the story is the same. Nativism conditions how we see our national tribe independent of context or country. Nativism is global in scope.

Table 8.1: Ipsos Polls Used in Data Analysis.

	2016	2019	2021	2023	2025
Number of Nativism Items	5	3	3	3	3
Number of Countries Employing Nativism Scale	21	27	25	28	31
Total Sample Size	16,069	18,528	19,017	20,630	23,789
Source	Ipsos Populism Survey	Ipsos Populism Survey	Ipsos Populism Survey	Ipsos Populism Survey	Ipsos Populism Survey

Like in Chapter 3, we assess the validity and reliability of our nativism index but at the global level. A sound performance in the US context does not mean the same across countries, languages, and different cultural contexts. Previous research has established the metric invariance of our nativism index, meaning that it works well across countries (Zhao, 2019). Here, Cronbach's alpha serves as our metric of internal consistency and reliability—an alpha of .65 or higher is considered a robust measure in the social sciences.

What do we find?

Nativism is indeed global in reach and statistically reliable. Across all countries in both the 2016 and 2025 surveys, the nativism index exceeds the .65 threshold. In fact, in the 2016 global poll across 20 countries, the five-item scale produced an alpha of .816.

Our 2025 three-item index performs similarly well with a Cronbach's Alpha of .801 (see Figure 8.1). When we take the 2025 questions and break them down by country, we find that the measure holds up across countries. At the high end, Italy, France, the UK, and Belgium all have an Alpha of .868 or greater. And at the low end, Switzerland, Indonesia, and Malaysia have Alpha's of .711 or lower *but* all above the .65 threshold. Our nativism index is a robust global measure.

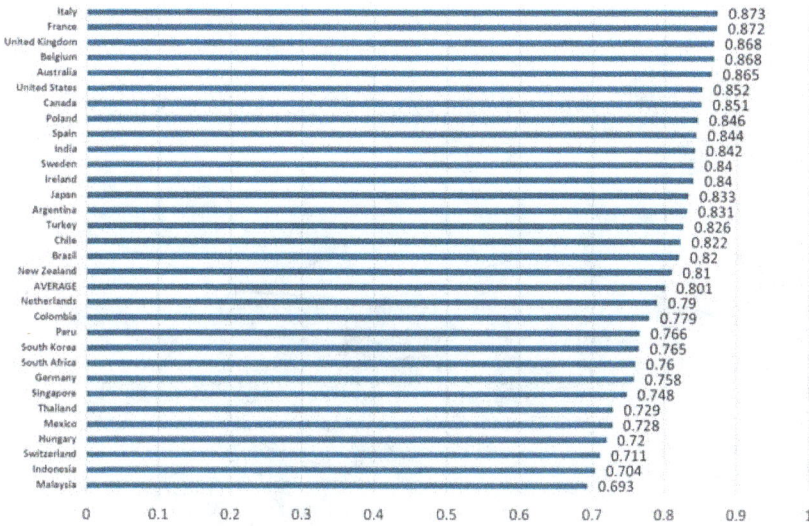

Figure 8.1: Cronbach's Alpha for Three-Item Nativism Scale by Country.
Source: Ipsos Populism Poll 2025.

Nativism Behaving in Sensible Ways Across Space and Time

So how does nativism trend overtime?

We see in Figure 8.2 that since 2016 nativism has been relatively stable at the global level. Here, for our analysis, we employ a single nativism item: "When jobs are scarce, employers should give priority to people of this country over immigrants." As noted in Chapter 4, we borrow this question from the world values survey (WVS).

As we saw in Chapter 6, nativism did show a slight decline over the last decade in the US. We find similar trends in Brazil, Argentina, Italy, and Spain. In contrast, countries like Hungary, Poland, and Sweden have shown increases in nativism in this same period. Nativism is a stable orientation globally and it behaves in predictable ways.

Nativism, however, is not a monolith globally. Some countries show higher levels and others lower levels of nativism. In Figure 8.3, we present the statement that "When jobs are scarce, employers should give priority to people of this country over immigrants." Twenty-five of the 31 countries in the 2025 Ipsos survey have more than half their population that agrees with greater nativist restrictions. At the high end, we find Indonesia, Hungary, Thailand, Malysia, and India. In contrast, at the low end, well below the average, we find Sweden, Spain,

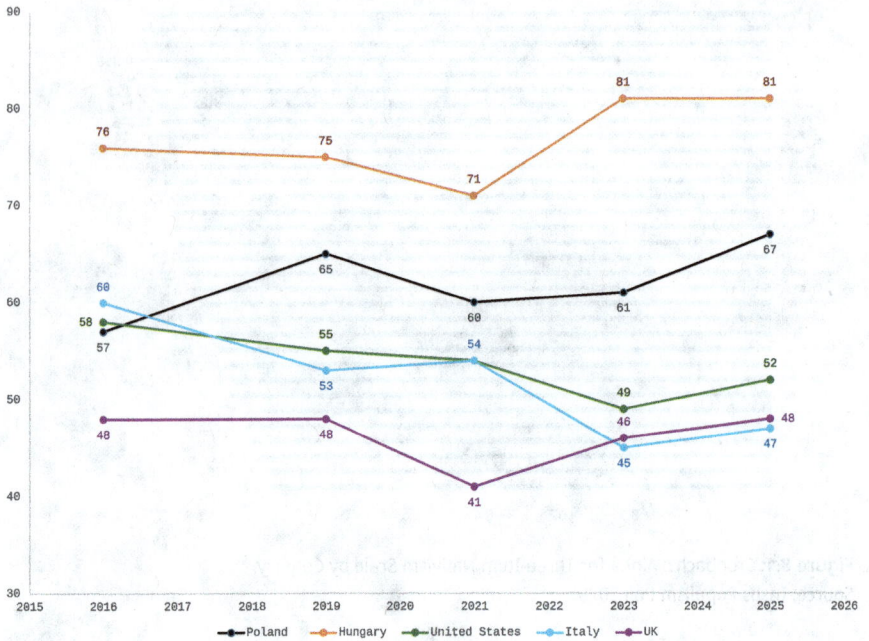

Figure 8.2: Percent Agreeing That When Jobs Are Scarce, Employers Should Give Priority to People of This Country over Immigrants.
Source: Ipsos Global Populism Poll 2016 to 2025.

Canada, Germany, and the Netherlands. Even those countries at the low end show strong plurality support for nativist restrictions. There is variability when it comes to nativism. But it is also everywhere.

Validity and Predictive Power

In terms of validity, we see a similar trend globally to that of the United States. From a convergent validity perspective, nativism is highly correlated with measures that are conceptually congruent, such as the belief that the system is broken, populism, authoritarianism, and nostalgia (feeling like a stranger in own land).

In terms of divergent validity, nativism is negatively correlated with congruent concepts such as beliefs that one is better off than one's parents, confidence in the political system, and there being more education. All these correlations show that nativism is measuring what it should be measuring and strongly mirrors what we found in the United States (see Table 8.2).

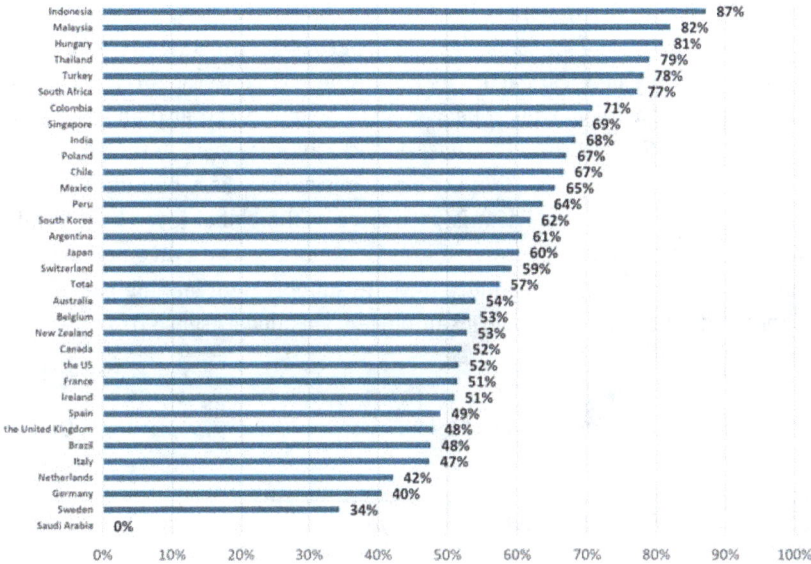

Figure 8.3: Percent Agree That When Jobs Are Scarce, Employers Should Prioritize People from This Country over Immigrants.
Source: Ipsos Global Populism 2025.

Table 8.2: Statistically Significant Pearson's Correlations with Nativism.

Convergent Validity	Divergent Validity
.412 System is Broken (2025)	−.027 Income (2025)
.340 System is Broken (2019)	−.066 Education (2025)
.208 Authoritarianism (2019)	−.121 College Degree (2019)
.352 Stranger in Own Land (2019)	−.060 Confidence in the System (2019)
.452 Populism	−.125 Better Off Than Parents (2019)

Source: 2019 and 2025 Ipsos Global Populism Surveys.

Nativism also has strong predictive properties at a global level. Our analyses below reinforce this point. We clearly find that nativism is a critical driver of politics globally. In the 2025 Global Populism Survey, our nativism index is positively correlated with two different outcome variables: support for the sitting government as well as identification with right leaning parties (see Table 8.3). Here, we define government as those parties in power at the time of the survey and right leaning parties as populist or anti-establishment parties in orientation.

Nativism has been shown to be a politically potent force cross-nationally, influencing support not only for right-wing populist parties but left-leaning as well (Davis et al., 2019b; Lubbers & Coenders, 2017). But anti-immigration rhetoric is not the sole province of extreme right-wing parties, it also emerges from mainstream and left-wing political parties as well (Alonso & Fonseca, 2012). According to Cas Mudde, right-wing parties appear to be the catalysts rather than innovators of nativist politics (Mudde, 2013). Nativist politics can arise even in the absence of right-wing populist parties and still play a role in contemporary politics.

So, what do we find? Nativism is predictive at the global level. Specifically, we find statistically significant correlations between our two outcome variables and nativism. Here, nativists are more likely to support right leaning parties and less likely to do the same with parties in power. This makes sense from a simple face validity perspective.

Table 8.3: Predictive Validity—Correlation Between Nativism and Political Outcomes at the National Level.

	Nativism	Party in Power	Right Leaning/Populist Parties
Nativism	1		
Party in Power	−.060	1	
Right Leaning/Populist Parties	.088	.163	1

** Correlations are significant at the .01 level (2-tailed).
Source: Ipsos Global Populism Poll 2025.

At the country level, we also find a strong correlation between nativism and other socio-political outcomes (see Table 8.4). This includes lower scores on indices for political participation, political cultural, social progress, corruption, and inequality. Nativism is more strongly correlated with outcomes than the index 'the system is broken' or populism; one more piece of evidence that shows Nativism's preeminence as a global explanatory variable.

Again, all these correlations are in the predicted direction and show that nativism is both a stable and highly ingrained belief system globally *but* also quite predictive of political and other socio-political outcomes. Nativism is global in its expanse.

Nativism as Identity: Ethnocultural vs. Civic

As discussed in Chapter 7, nativism is best understood as identity by another name. This holds true globally as it does in America. In our 2025 Global Populism poll, we fielded a seven-item national identity battery that included the importance of being born in the country, speaking the national language, voting, treating people equally,

Table 8.4: Country-Level Correlates of Nativism with Measures of Democracy and Economics.

	The Economist Economic Intelligence Index 2020					
	Overall Score 2020	Electoral Process and Pluralism	Functioning of Government	Political Participation	Political Cultural	Civil Liberties
Broken System Index	−.45	−.16	−.54	−.44	−.58	−.24
Populism Index	−.52	.24	−.57	−.55	−.59	.3
Nativism Index	−.73	.58	−.51	−.59	−.63	−.77
	Global Freedom (Freedom House)	2020 Social Progress Index	2020 Opportunity Score	Corruption Perceptions Index	Gross Domestic Product	GINI Index (Inequality)
Broken System Index	−.31	−.36	−.58	−.73	−.73	.68
Populism Index	−.41	−.55	−.57	−.7	−.69	.48
Nativism Index	−.79	−.61	−.85	−.71	−.66	.46

Source: Ipsos Global Populism Survey 2019.

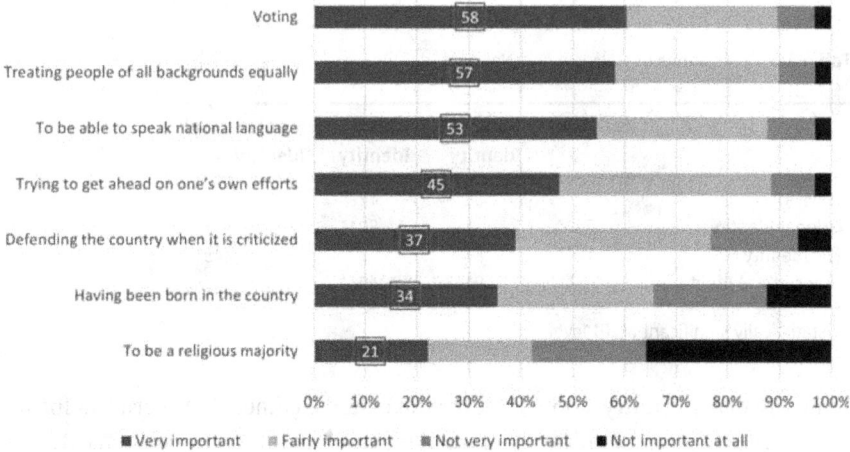

Figure 8.4: Characteristics Important to National Identity Across Countries.

and defending the country from criticism. The results across countries are presented in Figure 8.4.

These items form a reliable scale (Cronbach's alpha = .756) and correlate strongly with nativism. The connection is clear: the more exclusive one's definition of national identity, the more likely one is to embrace nativist politics. We grouped these into two national identity types using factors like we did in Chapter 7 on American identity.

- **Ethnocultural identity items:**
  - Speaking the national language.
  - Belonging to the national religion.
  - Being born in the country.
  - Defending the country no matter what.
- **Civic identity items:**
  - Voting in elections.
  - Treating people of all backgrounds equally.
  - Succeeding through individual effort.

In Table 8.5, we present bivariate correlations of nativism with measures of national identity, including a single measure as well as items gauging a civic or ethnocultural understanding of identity. Globally, the data show that civic national identity is strongly correlated with ethnocultural national identity (Pearson correlation = .362). Ethnocultural identity in turn is more strongly correlated with nativism than civic identity. We found the same in the US.

Table 8.5: Correlations of Nativism and National Identity.

	Nativism	National Identity	Civic Identity	Ethnocultural Identity
Nativism		.36**	.12**	.45**
National Identity	.36**		.80**	.91**
Civic Identity	.12**	.8**		.48*
Ethnocultural Identity	.45**	.91**	.48**	

** statistically significant at .01 level.

In nearly every country studied, those who endorse ethnocultural criteria for national belonging are significantly more likely to support nativist positions. By contrast, civic identity items—especially those tied to equality and participation—show a much weaker correlation with nativist attitudes. The strongest predictor among all identity items is being born in the country.

In Table 8.6, we examine the bivariate correlations between nativism and the characteristics individuals believe are important to national identity. The single strongest correlation ($r = .44$) is "having been born in the country" followed by "defending the country when it is criticized," being "the religious majority" and being "able to speak the language." Clearly, nativism is mostly a function of ethno-cultural identity.

Table 8.6: Correlations of Nativism with Characteristics Important to National Identity.

	Nativism
To be religious majority	.29**
Voting	.09**
To be able to speak the language	.25**
Trying to get ahead on one's own efforts	.22**
Treating people of all backgrounds equally	−.05**
Defending the country when it is criticized	.30**
Having been born in the country	.44**

The belief that being born in the country is essential to be a 'true' member of the nation is tightly linked to exclusionary politics. Religion and defending the country follow closely, especially in nations with dominant religious traditions. These findings suggest that nativism is not primarily about legal status or contribution —it is about cultural inheritance. It reflects an instinct to protect not just national boundaries, but a way of life and a sense of 'us' that feels imperiled.

Ultimately, like in the US, nativism globally is fundamentally about belonging. And this world view is restrictive in nature. From this lens, nativism is politically powerful because it cuts at national identity (Kešić & Duyvendak, 2019; Kim & Kim, 2021). Nativist politics are inevitable because the question '*who are we as a people?*' is never permanently settled. No matter where they reside, nativists answer this question by emphasizing birthplace and ancestry. They share an ethno-cultural, rather than a civic, understanding of national identity.

Nativism's Impact at a Global Level

Nativism is a stable deeply-ingrained belief system which is global in scale. It is a reliable and valid measure. It is also a very strong predictor of political attitudes at the global level. We ran a linear probability model with controls for age, education, income, respondent sex, belief that the system is broken as well as civic and

Table 8.7: Linear Probability Model of Right-Leaning or Populist Party Identification on Nativism.

	B	Std. Error	Beta
Attitudes			
Nativism	−.007**	.001	−.073
System is Broken	.001	.001	.008
Civic Identity	−.002^	.001	−.014
Ethnocultural Identity	−.007**	.001	−.067
Demographics			
Income	.012**	.003	.029
Education	−.025**	.003	−.052
Age	.001**	0	.065
Sex (Female)	−.03**	.005	−.044
Constant	.28**	.016	

ethnocultural identity. Here, our outcome variable is identification with a right-leaning or populist party.

So, what do we find? We present the results of the model in Table 8.7 and show the relative effect of each of the independent variables in Figure 8.5.

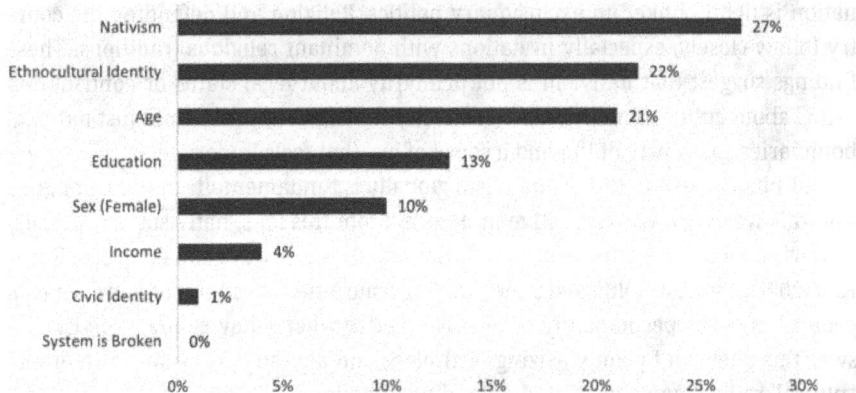

Figure 8.5: Relative Importance of Predictors of Right-Leaning or Populist Party Identification.

The biggest takeaway of all this analysis is that nativism is a significant and strong predictor of global politics.[131] Running this at the country level, we find a similar pattern: Nativism exerts an independent effect on politics. To exclude nativism in any substantive or statistical analysis is to misunderstand our world today.

---

131 In this model, nativism is coded so that higher scores indicate less nativist responses.

Nativism Takes On Different Forms and Flavors

This raises a fundamental question—how can nativism be so important globally when not all countries are experiencing massive immigration or suffering existential social change?

The answers to this question are both universal and particular. There are indeed macro forces that shape our world homogenizing us in the process. But there are also very specific idiosyncratic aspects of each place that makes nativism uniquely local.

Universal Forces

One of the unique features of the contemporary era is that politics are played in a flat world (Friedman, 2005). How is this so? Let us discuss below.

First, technological shifts have changed the way we communicate with each other and the way humans communicate about politics. Increasing political messaging is micro-targeted, appealing directly to groups of voters with related characteristics. Once upon a time, social norms limited the expression of ideas considered outside of the mainstream. Think of the 'spiral of silence' as a manifestation of this —the nasty things were kept inside (Noelle-Neumann, 1974). Social media, however, has allowed individuals with less desirable opinions to find each other and confirm their world view. The virtual world is the great aggregator and facilitator.

Second, the ability to move from place to place has never been easier. As a result, population shifts are continuous and dynamic with much of these shifts coming from areas experiencing violence, oppression, or economic hardship.[132] As a result, more people now live in urban areas than in the past, which are increasingly diverse and more economically vibrant. Rural communities, in contrast, struggle with aging populations, weak economies, and stagnant populations. These differences have played out in voting behavior (Gimpel et al., 2020; Huijsmans & Rodden, 2025; Rodden, 2010) and political attitudes (Huijsmans et al., 2021; Kenny & Luca, 2021). At least in the US context, there is evidence of place-based resentment (Cramer, 2016; Munis, 2022). Similarly, the movement of peoples across boarders has never been more pronounced. Indeed, as mentioned already, both Europe and the US are experiencing historically high levels of foreign-born residents.

Third, while globalization has arguably been a net positive for developed economies, it has nonetheless created winners and losers (Stiglitz, 2002) and has

---

[132] United Nations. (n.d.). Shifting demographics. https://www.un.org/en/un75/shifting-demo graphics#:~:text=URBAN%20FUTURE,and%20protecting%20our%20natural%20capital.

created a populist backlash against the forces of globalization (Rodrik, 2021; Walter, 2021). The losers share certain characteristics, they are older, live in rural communities, are less educated, and have less mobility (Margalit, 2012).

Throughout the world, these shifts are visible and inescapable, but even for individuals not directly experiencing the dislocations, they experience the shifts through mediated images and messages strategically communicated through social media by right-wing populist parties (Engesser et al., 2017; Heiss & Matthes, 2020; Ivarsflaten, 2008; Krämer, 2017; Krämer et al., 2021). As a result, population shifts are an important part of the story. But the larger story is that native populations perceive the world around them as changing due the forces of out of their control. And those changes challenge their understanding of their sense of belonging (Betz, 2022; Dancygier, 2010; Mudde, 2012; Norris, 2005). Nativist politics that define the contemporary era are rooted in questions of national identity and cultural change (Betz, 2019; Mutz, 2018; Sniderman et al., 2004). Our research in this chapter shows that this is global in scale

Idiosyncratic Context

Nativism, however, does not take a single form; it adapts to its environment, shaping itself according to a country's unique history, the ethnic heterogeneity of the population, the level and type of immigration, and the design of political institutions (Betz, 2017a). Central to the distinct forms of nativism around the world are the unique characteristics of the native population and the target of the nativist appeals (Betz, 2017a; Svraka, 2024). This will vary from place to place as will the relative power of the forces that give rise to nativism: the economic effects and population shifts due to globalism, the cultural shifts that give rise to perceptions of status threat, and the ability of right-wing populist candidates and parties to successfully appeal to voters (Green-Pedersen & Krogstrup, 2008; Odmalm & Bale, 2015).

Let's run a thought experiment to think through the idiosyncratic nature of nativism. To do this, we employ our Nativism Activation Model (NAM), introduced earlier. It provides a useful lens for understanding this variation. According to NAM, nativism becomes politically powerful when three core forces align:

- **Latent nativist beliefs:** Deep-seated attitudes within a population that favor native-born citizens over foreign-born ones.
- **Catalytic conditions:** External shocks or changes that activate latent beliefs, transforming them from quiet sentiments to public forces.
- **Political entrepreneur:** A leader who recognizes the opportunity to mobilize nativist sentiments.

But how these three forces interact and manifest is shaped by local context—by a country's history, the composition of its population, and the nature of its political system. Below, we examine how nativism takes on different forms in five countries: Hungary, India, Canada, Brazil, and the United Kingdom (see Table 8.8).

Table 8.8: Four Future Nativist Scenarios.

Country	Nativism Level	Primary Driver	Latent Beliefs (NAM)	Catalytic Conditions (NAM)	Political Entrepreneur (NAM)
Hungary	High	External Migration	Ethnic and cultural purity	2015 Migrant Crisis	Viktor Orban
India	High	Internal Religious Tensions	Hindu Nationalism	Rising Hindu-Muslim tensions	Narendra Modi
Canada	Low	External Migration	Multicultural Identity	Economic stability, points system	No dominant figure
Brazil	Moderate	Internal Stratification	Racial Hierarchies	Regional and Economic Inequality	Jair Bolsonaro (partial)
United Kingdom	Moderate High	Hybrid (Internal + External)	National Sovereignty	Brexit Campaign, EU Migration	Nigel Farage, Boris Johnson

Hungary: Fortress Nativism—External Threats

In Hungary, nativism is defined by fear of the outsider. The latent beliefs are rooted in ethnic and cultural purity—Hungary as a homogeneous Christian nation that must be defended. The catalytic condition was the 2015 migrant crisis, which brought asylum seekers to Europe. Prime Minister Viktor Orbán, acting as the political entrepreneur, seized on this moment, framing immigrants as an existential threat. His government built barbed-wire fences, ran anti-immigrant propaganda, and positioned Hungary as a bulwark against foreign influence.

India: Internal Sorting—Nativism as Religious Nationalism

In India, nativism is not about excluding foreigners—it is about defining who truly belongs within the nation. The latent beliefs are rooted in Hindu nationalism, a vision of India as a fundamentally Hindu country. The catalytic conditions include rising Hindu–Muslim tensions, religious violence, and the Citizenship Amendment Act, which grants citizenship based on religion. Prime Minister Narendra Modi and the Bharatiya Janata Party (BJP) serve as the political entrepreneurs, framing Muslims as outsiders even though they have lived in India for centuries.

Canada: The Outlier—Low Nativism Despite High Immigration

Canada defies the global trend. Despite high levels of immigration, nativism is weak. The latent beliefs are rooted in multiculturalism—Canada sees itself as a nation of immigrants. The catalytic conditions that might trigger nativism, such as economic insecurity or cultural loss, are largely absent thanks to a strong economy and a carefully managed immigration system. No dominant political entrepreneur has successfully mobilized nativism at the national level. However, the 2025 national election showed cracks in this monolith.

Brazil: Nativism as Social Hierarchy

In Brazil, nativism does not target immigrants but reinforces internal hierarchies. The latent beliefs are rooted in racial stratification and social inequality. The catalytic conditions include persistent economic inequality and regional disparities between the wealthy south and the impoverished north. While Jair Bolsonaro has used nativist rhetoric to attack left-wing politics, his appeal is more about cultural conservatism than pure nativism.

United Kingdom: Hybrid Nativism—External and Internal Divides

In the United Kingdom, nativism is a complex mix of external and internal drivers. The latent beliefs combine national sovereignty and cultural pride. The catalytic conditions include the Brexit referendum, which fueled fears of EU migration, and long-standing regional divides between London and economically struggling regions. Political entrepreneurs like Nigel Farage and Boris Johnson activated these sentiments with the promise of "taking back control."[133] UK nativism is a hybrid—both a rejection of external influence and a struggle over internal identity.

Why Context Matters

While the instinct to protect or reclaim a national identity is constant, its expression depends on local conditions. Some countries, like Hungary, experience nativ-

---

133 Farage, N. (2016, June). Nigel Farage: Why you should vote for Brexit this Thursday. The Independent.
   https://www.independent.co.uk/voices/eu-referendum-brexit-nigel-farage-on-why-you-should-vote-to-leave-a7091021.html.

ism as a reaction to external threats. Others, like India, use nativism to sort and exclude populations from within. Canada's experience suggests that strong institutions and inclusive national narratives can neutralize nativism, while Brazil shows that even in the absence of immigration, nativist attitudes can reinforce social hierarchies.

Our framework—Nativism Activation Model (NAM)—reveals that while the triggers and targets of nativism vary, the underlying structure remains consistent. This model allows us to see beyond local color to the deeper dynamics that drive nativism as a global phenomenon.

Bringing It All Together

In this chapter, we have shown that nativism is not a uniquely American phenomenon. It is not a passing phase. It is a global force—deep, persistent, and politically potent.

It emerges wherever people feel dislocated by cultural change, unmoored by globalization, or alienated by a political system they no longer trust. It draws strength not only from grievance, but from identity—a belief that the nation is 'ours,' and that 'they' are changing it beyond recognition. Nativism adapts. It can be religious or secular. It can oppose immigrants or internal minorities. It can wear the garb of populism, nationalism, or even democracy. But at its heart, it is always about belonging—and the belief that that belonging must be protected, policed, and preserved.

The 2024 global election cycle laid bare the rising influence of this force. In country after country, voters rallied around nativist parties and platforms—not as fringe actors, but as central contenders for power. In the United States, Donald Trump returned to the presidency riding a wave of cultural grievance, promising to restore the nation by excluding those deemed outsiders. In Europe, parties once dismissed as far-right consolidated into powerful regional blocs, winning seats and setting agendas. From the Netherlands to Argentina, immigration, national identity, and cultural integrity dominated the political conversation—regardless of who was on the ballot.

Elections are no longer just contests between left and right—they are referenda on identity, on who belongs, and whose voice counts. And the results show that the nativist instinct is not only resilient but increasingly mainstream. What was once coded language is now explicit: 'protect our borders,' 'defend our culture,' 'reclaim our country.' These are not just slogans; they are expressions of a deeper desire to preserve a bounded, inherited sense of nationhood against the fluidity of modern life.

This chapter has shown that nativism only comes to the fore under the unique mix of three factors: engrained nativist beliefs, a political entrepreneur, and catalytic conditions. We deployed our NAM framework to show how nativism could manifest itself idiosyncratically from context to context. America and Donald Trump are different than Narendra Modi and India, which, in turn, are different from Viktor Orbán and Hungry. But while the proximate causes of nativism manifest might be different, nativism itself is about meaning and belonging.

To navigate this age of nativism, we must understand its reach, its roots, and its remarkable ability to adapt to—and transform—the societies it touches. In a world where more voters are choosing leaders based on who they exclude rather than what they build, the future of pluralism may depend less on ideology than on identity—and whether our democracies can forge a shared 'we' broad enough to survive.

Chapter 9
Conclusions: The Future of Nativism

Nativism Is a Driver of Contemporary Politics

We began this project with a simple observation. Donald Trump's 'Build a Wall' nativist appeals were not just a sideshow—they were a signal of something deeper. Nativism was not just a campaign tactic; it was reshaping the political landscape.

One of the authors, Cliff Young, as President of Ipsos at the time, had a front-row seat to these shifts. As the polling data came in, patterns began to emerge. Too often, polling is reduced to a horse race—who is winning and who is not—rather than a tool for uncovering deeper patterns. But good polling reveals underlying structures. Recognizing this, Young developed the nativist index (as described in Chapter 3).[134] With it, he systematically measured nativist sentiment and explored how it correlated with other attitudes—populism, authoritarianism, and White grievance—each a critical pillar of Donald Trump's appeal to the White working class.

The conclusion was simple but profound. Nativism was not just a factor or correlate—it was the central force driving support for Donald Trump's hostile takeover of the Republican Party. It was the backbone of his successful 2016 presidential run and, more broadly, a central pillar of Republican identity. Even in its earliest form, the analysis showed that nativism was responsible for critical political cleavage.

Nativism did not win every election, but after 2016, it became an organizing principle of the American right. Many attributed Trump's hold on the Republican Party to his nativist appeals, but this misses the larger truth. Trump did not create nativism—he recognized it, leveraged it, and amplified it. Nativism existed before Trump; it did not begin with him.

But there was more to this story. Nativism was not an isolated attitude—it was the lynchpin in a broader belief ecosystem. In June 2016, Young demonstrated the effect of nativism on primary support for Donald Trump using Bayes Net, a sophisticated technique designed to capture complex relationships within a set of data. As shown in Figure 9.1 below, nativism was central to Republican

---

134 Young, C. (2024, May 1). Why getting the numbers right isn't enough for pollsters to be credible in today's polarized climate. The Conversation. https://theconversation.com/why-getting-the-numbers-right-isnt-enough-for-pollsters-to-be-credible-in-todays-polarized-climate-247955.

https://doi.org/10.1515/9783111384047-009

identification. Because the data were cross-sectional, we cannot make strong causal claims. But again, the analysis revealed that nativism was an essential organizing principle of politics today.

America First & System is Broken: Increasingly Key Political Drivers (Neuro Networks)

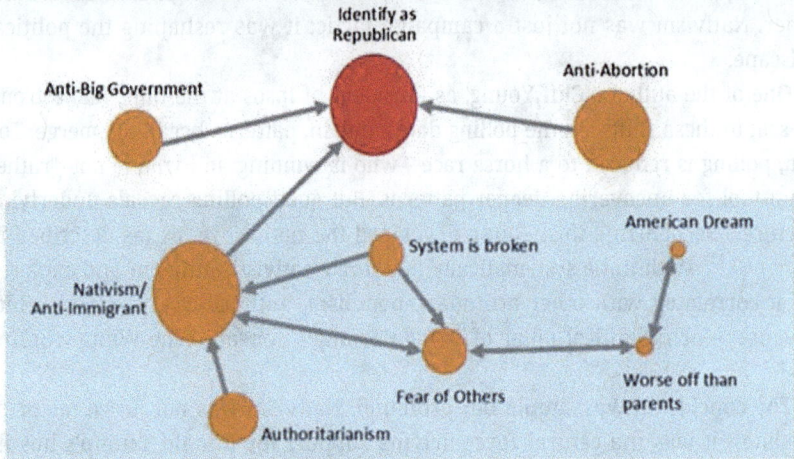

Figure 9.1: Neuro Net of Republican Identification.

The analysis showed that other attitudes—cynicism about the system, fear of social change, and even authoritarianism—were drawn into nativism's gravitational field. It was not just another issue—it was the centrifugal force of American politics, pulling in and aligning related beliefs.

Politically, nativism allowed Trump to separate from his primary challengers in 2016 and propelled him to the White House. It became the most important determinant of Republican identity—defining who belonged in the party and who did not. Critically, it cuts to a fundamental question of democracy: Who counts?

At the same time, Democrats moved in the opposite direction. As the GOP became a nativist political party, the Democrats became more pro-immigrant. The paradox was clear: Even as Americans became less nativist overall, nativism became more important to electoral outcomes. Some might call this an anomaly—it was not.

As we show in Chapter 5, nativism was a central theme of the 2018 and 2022 midterm elections, with Republican candidates running on border security. In

2020, the presidential election was shaped mostly by Trump's failed management of the COVID-19 pandemic. But had the pandemic not emerged, it is likely Trump would have won re-election, fueled by a strong economy (prior to COVID) and his nativist appeals to secure the border.

In 2024, the primary issue was cost of living. Ultimately, Biden bowed out, and Trump rode the inflation wave to victory over Harris. Immigration, while not the primary issue, remained a powerful secondary theme—an enduring cultural genome.

Here, nativism should be seen as the sinew that binds the Republican coalition. Yes, inflation was a critical issue, but Republicans continued to define themselves with more restrictive notions of American identity. This cultural glue gave the coalition coherence and longevity. Nativism was not just another issue—it was a marker of identity, a shared belief that provided both purpose and meaning.

When the history of this period is written, we believe that nativism will be the major character in the story—defining the right and reshaping American politics. Again, nativism might ebb and flow. But it is ever-present just below the surface until the time is right.

Nativism Is a Global Phenomenon

But America is not an exception. As we have seen, nativism is a global force, with local flare. It takes on different flavors and forms from context to context.

Nativism is not about geography or borders. Instead, nativism is fundamentally about belonging—who is considered part of the nation, who is excluded, and what defines membership. Critically, this sense of belonging is shaped by local histories, social tensions, and cultural conflicts. Each country's nativism is a product of its unique context, but the underlying logic is always the same: a fear that something essential is being lost, and a desire to defend what is seen as the 'true' nation.

In the United States, nativism is deeply intertwined with the nation's identity as a country of immigrants. It is a story of tension between the Statue of Liberty's welcoming promise and the persistent fear of cultural dilution. American nativism carries racial and cultural undertones, often focusing on the perceived threat posed by newcomers who are seen as not fully 'American.'

In Europe, nativism has long been defined by cultural and religious identity. In France, it is inseparable from the idea of laïcité—the secular state. For Marine Le Pen and her supporters, nativism is a defense against the perceived threat of cultural erosion, especially from Muslim immigrants who are portrayed as being incompatible with French values. The debate is not just about immigration but about what it means to be French—whether French identity is defined by citizenship or by cultural heritage. In Germany, the rise of the Alternative for Germany (AfD) reflects a similar anxiety, where the fear is not just of newcomers but of losing a cultural identity rooted in European Christian civilization.

In India, nativism is a rejection of secularism and a defense of Hindu nationalism. Under Narendra Modi and the Bharatiya Janata Party (BJP), Indian identity has been increasingly defined in religious terms, with Hindu heritage positioned as the core of the nation. Here, nativism is not just a reaction to demographic change but a claim that India's true character is being undermined by secular intellectuals, Muslim minorities, and leftist elites. This is not a rejection of all diversity—India is a profoundly diverse society—but a rejection of those who are seen as disrespecting Hindu culture and values.

In Latin America, nativism takes on a different form, often merging with anti-globalism and cultural conservatism. In Brazil, Jair Bolsonaro has used nativist rhetoric to portray global elites, environmentalists, and progressive educators as threats to 'real Brazilians.' For his supporters, the 'communists' are not just Marxists but anyone who is seen as trying to impose foreign values on Brazil's traditional way of life. Nativism here is a defense against cultural change perceived as coming from outside—whether from the United Nations, human rights organizations, or liberal media.

But nativism is not just a rejection of outsiders—it is also a rejection of elites who are seen as out of touch with ordinary citizens. This is why nativism thrives not only on the right but also in societies where resentment is directed upward at political, economic, and cultural elites. Across the world, nativism is an expression of this basic tension: a desire to protect the nation from those who are seen as corrupting it, whether they are immigrants, cosmopolitans, or domestic elites.

Finally, nativism is not merely a reaction; it is also a claim. It is a demand for recognition, for a voice, for a say in the future of the nation. Who belongs? Who counts? Who decides—and who does not?

Nativists Define National Identity in Ethnocultural Terms

Nativism is rooted in cultural change and the feeling among native populations that they are losing their national identity, and their collective and individual sense of who they are as people (Margalit et al., 2022). For the nativist, the world is changing in ways that are uncertain and/or undesirable. They notice their communities are growing more diverse and that newly arrived immigrants do not appear to share the same set of values.

Competing understandings of national identity shape these perceptions. Nativists adopt an ethnocultural understanding, meaning that they define identity largely in terms of ancestry, language, and birth. Within the US context, nativists define national identity as being born in the United States, sharing a Western European heritage, or preferably both. Non-nativists, in contrast, define national identity in civic terms. Being American means embracing a core set of American ideals (e.g., individualism, personal and economic freedom, and support for free markets and the rule of law). It can extend to beliefs about citizenship, specifically that being American means engaging in the political process through voting and community service.

Ethnocultural and civic Americanism posit two very different worlds. Those who lean toward a more restrictive view see external groups as incapable of becoming American. It simply isn't in their nature to do so. Muslims cannot be fully American because of their religion, Latinos because of their language. Nor is politics removed from the equation. In March 2025, when the Trump Administration began revoking student visas, they did so with the stated rationale that the students in question supported a terrorist organization (Hamas).[135] Other deportations were based on the 1798 Alien Enemies Act, allowing the president to deport immigrants from enemy nations during times of war without due process. The immigrants in question, the Trump Administration argued, were members of Venezuelan gangs and presented a threat to the United States.[136] Populist appeals trigger our most base fears.

Nativism and populism are closely connected, but it is nativism that gives rise to right-wing populism. Increases in immigration alone are not enough, instead immigration must be salient as a political issue and framed as a cultural threat (Ivarsflaten, 2008; Norris, 2005; Shehaj et al., 2021).

Nativism is also closely connected to the politics of racial grievance. Indeed, the version of nativism that defines contemporary American politics is a form of racial nativism directed at ethnicity rather than religion or political ideology.

---

135 Melton, B. (2025, March 28). Up First briefing: Health and Human Services job cuts; Elise Stefanik. NPR. https://www.npr.org/2025/03/28/g-s1-56863/up-first-newsletter-visas-student-activism-health-human-services-job-cuts.

136 Garrett, L. (2025, March 16). U.S. deports hundreds of Venezuelans to El Salvador, despite court order. NPR. https://www.npr.org/2025/03/16/g-s1-54154/alien-enemies-el-salvador-trump.

This gives nativist appeals resonance as they tap into implicit and explicit resentment. But nativism, as we have argued, is not racism by another name. It is a distinct belief system.

Nativism intersects with authoritarianism and nostalgia as well. Returning to a simpler time requires a strong leader who can ignore Congress, the courts, and the Constitution to 'make America great again.' Nativists see the rapid pace of cultural change and a feel a sense of loss for their communities and for their way of life. The same forces are at play across the globe and define much of the contemporary moment. At its core, nativism cuts to the essence of how humans identify with themselves and others.

The Future of Nativism

Nativism is an enduring force in American and global politics—an instinct rooted in the desire to protect identity, belonging, and cultural heritage against perceived threats. Throughout this book, we have examined how nativism rises and falls based on shifting contexts and political dynamics. Our Nativism Activation Model (NAM), introduced at the outset, has helped us understand how nativism becomes politically powerful when three core forces align: **Latent Nativist Beliefs, Catalytic Conditions, and Political Entrepreneurs** (see Figure 1.1). As we look to the future, these forces will not disappear. Instead, they may adapt to new realities—particularly declining birth rates, the rise of artificial intelligence, and long-term demographic changes.

But while the core drivers of nativism remain constant, their triggers and targets are always evolving. Nativism thrives on cultural anxiety—on the fear that something essential is being lost. As the United States becomes more diverse, as technology transforms work and identity, and as the politics of belonging become more contested, these anxieties will not simply disappear. If anything, they will find new forms and new voices.

Yet one crucial factor shapes the potency of nativism: its political representation. Latent beliefs, no matter how strong, only become powerful when they are mobilized—when they are given a voice, an agenda, and a party that represents them. We have seen this with Trump over the last decade. This is why the structure of political competition is so critical. A latent belief is a quiet fear, but a politically mobilized belief is a force. In the future, nativism will not just survive—it will adapt, find new champions, and take on new forms.

Will Nativism Simply Die Out?

A counter-argument suggests that nativism will fade as younger, more diverse generations become the majority. Catalytic show that younger Americans, especially Democrats, are significantly less likely to hold nativist views. However, this transition will not be smooth. Generational change is gradual and often accompanied by intense backlash from older or more conservative groups. Furthermore, as the Democratic Party becomes less nativist, the Republican Party may continue to mobilize nativist sentiments, ensuring that these ideas do not simply disappear with the passing of older generations. Critically, we should always be cautious of demographic determinism.

From Analysis to Possibility: Four Scenarios for the Future of Nativism

Our NAM framework offers more than a retrospective tool—it also helps us forecast. When latent beliefs, catalytic conditions, and political entrepreneurs interact under different configurations, distinct futures emerge. Below, we outline four plausible scenarios, drawing on the demographic and technological pressures discussed above.

Four Scenarios for the Future of Nativism

Catalytic forces—demographic decline, cultural anxiety, and technological disruption—do not operate in isolation. Instead, they will interact, creating a range of possibilities for the future of nativism. We detail four such scenarios (see Table 9.1).

In the first scenario, nativism intensifies as an aging population becomes more protective of cultural heritage, even as the country becomes more diverse. The demand for cheap and qualified labor only amplifies the contextual triggers. In the second scenario, nativism evolves into a defense of human skills and creativity against the rise of artificial intelligence, potentially coalescing into an explicit Anti-AI Party. AI populism becomes a driving political force of the 21st century. In scenario three, nativism shifts to a 'good immigrant/bad immigrant' narrative, where economic necessity forces even nativist parties to accept some migrants while demonizing others. Finally, in the last scenario, if demographic change reaches a tipping point, nativism may temporarily weaken as younger, diverse generations embrace multiculturalism. But cultural anxiety could still reactivate nativism.

Table 9.1: Four Possible Scenarios for the Future of Nativism.

Scenario #	Scenario Name	Latent Beliefs	Catalytic Conditions	Political Entrepreneurs	Political Representation
1	Demographic Decline and Cultural Panic	Cultural preservation in an aging society	Falling birth rates, aging population	Nativist politicians emphasizing cultural decline	Republican Party doubling down on nativism
2	AI-Driven Displacement and Cultural Purism	Human uniqueness vs. AI domination	AI-driven job losses, cultural anxiety	Anti-AI Party or leaders opposing automation	Emergence of an Anti-AI Party or movement
3	Economic Pressures and Selective Acceptance	Selective openness to 'good' immigrants	Labor shortages, economic necessity	Politicians balancing economic need with nativist rhetoric	Parties adopting a 'good immigrant/ bad immigrant' narrative
4	Nativism Recedes (Temporarily) in a Multiracial America	Multicultural identity as a norm	Majority-minority demographic tipping point	Progressive leaders promoting multiculturalism	Progressive and multicultural coalitions

Nativism in a World of Constant Anxiety

Nativism is not just a reaction to specific threats—it is an adaptive force that emerges wherever cultural, economic, or demographic stability feels threatened. But its potency is magnified when it finds a political voice—when a party, movement, or leader claims it as their cause. As long as there are latent beliefs, catalytic conditions, and political entrepreneurs, nativism will persist.

Whether driven by demographic decline, AI-induced displacement, or economic necessity, nativism will continue to be a defining feature of American politics for decades to come. And because the definition of who truly 'belongs' is never fully settled, nativism will remain a potent, adaptable force in a world of constant anxiety

Closing Thoughts: Nativism's Embeddedness

In Chapter 7 we discuss two symbolic places—Potomac and Front Royal—separated by about an hour of highway, yet worlds apart in political imagination. One reflects a cosmopolitan ideal, where identity is fluid and inclusive. The other reflects a more bounded vision of belonging, rooted in place, ancestry, and tradition. What *Nativist Nation* has shown is that these are not just local variations—they are the tectonic plates of American political life. Whether the future looks more like Potomac or Front Royal will depend on how we, as a nation, answer a deceptively simple question: Who gets to be American?

Nativism is not the shadow of American politics—it is part of its architecture. It emerges not only in moments of fear, but also in moments of redefinition, when the boundaries of citizenship and belonging are contested. The central question should not be whether nativism is right or wrong, but what kind of nativism emerges: inclusive or exclusive, hopeful or punitive, nostalgic or adaptive. As America continues to wrestle with its identity, the debate over who belongs will remain—sometimes quiet, sometimes loud, but never fully resolved. In that sense, the nativist nation is not an aberration. It is one of America's enduring truths.

In the end, nativism is not simply another episode in America's long culture wars, nor merely one of many grievances competing for political attention. It is the structural constraint of our political age. Nativism is not a passing fever but a structural force that will continue to shape legitimacy, identity, and democracy. The politics of belonging is the politics of our time, and it is here to stay. Ultimately, nativism is not a dirty word. It is a core feature of American identity, as American as mom, baseball, and apple pie.

Epilogue: The Pollster's Responsibility

Nativist Nation is not just a book about nativism—it is a testament to the power of the pollster. It is a work born of data, yet it is driven by something deeper: The quest to understand who we are, what we believe, and how those beliefs shape our shared world. In an era of ideological fragmentation, where competing voices drown out clarity, the pollster is more than a technician. The pollster is a guardian of public truth—a listener at scale, a cartographer of collective identity.

Polling is often dismissed as mere measurement, a numerical snapshot of public opinion at a moment in time. But this is a profound misunderstanding. Properly done, polling is a philosophical endeavor—a disciplined attempt to capture the beliefs, fears, hopes, and anxieties that define a society. It is an act of listening at scale, of giving voice to the voiceless, and of revealing the silent majority or the vocal minority. It is a mirror held up to the nation, but also a window through which we glimpse the future.

This book is the product of that discipline, a demonstration of what is possible when the pollster goes beyond surface impressions to uncover deeper truths. It shows that nativism is not just a reactionary impulse or a passing trend. It is an ingrained belief system, a powerful force that defines who we are and who we aspire to be. But more than that, it shows that the pollster is uniquely positioned to uncover this force—not by speculating, but by listening, measuring, and understanding.

But polling is not just a craft—it is a responsibility. The pollster is entrusted with more than just data. They are entrusted with truth. In an age of tribalization, polarization, and ideological warfare, the pollster's work is more critical than ever. It is the pollster who can tell the difference between noise and signal, who can reveal not just what people say but what they believe. It is the pollster who can separate the fleeting passions of the moment from the enduring beliefs that shape a nation's soul.

Nativist Nation is not only a study of American politics—it is a study of belonging, of who counts and who is cast aside, of who gets to define the nation and who is left on the margins. To be a pollster in this context is not just to count opinions—it is to navigate the depths of identity, to reveal the hidden patterns that define a people.

And it is a shared endeavor. This book is not the work of a single voice, but of two—an intellectual partnership between two pollsters who brought together different skills, experiences, and insights, united by a shared commitment to truth. It is a reminder that even in a divided world, it is possible to find common ground in the pursuit of understanding.

At its heart, this is not just a book about nativism but a defense of the pollster's highest calling: to understand who we are and who we are becoming.

References

Abrajano, M. A. and Hajnal, Z. (2015). *White Backlash: Immigration, Race, and American Politics*, Princeton, NJ: Princeton University Press.

Abramowitz, A., & McCoy, J. (2019). United States: Racial resentment, negative partisanship, and polarization in Trump's America. *The Annals of the American Academy of Political and Social Science*, *681*(1), 137–156.

Abramowitz, A. I. (2018). *The Great Alignment: Race, Party Transformation, and the Rise of Donald Trump*. Yale University Press.

Abramowitz, A. I., & Knotts, H. G. (2006). Ideological realignment in the American electorate: A comparison of northern and southern white voters in the pre-Reagan, Reagan, and post-Reagan eras. *Politics & Policy*, *34*(1), 94–108.

Abramowitz, A. I., & Stone, W. J. (2006). The Bush effect: Polarization, turnout, and activism in the 2004 presidential election. *Presidential Studies Quarterly*, *36*(2), 141–154.

Alexander, E. C. (2018). Don't know or won't say? Exploring how colorblind norms shape item nonresponse in social surveys. *Sociology of Race and Ethnicity*, *4*(3), 417–433.

Alonso, S., & Fonseca, S. C. d. (2012). Immigration, left and right. *Party Politics*, *18*(6), 865–884.

Anbinder, T. (2006). Nativism and prejudice against immigrants. In Ueda, R. (ed.), *A Companion to American Immigration*. Oxford: Blackwell. pp. 177–201.

Arceneaux, K., & Nicholson, S. P. (2012). Who wants to have a tea party? The who, what, and why of the tea party movement. *PS: Political Science & Politics*, *45*(4), 700–710.

Baer, K. S. (2000). *Reinventing Democrats: The Politics of Liberalism from Reagan to Clinton*. University Press of Kansas.

Bai, H., & Federico, C. M. (2020). Collective existential threat mediates white population decline's effect on defensive reactions. *Group Processes & Intergroup Relations*, *23*(3), 361–377.

Bai, H., & Federico, C. M. (2021). White and minority demographic shifts, intergroup threat, and right-wing extremism. *Journal of Experimental Social Psychology*, *94*, 104114.

Baker, P., & Glasser, S. (2023). *The Divider: Trump in the White House, 2017–2021*. Anchor.

Bartels, L. M. (2016). Failure to converge: Presidential candidates, core partisans, and the missing middle in American electoral politics. *The Annals of the American Academy of Political and Social Science*, *667*(1), 143–165.

Bergan, D. E., Gerber, A. S., Green, D. P., & Panagopoulos, C. (2005). Grassroots mobilization and voter turnout in 2004. *Public Opinion Quarterly*, *69*(5), 760–777.

Bergquist, J. M. (1986). The concept of nativism in historical study since "Strangers in the Land". *American Jewish History*, *76*(2), 125–141.

Berinsky, A. J. (2002). Political context and the survey response: The dynamics of racial policy opinion. *Journal of Politics*, *64*(2), 567–584.

Berry, J. M., Glaser, J. M., & Schildkraut, D. J. (2021). Race and gender on Fox and MSNBC. *The Forum*.

Betz, H.-G. (2017a). Nativism across time and space. *Swiss Political Science Review*, *23*(4), 335–353.

Betz, H.-G. (2017b). Nativism and the success of populist mobilization. *Revista Internacional Pensamiento Politico*, *12*, 169.

Betz, H.-G. (2019). Facets of nativism: a heuristic exploration. *Patterns of prejudice*, *53*(2), 111–135.

Betz, H.-G. (2022). Economic resentment or cultural malaise: What accounts for nativist sentiments in contemporary liberal democracies. In *Handbook on Migration and Welfare*. Edward Elgar Publishing. pp. 351–366.

https://doi.org/10.1515/9783111384047-010

Bloch, K. R., Taylor, T., & Martinez, K. (2020). Playing the race card: White injury, white victimhood and the paradox of colour-blind ideology in anti-immigrant discourse. *Ethnic and Racial Studies*, *43*(7), 1130–1148.

Blumer, H. (1958). Race prejudice as a sense of group position. *Pacific Sociological Review*, *1*(1), 3–7.

Bobo, L., & Hutchings, V. L. (1996). Perceptions of racial group competition: Extending Blumer's theory of group position to a multiracial social context. *American Sociological Review*, 951–972.

Bonikowski, B., & Zhang, Y. (2023). Populism as dog-whistle politics: Anti-elite discourse and sentiments toward minority groups. *Social Forces*, *102*(1), 180–201. https://doi.org/10.1093/sf/soac147.

Boot, M. (2024). *Reagan: His Life and Legend*. Liverlight Publishing.

Bowler, S., Nicholson, S. P., & Segura, G. M. (2006). Earthquakes and aftershocks: Race, direct democracy, and partisan change. *American Journal of Political Science*, *50*(1), 146–159.

Brader, T., Valentino, N. A., & Suhay, E. (2008). What triggers public opposition to immigration? Anxiety, group cues, and immigration threat. *American Journal of Political Science*, *52*(4), 959–978.

Brown, H. E. (2013). Race, legality, and the social policy consequences of anti-immigration mobilization. *American Sociological Review*, *78*(2), 290–314.

Brubaker, W. R. (1990). Immigration, citizenship, and the nation-state in France and Germany: a comparative historical analysis. *International Sociology*, *5*(4), 379–407.

Bui, P. (2024). Defining American national identity: An exploration into measurement and its outcomes. *Nationalities Papers*, *52*(1), 3–21.

Butcher, K. F., & Card, D. (1991). Immigration and wages: Evidence from the 1980's. *The American Economic Review*, *81*(2), 292–296.

Buyuker, B., D'Urso, A. J., Filindra, A., & Kaplan, N. J. (2021). Race politics research and the American presidency: thinking about white attitudes, identities and vote choice in the Trump era and beyond. *Journal of Race, Ethnicity, and Politics*, *6*(3), 600–641.

Campbell, A. (1954). *The Voter Decides*. Row, Peterson.

Campbell, A., Converse, P., Miller, W., & Stokes, D. (1960). *The American Voter*. John Wiley & Sons.

Campbell, C., & Rockman, B. A. (2001). Third way leadership, old way government: Blair, Clinton and the power to govern. *The British Journal of Politics and International Relations*, *3*(1), 36–48.

Card, D. (2009). Immigration and inequality. *American Economic Review*, *99*(2), 1–21.

Carnes, N., & Lupu, N. (2021). The white working class and the 2016 election. *Perspectives on Politics*, *19*(1), 55–72.

Ceobanu, A. M., & Escandell, X. (2008). East is West? National feelings and anti-immigrant sentiment in Europe. *Social Science Research*, *37*(4), 1147–1170.

Citrin, J., Reingold, B., & Green, D. P. (1990). American identity and the politics of ethnic change. *The Journal of Politics*, *52*(4), 1124–1154.

Citrin, J., Wong, C., & Duff, B. (2001). The meaning of American national identity. *Social Identity, Intergroup Conflict, and Conflict Reduction*, *3*, 71.

Clayton, K., Davis, N. T., Nyhan, B., Porter, E., Ryan, T. J., & Wood, T. J. (2021). Elite rhetoric can undermine democratic norms. *Proceedings of the National Academy of Sciences*, *118*(23), e2024125118.

Craig, M. A., & Richeson, J. A. (2014). On the precipice of a "majority-minority" America: Perceived status threat from the racial demographic shift affects white Americans' political ideology. *Psychological Science*, *25*(6), 1189–1197.

Craig, M. A., & Richeson, J. A. (2017). Information about the US racial demographic shift triggers concerns about anti-white discrimination among the prospective white "minority". *PloS one*, *12*(9), e0185389.

Cramer, K. J. (2016). *The Politics of Resentment: Rural Consciousness in Wisconsin and the Rise of Scott Walker*. University of Chicago Press.

Curran, P. J., & Bauer, D. J. (2011). The disaggregation of within-person and between-person effects in longitudinal models of change. *Annual Review of Psychology, 62*(1), 583–619.

Dahl, R. A. (2008). *Democracy and its Critics*. Yale University Press.

Dancygier, R. M. (2010). *Immigration and Conflict in Europe*. Cambridge University Press.

Davidson, T., & Burson, K. (2017). Keep those kids out: Nativism and attitudes toward access to public education for the children of undocumented immigrants. *Journal of Latinos and Education, 16*(1), 41–50.

Davis, D. W., & Wilson, D. C. (2022). *Racial Resentment in the Political Mind*. The University of Chicago Press.

Davis, N. T., Goidel, K., Lipsmeyer, C. S., Whitten, G. D., & Young, C. (2019a). Economic vulnerability, cultural decline, and nativism: contingent and indirect effects. *Social Science Quarterly, 100*(2), 430–446.

Davis, N. T., Goidel, K., Lipsmeyer, C. S., Whitten, G. D., & Young, C. (2019b). The political consequences of nativism: The impact of nativist sentiment on party support. *Social Science Quarterly, 100*(2), 466–479.

DeVellis, R. F. (2017). *Scale Development: Theory and Applications*. (4th ed.). Sage.

Devine, C. J. (2018). What if Hillary Clinton had gone to Wisconsin? Presidential campaign visits and vote choice in the 2016 election. *The Forum*.

Dickey, C. (2023). *Under the Eye of Power: How Fear of Secret Societies Shapes American Democracy*. Viking.

Downs, A. (1957). *An Economic Theory of Democracy*. Harper and Brothers.

Dustmann, C., Frattini, T., & Preston, I. P. (2013). The effect of immigration along the distribution of wages. *Review of Economic Studies, 80*(1), 145–173.

Enelow, J. M., & Hinich, M. J. (1984). *The Spatial Theory of Voting: An Introduction*. CUP Archive.

Engesser, S., Ernst, N., Esser, F., & Büchel, F. (2017). Populism and social media: How politicians spread a fragmented ideology. *Information, Communication & Society, 20*(8), 1109–1126.

Enns, P. K., & Jardina, A. (2021). Complicating the role of white racial attitudes and anti-immigrant sentiment in the 2016 US presidential election. *Public Opinion Quarterly, 85*(2), 539–570.

Erisen, C., & Vasilopoulou, S. (2022). The affective model of far-right vote in Europe: Anger, political trust, and immigration. *Social Science Quarterly, 103*(3), 635–648.

Farris, E. M., & Silber Mohamed, H. (2018). Picturing immigration: How the media criminalizes immigrants. *Politics, Groups, and Identities, 6*(4), 814–824.

Feldman, S., & Huddy, L. (2005). Racial resentment and white opposition to race-conscious programs: Principles or prejudice? *American Journal of Political Science, 49*(1), 168–183.

Firebaugh, G. (1978). A rule for inferring individual-level relationships from aggregate data. *American Sociological Review*, 557–572.

Flores-González, N., & Salgado, C. D. (2022). Shifting racial schemas: From post-racial to new "old-fashioned" racism. *Sociological Inquiry, 92*(2), 341–363.

Ford, P. K., Maxwell, A., & Shields, T. (2010). What's the matter with Arkansas? Symbolic racism and 2008 presidential candidate support. *Presidential Studies Quarterly, 40*(2), 286–302.

Fording, R. C., & Schram, S. F. (2020). *Hard White: The Mainstreaming of Racism in American Politics*. Oxford University Press.

Forgas, J. P., & Crano, W. D. (2021). The psychology of populism: The tribal challenge to liberal democracy. In *The Psychology of Populism*. Routledge. pp. 1–19.

Friedman, N. L. (1967). Nativism. *Phylon, 28*(4), 408–415.

Friedman, T. L. (2005). *The World Is Flat: A Brief History of the Twenty-first Century*. Macmillan.

Frost, A. (2021). *You Are Not American: Citizenship Stripping from Dred Scott to the Dreamers*. Beacon Press.

Gadarian, S. K. (2014). Scary pictures: How terrorism imagery affects voter evaluations. *Political Communication, 31*(2), 282–302.

Gaston, S., & Uscinski, J. (2018). Out of the shadows: conspiracy thinking on immigration. *The Henry Jackson Society, 60*.

Gerber, D. A., & Kraut, A. M. (2005). Nativism, an American perennial. In *American Immigration and Ethnicity: A Reader*. Springer. pp. 126–160.

Gerstle, G. (2017). *American Crucible: Race and Nation in the Twentieth Century*. Princeton University Press.

Gienapp, W. (1987). *The Origins of the Republican Party, 1852–1856*. Oxford University Press.

Gienapp, W. E. (1985). Nativism and the creation of a Republican majority in the north before the Civil War. *The Journal of American History, 72*(3), 529–559.

Gil de Zúñiga, H., Correa, T., & Valenzuela, S. (2012). Selective exposure to cable news and immigration in the US: The relationship between FOX News, CNN, and attitudes toward Mexican immigrants. *Journal of Broadcasting & Electronic Media, 56*(4), 597–615.

Gilens, M. (1999). *Why Americans Hate Welfare: Race, Media, and the Politics of Antipoverty Policy*. Chicago: University of Chicago Press.

Gimpel, J. G. (2019). From wedge issue to partisan divide: The development of immigration policy opinion after 2016. *The Forum*.

Gimpel, J. G., Lovin, N., Moy, B., & Reeves, A. (2020). The urban–rural gulf in American political behavior. *Political Behavior, 42*, 1343–1368.

Gleason, P. (1964). The melting pot: Symbol of fusion or confusion? *American Quarterly, 16*(1), 20–46.

Goidel, S., Goidel, K., & Kellstedt, P. M. (2025). Nostalgia in politics. *Public Opinion Quarterly*, nfae054.

Goidel, S., Goidel, K., & Madsen, B. (2024). Longing for the "good old days" or longing for a racist and sexist past? *Research & Politics, 11*(2).

Goidel, S., Moreira, T., & Armstrong, B. (2024). Party realignment, education, and the turnout advantage: Revisiting the partisan effect of turnout. *American Politics Research, 52*(1), 23–29.

Goldstein, J. A. (2018) Unfit for the constitution: Nativism and the constitution, from the Founding Fathers to Donald Trump. *University of Pennsylvania Journal of Constitutional Law, 20*(3), 489–560. Available at: https://search.ebscohost.com/login.aspx?direct=true&db=lgs&AN=129616288&site=ehost-live&scope=site (accessed: June 8, 2025).

Goldstein, J. L., & Peters, M. E. (2014). Nativism or economic threat: Attitudes toward immigrants during the great recession. *International Interactions, 40*(3), 376–401.

Gomez, B. T., Hansford, T. G., & Krause, G. A. (2007). The Republicans should pray for rain: Weather, turnout, and voting in US presidential elections. *The Journal of Politics, 69*(3), 649–663.

Gordon, M. M. (2010). *Assimilation in American Life: The Role of Race, Religion and National Origins*. Oxford University Press.

Green-Pedersen, C., & Krogstrup, J. (2008). Immigration as a political issue in Denmark and Sweden. *European Journal of Political Research, 47*(5), 610–634.

Heiss, R., & Matthes, J. (2020). Stuck in a nativist spiral: Content, selection, and effects of right-wing populists' communication on Facebook. *Political Communication, 37*(3), 303–328.

Hellwig, D. J. (1982). Strangers in their own land: Patterns of Black nativism, 1830–1930. *American Studies, 23*(1), 85–98.

Herrnson, P. S., & Stewart III, C. (2023). The impact of COVID-19, election policies, and partisanship on voter participation in the 2020 US election. *Election Law Journal: Rules, Politics, and Policy, 22*(2), 129–144.

Hervik, P. (2015). Xenophobia and nativism. *International Encyclopedia of the Social & Behavioral Sciences, 2*, 796–801.

Hewitt, R. (2005). *White Backlash and the Politics of Multiculturalism*. Cambridge University Press.

Hibbing, J. R. (2020). *The Securitarian Personality: What Really Motivates Trump's Base and Why It Matters for the Post-Trump Era*. Oxford University Press.

Hibbing, J. R. (2022). Why do Trump's authoritarian followers resist COVID-19 authorities? Because they are not really authoritarian followers. *Frontiers in Political Science, 4*.

Higham, J. (1955). *Strangers in the Land: Patterns of American Nativism, 1860–1925*. Rutgers University Press.

Hillygus, D. S., & Shields, T. G. (2008). *The Persuadable Voter: Wedge Issues in Presidential Campaigns*. Princeton University Press.

Hirschman, C., & Mogford, E. (2009). Immigration and the American Industrial Revolution from 1880 to 1920. *Social Science Research, 38*(4), 897–920.

Hoewe, J., Peacock, C., Kim, B., & Barnidge, M. (2020). The relationship between Fox News use and Americans' policy preferences regarding refugees and immigrants. *International Journal of Communication, 14*, 21.

Hofstadter, R. (2011). *The Age of Reform*. Vintage.

Hughey, M. W. (2014). White backlash in the 'post-racial' United States. *Ethnic and Racial Studies, 37*(5), 721–730.

Huijsmans, T., Harteveld, E., Van der Brug, W., & Lancee, B. (2021). Are cities ever more cosmopolitan? Studying trends in urban-rural divergence of cultural attitudes. *Political Geography, 86*, 102353.

Huijsmans, T., & Rodden, J. (2025). The great global divider? A comparison of urban-rural partisan polarization in western democracies. *Comparative Political Studies, 58*(2), 261–290.

Huntington, S. P. (2004). *Who Are We? The Challenges to America's National Identity*. Simon and Schuster.

Hurwitz, J., & Peffley, M. (2005). Playing the race card in the post–Willie Horton era: The impact of racialized code words on support for punitive crime policy. *Public Opinion Quarterly, 69*(1), 99–112.

Iakhnis, E., Rathbun, B., Reifler, J., & Scotto, T. J. (2018). Populist referendum: Was 'Brexit' an expression of nativist and anti-elitist sentiment? *Research & Politics, 5*(2).

Ignatiev, N. (1994). *How The Irish Became White*. Harvard University.

Inglehart, R. H., C., Moreno, A., Welzel, C., Kizilova, K., Diez-Medrano, M., Lagos, P., Norris, P., Ponarin, E., and Puranend, B. (2014). *World Values Survey*. JD Systems Institute.

Ivarsflaten, E. (2008). What unites right-wing populists in Western Europe? Re-examining grievance mobilization models in seven successful cases. *Comparative Political Studies, 41*(1), 3–23.

Jacobson, G. C. (2003). Terror, terrain, and turnout: Explaining the 2002 midterm elections. *Political Science Quarterly, 118(1)*, 1–22. https://doi.org/10.1002/j.1538-165X.2003.tb00384.x.

Johnson, K. R. (2019). Proposition 187 and its political aftermath: Lessons for US immigration politics after Trump. UC Davis School of Law. http://dx.doi.org/10.2139/ssrn.3564751.

Kam, C. D., & Kinder, D. R. (2012). Ethnocentrism as a short-term force in the 2008 American presidential election. *American Journal of Political Science, 56*(2), 326–340.

Kaufman, R. R., & Haggard, S. (2019). Democratic decline in the United States: What can we learn from middle-income backsliding? *Perspectives on Politics, 17*(2), 417–432.

Kelley-Romano, S., & Carew, K. L. (2017). Make America hate again: Donald Trump and the birther conspiracy. *Journal of Hate Studies, 14*, 33.

Kenny, M., & Luca, D. (2021). The urban-rural polarisation of political disenchantment: An investigation of social and political attitudes in 30 European countries. *Cambridge Journal of Regions, Economy and Society, 14*(3), 565–582.

Kešić, J., & Duyvendak, J. W. (2019). The nation under threat: secularist, racial and populist nativism in the Netherlands. *Patterns of Prejudice, 53*(5), 441–463.

Kešić, J., Frenkel, S. C., Speelman, I., & Duyvendak, J. W. (2022). Nativism and nostalgia in the Netherlands *Sociological Forum*. https://doi.org/10.1111/socf.12841.

Key, V.O. (1966). *The Responsible Electorate: Rationality in Presidential Voting, 1936-1960*. Cummings, M.C. (ed.). Cambridge, MA: Harvard University Press.

Kim, H. H.-s., & Kim, H. J. K. (2021). National pride, social trust, and cultural nativism: Findings from East and Southeast Asia. *International Journal of Intercultural Relations, 84*, 251–263.

Kim, S.-h., Carvalho, J. P., Davis, A. G., & Mullins, A. M. (2011). The view of the border: News framing of the definition, causes, and solutions to illegal immigration. *Mass Communication and Society, 14*(3), 292–314.

Kinder, D. R. (1986). The continuing American dilemma: White resistance to racial change 40 years after Myrdal. *Journal of Social Issues, 42*(2), 151–171.

Kinder, D. R., & Sanders, L. M. (1996). *Divided by Color: Racial Politics and Democratic Ideals*. University of Chicago Press.

Kinder, D. R., & Sears, D. O. (1981). Prejudice and politics: Symbolic racism versus racial threats to the good life. *Journal of Personality and Social Psychology, 40*(3), 414.

Kingzette, J., Druckman, J. N., Klar, S., Krupnikov, Y., Levendusky, M., & Ryan, J. B. (2021). How affective polarization undermines support for democratic norms. *Public Opinion Quarterly, 85*(2), 663–677.

Klarman, M. J. (1994). How Brown changed race relations: The backlash thesis. *Journal of American History, 81*(1), 81–118.

Knoll, B. R. (2012). ¿Compañero o Extranjero? Anti-immigrant nativism among Latino Americans. *Social Science Quarterly, 93*(4), 911–931.

Knoll, B. R. (2013). Implicit nativist attitudes, social desirability, and immigration policy preferences. *International Migration Review, 47*(1), 132–165.

Knuckey, J., & Hassan, K. (2022). Authoritarianism and support for Trump in the 2016 presidential election. *The Social Science Journal, 59*(1), 47–60.

Knuckey, J., & Kim, M. (2015). Racial resentment, old-fashioned racism, and the vote choice of southern and nonsouthern whites in the 2012 US presidential election. *Social Science Quarterly, 96*(4), 905–922.

Krämer, B. (2017). Populist online practices: The function of the internet in right-wing populism. *Information, Communication & Society, 20*(9), 1293–1309.

Krämer, B., Fernholz, T., Husung, T., Meusel, J., & Voll, M. (2021). Right-wing populism as a worldview and online practice: Social media communication by ordinary citizens between ideology and lifestyles. *European Journal of Cultural and Political Sociology, 8*(3), 235–264.

Ladd, E. C. (1993). The 1992 vote for President Clinton: Another brittle mandate? *Political Science Quarterly, 108*(1), 1–28.

Lazarsfeld, P. F., Berelson, B., & Gaudet, H. (1968). *The People's Choice: How the Voter Makes Up His Mind in a Presidential Campaign*. New York Chichester, West Sussex: Columbia University Press.

Levy, M., & Wright, M. (2020). *Immigration and the American Ethos*. Cambridge University Press.

Lewis-Beck, M. S., Tien, C., & Nadeau, R. (2010). Obama's missed landslide: a racial cost? *PS: Political Science & Politics*, *43*(1), 69–76.

Lippard, C. D. (2011). Racist nativism in the 21st century. *Sociology Compass*, *5*(7), 591–606.

Lipset, S. M. (1960). *Political Man; The Social Bases of Politics*. (1st ed.). Doubleday.

Lipset, S. M. (1979). *The First New Nation: The United States in Historical and Comparative Perspective*. Norton.

Lipset, S. M. (1996). *American Exceptionalism: A Double-Edged Sword*. WW Norton & Company.

Lubbers, M., & Coenders, M. (2017). Nationalistic attitudes and voting for the radical right in Europe. *European Union Politics*, *18*(1), 98–118.

Lyons, W., & Scheb, J. M. (1992). Ideology and candidate evaluation in the 1984 and 1988 presidential elections. *The Journal of Politics*, *54*(2), 573–584.

MacKuen, M., Wolak, J., Keele, L., & Marcus, G. E. (2010). Civic engagements: Resolute partisanship or reflective deliberation. *American Journal of Political Science*, *54*(2), 440–458.

MacWilliams, M. C. (2016). *The Rise of Trump: America's Authoritarian Spring*. Amherst College Press.

Major, B., Blodorn, A., & Major Blascovich, G. (2018). The threat of increasing diversity: Why many white Americans support Trump in the 2016 presidential election. *Group Processes & Intergroup Relations*, *21*(6), 931–940.

Mansfield, E. D., & Mutz, D. C. (2009). Support for free trade: Self-interest, sociotropic politics, and out-group anxiety. *International Organization*, *63*(3), 425–457.

Marcus, G. E., Valentino, N. A., Vasilopoulos, P., & Foucault, M. (2019). Applying the theory of affective intelligence to support for authoritarian policies and parties. *Political Psychology*, *40*, 109–139.

Margalit, Y. (2012). Lost in globalization: International economic integration and the sources of popular discontent. *International Studies Quarterly*, *56*(3), 484–500.

Margalit, Y., Raviv, S., & Solodoch, O. (2022). The cultural origins of populism.

Massey, D. S. (2021). The bipartisan origins of white nationalism. *Daedalus*, *150*(2), 5–22.

Massey, D. S., & Pren, K. A. (2012). Unintended consequences of US immigration policy: explaining the post-1965 surge from Latin America. *Population and Development Review*, *38*(1), 1–29.

Maxwell, A., & Shields, T. G. (2019). *The Long Southern Strategy: How Chasing White Voters in the South Changed American Politics*. Oxford University Press, USA.

Mayhew, D. R. (2008). *Electoral Realignments: A Critique of an American Genre*. Yale University Press.

McDonald, L. E., & Morgaine, K. (2016). Progressive and conservative "freedom" through the lens of Fox and MSNBC. *Sage Open*, *6*(3).

McDonald, M. P. (2022). *From Pandemic to Insurrection: Voting in the 2020 US Presidential Election*. Walter de Gruyter GmbH & Co KG.

McDonald, M. P., Mucci, J. K., Shino, E., & Smith, D. A. (2024). Mail voting and voter turnout. *Election Law Journal: Rules, Politics, and Policy*, *23*(1), 1–18.

McIlwain, C., & Caliendo, S. M. (2011). *Race Appeal: How Candidates Invoke Race in US Political Campaigns*. Temple University Press.

Meffert, M. F., Norpoth, H., & Ruhil, A. V. (2001). Realignment and macropartisanship. *American Political Science Review*, *95*(4), 953–962.

Mendelberg, T. (2001). *The Race Card: Campaign Strategy, Implicit Messages, and the Norm of Equality*. Princeton University Press.

Moench, D. (2018). Anti-German hysteria and the making of the "Liberal Society". *American Political Thought*, *7*(1), 86–123.

Monogan III, J. E., & Doctor, A. C. (2017). Immigration politics and partisan realignment: California, Texas, and the 1994 election. *State Politics & Policy Quarterly*, *17*(1), 3–23.

Morgan, S. L., & Lee, J. (2017). The white working class and voter turnout in US presidential elections, 2004 to 2016. *Sociological Science, 4*, 656–685.

Morris, D. (1997). *Behind the Oval Office: Winning the Presidency in the Nineties*. (1st ed.). Random House.

Moslimani, M., & Passel, J. (2024). What the data says about immigrants in the U.S. https://www.pewresearch.org/short-reads/2024/07/22/key-findings-about-us-immigrants/.

Mudde, Cas. (2007). *Populist Radical Right Parties in Europe*. New York: Cambridge University Press.

Mudde, C. (2012). The Relationship Between Immigration and Nativism in Europe and North America. Migration Policy Institute. https://www.migrationpolicy.org/sites/default/files/publications/Immigration-Nativism.pdf.

Mudde, C. (2013). Three decades of populist radical right parties in Western Europe: So what? *European Journal of Political Research, 52*(1), 1–19.

Mudde, C. (2019). *The Far Right Today*. John Wiley & Sons.

Mudde, C., & Kaltwasser, C. R. (2017). *Populism: A Very Short Introduction*. Oxford University Press.

Munis, B. K. (2022). Us over here versus them over there . . . literally: Measuring place resentment in American politics. *Political Behavior, 44*(3), 1057–1078.

Mutz, D. C. (2018). Status threat, not economic hardship, explains the 2016 presidential vote. *Proceedings of the National Academy of Sciences, 115*(19), E4330–E4339.

Mylonas, H., & Tudor, M. (2021). Nationalism: What we know and what we still need to know. *Annual Review of Political Science, 24*, 109–132.

Nagel, J. H., & McNulty, J. E. (1996). Partisan effects of voter turnout in senatorial and gubernatorial elections. *American Political Science Review, 90*(4), 780–793.

Nagel, J. H., & McNulty, J. E. (2000). Partisan effects of voter turnout in presidential elections. *American Politics Quarterly, 28*(3), 408–429.

Neundorf, A., & Pardos-Prado, S. (2022). The impact of COVID-19 on Trump's electoral demise: the role of economic and democratic accountability. *Perspectives on Politics, 20*(1), 170–186.

Ngai, M. M. (2014). *Impossible Subjects: Illegal Aliens and the Making of Modern America*. Princeton University Press.

Noelle-Neumann, E. (1974). The spiral of silence a theory of public opinion. *Journal of Communication, 24*(2), 43–51.

Norris, P. (2005). *Radical Right: Voters and Parties in the Electoral Market*. Cambridge University Press.

Norris, P., & Inglehart, R. (2019). *Cultural Backlash: Trump, Brexit, and Authoritarian Populism*. Cambridge University Press.

Nteta, T. M., & Rice, D. (2021). Driving a Wedge? Republicans, immigration, and the impact of substantive appeals on African American vote choice. *Political Research Quarterly, 74*(1), 228–242.

Obama, B. (2020). *A Promised Land*. Penguin UK.

Odmalm, P., & Bale, T. (2015). Immigration into the mainstream: Conflicting ideological streams, strategic reasoning and party competition. *Acta Politica, 50*, 365–378.

Oliver, J. E., & Rahn, W. M. (2016). Rise of the Trumpenvolk: Populism in the 2016 election. *The Annals of the American Academy of Political and Social Science, 667*(1), 189–206.

Ollerenshaw, T., & Jardina, A. (2023). The asymmetric polarization of immigration opinion in the United States. *Public Opinion Quarterly, 87*(4), 1038–1053. https://doi.org/10.1093/poq/nfad048.

Panagopoulos, C. (2016). All about that base: Changing campaign strategies in U.S. presidential elections. *Party Politics, 22*(2), 179–190.

Panagopoulos, C. (2020). *Bases Loaded: How US Presidential Campaigns Are Changing and Why It Matters*. Oxford University Press.

Parker, C. S. (2021). Status threat: Moving the right further to the right? *Daedalus, 150*(2), 56–75.

Parker, C. S., & Barreto, M. A. (2014). *Change They Can't Believe In: The Tea Party and Reactionary Politics in America*. (updated edition). Princeton University Press.

Payne, Rodger M. (2017). Nativism and religion in America. In *Oxford Research Encyclopedia of Religion*. New York: Oxford University Press.

Pegram, T. R. (2011). *One Hundred Percent American: The Rebirth and Decline of the Ku Klux Klan in the 1920s*. Rowman & Littlefield.

Pehrson, S., Vignoles, V. L., & Brown, R. (2009). National identification and anti-immigrant prejudice: Individual and contextual effects of national definitions. *Social Psychology Quarterly*, *72*(1), 24–38.

Perea, J. F. (1997). *Immigrants Out! The New Nativism and the Anti-Immigrant Impulse in the United States* (Vol. 76). NYU Press.

Persily, N., & Stewart III, C. (2021). The miracle and tragedy of the 2020 US election. *Journal of Democracy*, *32*(2), 159–178.

Petrocik, J. R. (1987). Realignment: New party coalitions and the nationalization of the South. *The Journal of Politics*, *49*(2), 347–375.

Piston, S. (2010). How explicit racial prejudice hurt Obama in the 2008 election. *Political Behavior*, *32*, 431–451.

Ramsey, P. J. (2002). The war against German-American culture: The removal of German-language instruction from the Indianapolis schools, 1917–1919. *The Indiana Magazine of History*, 285–303.

Reber, S. J. (2011). From separate and unequal to integrated and equal? School desegregation and school finance in Louisiana. *The Review of Economics and Statistics*, *93*(2), 404–415.

Riedel, R. (2018). Nativism versus nationalism and populism–bridging the gap. *Central European Papers*, *6*(2), 18–28.

Rodden, J. (2010). The geographic distribution of political preferences. *Annual Review of Political Science*, *13*(1), 321–340.

Rodrik, D. (2021). Why does globalization fuel populism? Economics, culture, and the rise of right-wing populism. *Annual Review of Economics*, *13*, 133–170.

Rooduijn, M., Bonikowski, B., & Parlevliet, J. (2021). Populist and nativist attitudes: Does ingroup-outgroup thinking spill over across domains? *European Union Politics*, *22*(2), 248–265.

Rosenstone, S. J., & Hansen, J. M. (1993). *Mobilization, Participation, and Democracy in America*. Macmillan.

Sabato, L. (2003). *Midterm Madness: The Elections of 2002*. Rowman & Littlefield.

Schaffner, B. F., MacWilliams, M., & Nteta, T. (2018). Understanding white polarization in the 2016 vote for president: The sobering role of racism and sexism. *Political Science Quarterly*, *133*(1), 9–34.

Schildkraut, D. J. (2013a). Immigrant resentment and American identity in the twenty-first century. In *American Identity in the Age of Obama*. Routledge. pp. 100–132.

Schildkraut, D. J. (2013b). *Press "One" for English: Language Policy, Public Opinion, and American Identity*. Princeton University Press.

Schildkraut, D. J. (2014). Boundaries of American identity: Evolving understandings of "us". *Annual Review of Political Science*, *17*(1), 441–460.

Schneider, W. (1982). Realignment: the eternal question. *PS: Political Science & Politics*, *15*(3), 449–458.

Schrag, P. (2010). *Not Fit for Our Society: Immigration and Nativism in America*. University of California Press.

Shafer, B. E. (1991). *The End of Realignment? Interpreting American Electoral Eras*. University of Wisconsin Press.

Shafer, B. E. (1999). American exceptionalism. *Annual Review of Political Science*, *2*(1), 445–463.

Shaw, D. R., & Petrocik, J. R. (2020). *The Turnout Myth: Voting Rates and Partisan Outcomes in American National Elections*. Oxford University Press.

Shehaj, A., Shin, A. J., & Inglehart, R. (2021). Immigration and right-wing populism: An origin story. *Party Politics, 27*(2), 282–293.

Shino, E., McKee, S. C., & Smith, D. A. (2024). The fall of Trump: mobilization and vote switching in the 2020 presidential election. *Political Science Research and Methods, 12*(2), 229–248.

Sides, J. (2006). The origins of campaign agendas. *British Journal of Political Science, 36*(3), 407–436.

Sides, J., Tesler, M., & Vavreck, L. (2017). The 2016 US election: How Trump lost and won. *Journal of Democracy, 28*(2), 34–44.

Sides, J., Tesler, M., & Vavreck, L. (2019). *Identity Crisis: The 2016 Presidential Campaign and the Battle for the Meaning of America*. Princeton University Press.

Simon, H. A. (1955). A behavioral model of rational choice. *The Quarterly Journal of Economics*, 99–118.

Skinner, A. L., & Cheadle, J. E. (2016). The "Obama effect"? Priming contemporary racial milestones increases implicit racial bias among Whites. *Social Cognition, 34*(6), 544–558.

Skocpol, T., & Williamson, V. (2016). *The Tea Party and the Remaking of Republican Conservatism*. Oxford University Press.

Smith, D. N., & Hanley, E. (2020). The heart of whiteness: Patterns of race, class, and prejudice in the divided Midwest. In *Political Landscapes of Donald Trump*. Routledge. pp. 111–128.

Smith, R. M. (1993). Beyond Tocqueville, Myrdal, and Hartz: the multiple traditions in America. *American Political Science Review, 87*(3), 549–566.

Smith, R. M. (1997). *Civic Ideals: Conflicting Visions of Citizenship in US History*. Yale University Press.

Smith, T. W., Davern, M., Freese, J., & Hout, M. (2018). *General Social Surveys*. NORC at the University of Chicago.

Sniderman, P. M. (1997). *Reaching Beyond Race*. Harvard University Press.

Sniderman, P. M., Hagendoorn, L., & Prior, M. (2004). Predisposing factors and situational triggers: Exclusionary reactions to immigrant minorities. *American Political Science Review, 98*(1), 35–49.

Soss, J., Fording, R. C., & Schram, S. F. (2008). The color of devolution: race, federalism, and the politics of social control. *American Journal of Political Science, 52*(3), 536–553.

Soss, J., Schram, S. F., Vartanian, T. P., & O'Brien, E. (2001). Setting the terms of relief: Explaining state policy choices in the devolution revolution. *American Journal of Political Science*, 378–395.

Stenner, K. (2005). *The Authoritarian Dynamic*. Cambridge University Press. https://doi.org/10.1017/CBO9780511614712.

Stenner, K. (2008). The authoritarian dynamic: racial, political and moral intolerance under conditions of societal threat. In *Toleration on Trial*, Lexington Books. p. 225.

Stern, L. M. (1981). Response to Vietnamese refugees: Surveys of public opinion. *Social Work, 26*(4), 306–311.

Stiglitz, J. E. (2002). *Globalization and its Discontents* (1st ed.). W. W. Norton. Table of contents http://www.loc.gov/catdir/toc/fy035/2002023148.html.

Strach, P., & Sapiro, V. (2011). Campaigning for Congress in the "9/11" era: Considerations of gender and party in response to an exogenous shock. *American Politics Research, 39*(2), 264–290.

Sundquist, J. L. (1973). *Dynamics of the Party System: Alignment and Realignment of Political Parties in the United States*. The Brookings Institution.

Svraka, D. (2024). Targeted nativism: ethnic diversity and radical right parties in Europe. *Government and Opposition, 59*(2), 360–381.

Tajfel, H. (1981). *Human Groups and Social Categories: Studies in Social Psychology*. Cambridge University Press.

Tesler, M. (2013). The return of old-fashioned racism to White Americans' partisan preferences in the early Obama era. *The Journal of Politics, 75*(1), 110–123.

Tesler, M. (2015). The conditions ripe for racial spillover effects. *Political Psychology, 36*, 101–117.

Tesler, M. (2016). Views about race mattered more in electing Trump than in electing Obama. *Washington Post, 22.*

Tesler, M. (2019). Racial attitudes and American politics. In *New Directions in Public Opinion* Routledge. pp. 118–136.

Theiss-Morse, E. (2009). *Who Counts as an American? The Boundaries of National Identity.* Cambridge University Press.

Tocqueville, Alexis de. (2000). *Democracy in America.* Translated by Mansfield, Harvey C. and Winthrop, Delba. Chicago: University of Chicago Press.

Tolbert, C. J., Redlawsk, D. P., & Gracey, K. J. (2018). Racial attitudes and emotional responses to the 2016 Republican candidates. *Journal of Elections, Public Opinion and Parties, 28*(2), 245–262.

Turner, J. C. (1975). Social comparison and social identity: Some prospects for intergroup behaviour. *European Journal of Social Psychology, 5*(1), 1–34.

Uscinski, J. E., & Enders, A. M. (2023). What is a conspiracy theory and why does it matter? *Critical Review, 35*(1–2), 148–169.

Valentino, N. A., Neuner, F. G., & Vandenbroek, L. M. (2018). The changing norms of racial political rhetoric and the end of racial priming. *The Journal of Politics, 80*(3), 757–771.

Vespa, J., Medina, L., & Amstrong, D. (2018). *Demographic Turning Points for the United States: Population Projections for 2020 to 2060.* Current Population Reports.

Vonnegut, Kurt. (1981). *Palm Sunday: An Autobiographical Collage.* New York, N.Y.: Delacorte Press. p. 21.

Walter, S. (2021). The backlash against globalization. *Annual Review of Political Science, 24*(1), 421–442.

White, J. K. (2016). Donald Trump and the Scourge of Populism. *The Forum, 14*(3), 265–279.

Whitehead, A. L., Perry, S. L., & Baker, J. O. (2018). Make America Christian again: Christian nationalism and voting for Donald Trump in the 2016 presidential election. *Sociology of religion, 79*(2), 147–171.

Whiteley, P., Clarke, H. D., & Stewart, M. C. (2020). Populism plus: Voting for Donald Trump and Hillary Clinton in the 2016 US presidential election. In *Authoritarian Populism and Liberal Democracy,* 87–105.

Wilkins, C. L., Hirsch, A. A., Kaiser, C. R., & Inkles, M. P. (2017). The threat of racial progress and the self-protective nature of perceiving anti-white bias. *Group Processes & Intergroup Relations, 20*(6), 801–812.

Wilkins, C. L., & Kaiser, C. R. (2014). Racial progress as threat to the status hierarchy: Implications for perceptions of anti-white bias. *Psychological Science, 25*(2), 439–446.

Williamson, V., Skocpol, T., & Coggin, J. (2011). The Tea Party and the remaking of Republican conservatism. *Perspectives on Politics, 9*(1), 25–43.

Wright, M. (2011). Diversity and the imagined community: Immigrant diversity and conceptions of national identity. *Political Psychology, 32*(5), 837–862.

Wright, M., Citrin, J., & Wand, J. (2012). Alternative measures of American national identity: Implications for the civic-ethnic distinction. *Political Psychology, 33*(4), 469–482.

Yang, Y. (2013). *Age-Period-Cohort Analysis: New Models, Methods, and Empirical Applications.* (Vol. 1). CRC Press.

Young, C. (2016). *It's Nativism: Explaining the Drivers of Trump's Popular Support.* https://www.ipsos.com/en/its-nativism-explaining-drivers-trumps-popular-support.

Young, C., Ziemer, K., & Jackson, C. (2019). Explaining Trump's popular support: Validation of a nativism index. *Social Science Quarterly, 100*(2), 412–418.

Young, J. G. (2017). Making America 1920 again? Nativism and US immigration, past and present. *Journal on Migration and Human Security, 5*(1), 217–235.

Zaller, J. R. (1998). Monica Lewinsky's contribution to political science. *PS: Political Science & Politics, 31*(2), 182–189.

Zhao, Y. (2019). Testing the measurement invariance of nativism. *Social Science Quarterly, 100*(2), 419–429.

Index

Note: Page numbers in *italics* indicate figures, **bold** indicate tables in the text, and references following "n" refer notes.

https://doi.org/10.1515/9783111384047-011

www.ingramcontent.com/pod-product-compliance
Lightning Source LLC
Chambersburg PA
CBHW071743270326
41928CB00013B/2786